A WALK THROUGH HELL ™

VOLUME 1

THE WAREHOUSE

GARTH ENNIS

GORAN SUDŽUKA

IVE SVORCINA

ROB STEEN

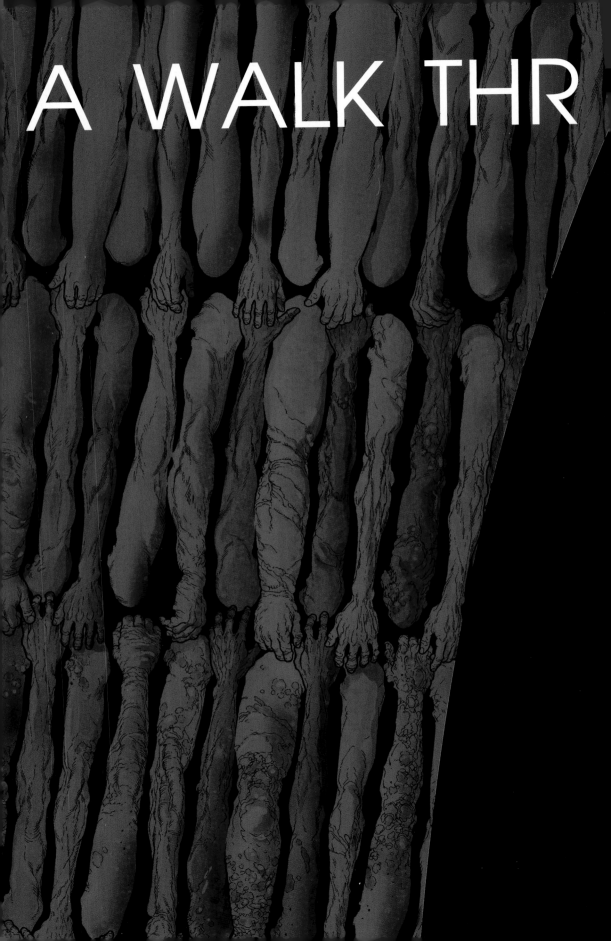

A WALK THR

OUGH HELL
VOLUME 1
THE WAREHOUSE

GARTH ENNIS co-creator & writer

GORAN SUDŽUKA co-creator & artist

IVE SVORCINA colorist

ROB STEEN letterer

ANDY CLARE w/ JOSE VILLARRUBIA front & original covers

ANDY CLARKE, FRANCESCO FRANCAVILLA, ROBERT HACK, HOYT SILVA, GORAN SUDŽUKA w/ IVE SVORCINA & BEN TEMPLESMITH variant covers

COREY BREEN book designer

JARED K. FLETCHER logo designer

MIKE MARTS editor

AFTERSHOCK™

MIKE MARTS - Editor-in-Chief • JOE PRUETT - Publisher/CCO • LEE KRAMER - President • JON KRAMER - Chief Executive Officer
STEVE ROTTERDAM - SVP, Sales & Marketing • LISA Y. WU - Retailer/Fan Relations Manager
CHRISTINA HARRINGTON - Managing Editor • JAY BEHLING - Chief Financial Officer • JAWAD QURESHI - SVP, Investor Relations
AARON MARION - Publicist • CHRIS LA TORRE - Sales Associate • LISA MOODY - Finance
CHARLES PRITCHETT - Comics Production • COREY BREEN - Collections Production • TEDDY LEO - Editorial Assistant
STEPHANIE CASEBIER & SARAH PRUETT - Publishing Assistants

AfterShock Logo Design by COMICRAFT
Publicity: contact AARON MARION (aaron@publichausagency.com) & RYAN CROY (ryan@publichausagency.com) at PUBLICHAUS
Special thanks to: IRA KURGAN, STEPHAN NILSON & JULIE PIFHER

First Printing: October 2018. 10 9 8 7 6 5 4 3 2 1

AFTERSHOCKCOMICS.COM Follow us on social media

A WALK THROUGH HELL ™

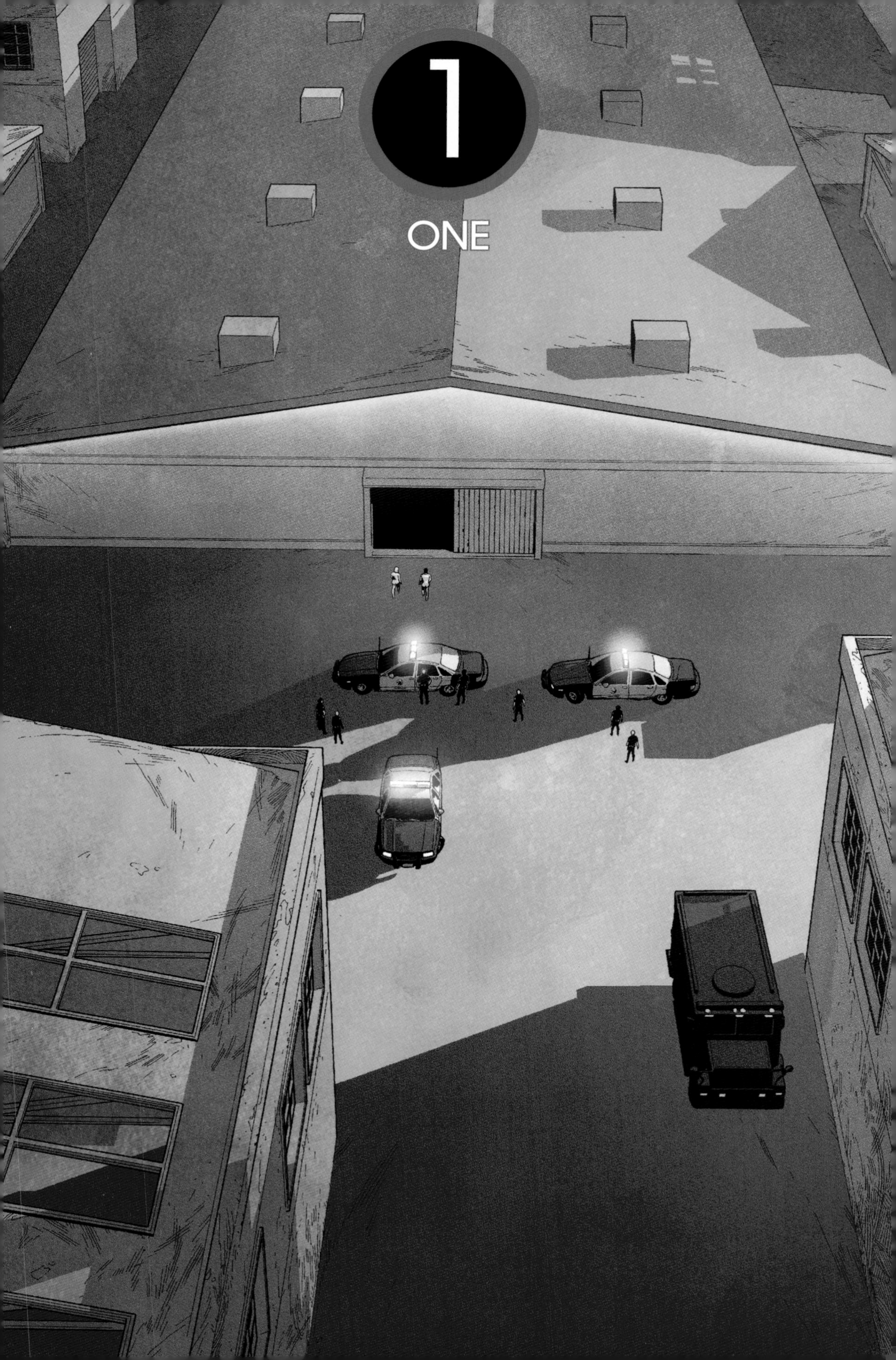
1
ONE

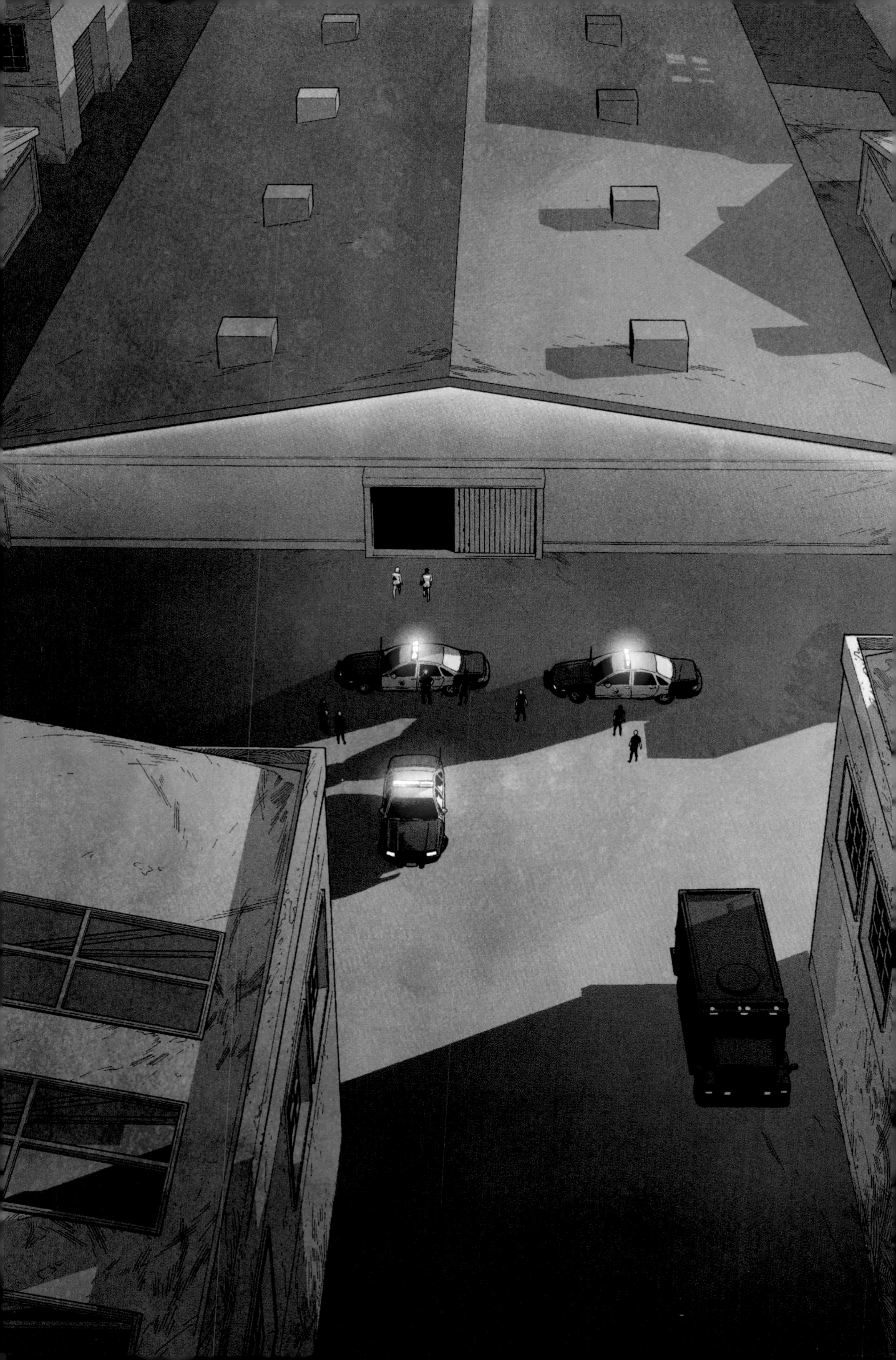

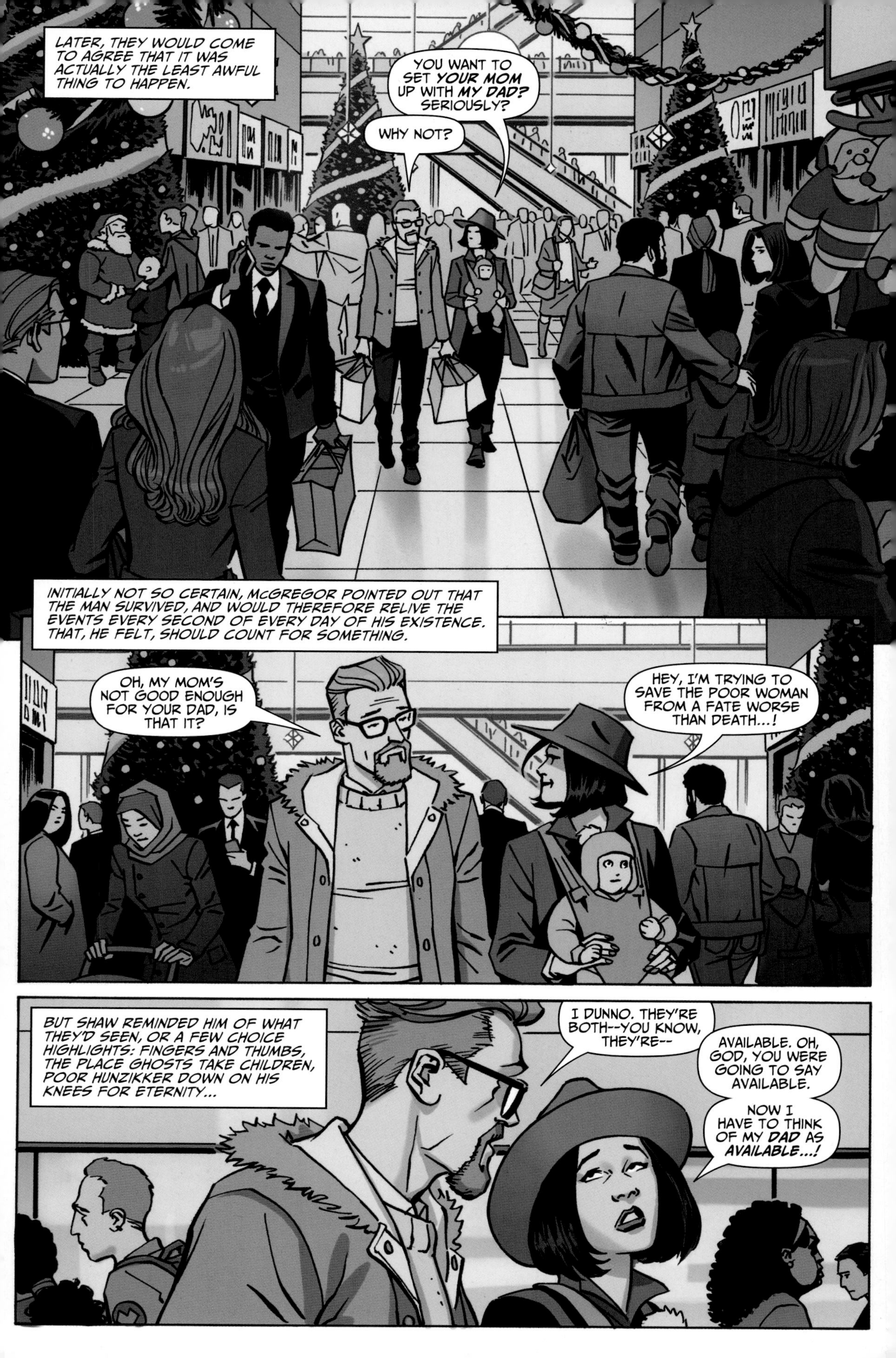
LATER, THEY WOULD COME TO AGREE THAT IT WAS ACTUALLY THE LEAST AWFUL THING TO HAPPEN.
YOU WANT TO SET YOUR MOM UP WITH MY DAD? SERIOUSLY?
WHY NOT?
INITIALLY NOT SO CERTAIN, McGREGOR POINTED OUT THAT THE MAN SURVIVED, AND WOULD THEREFORE RELIVE THE EVENTS EVERY SECOND OF EVERY DAY OF HIS EXISTENCE. THAT, HE FELT, SHOULD COUNT FOR SOMETHING.
OH, MY MOM'S NOT GOOD ENOUGH FOR YOUR DAD, IS THAT IT?
HEY, I'M TRYING TO SAVE THE POOR WOMAN FROM A FATE WORSE THAN DEATH...!
BUT SHAW REMINDED HIM OF WHAT THEY'D SEEN, OR A FEW CHOICE HIGHLIGHTS: FINGERS AND THUMBS, THE PLACE GHOSTS TAKE CHILDREN, POOR HUNZIKKER DOWN ON HIS KNEES FOR ETERNITY...
I DUNNO. THEY'RE BOTH--YOU KNOW, THEY'RE--
AVAILABLE. OH, GOD, YOU WERE GOING TO SAY AVAILABLE.
NOW I HAVE TO THINK OF MY DAD AS AVAILABLE...!

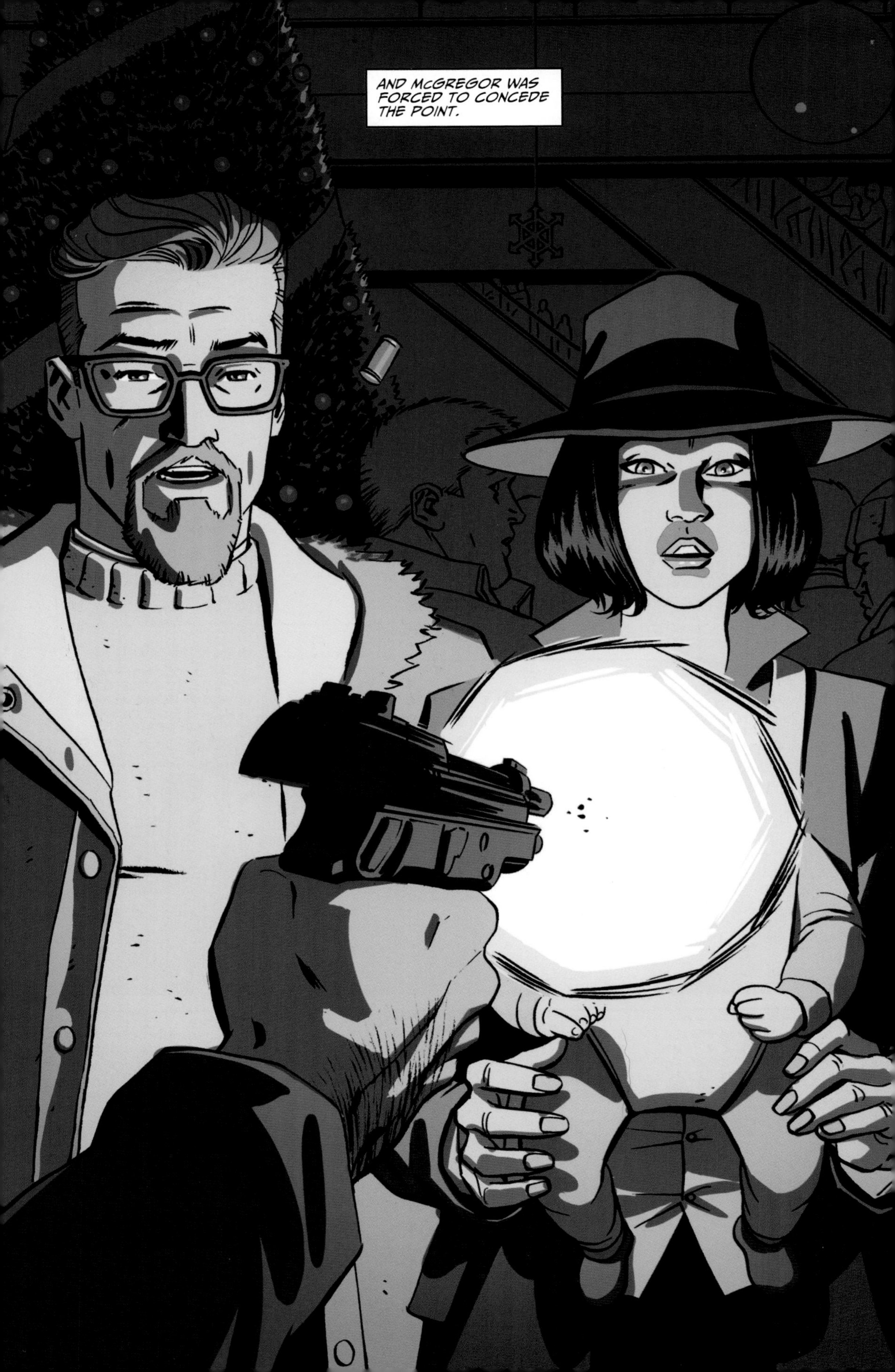
AND McGREGOR WAS FORCED TO CONCEDE THE POINT.

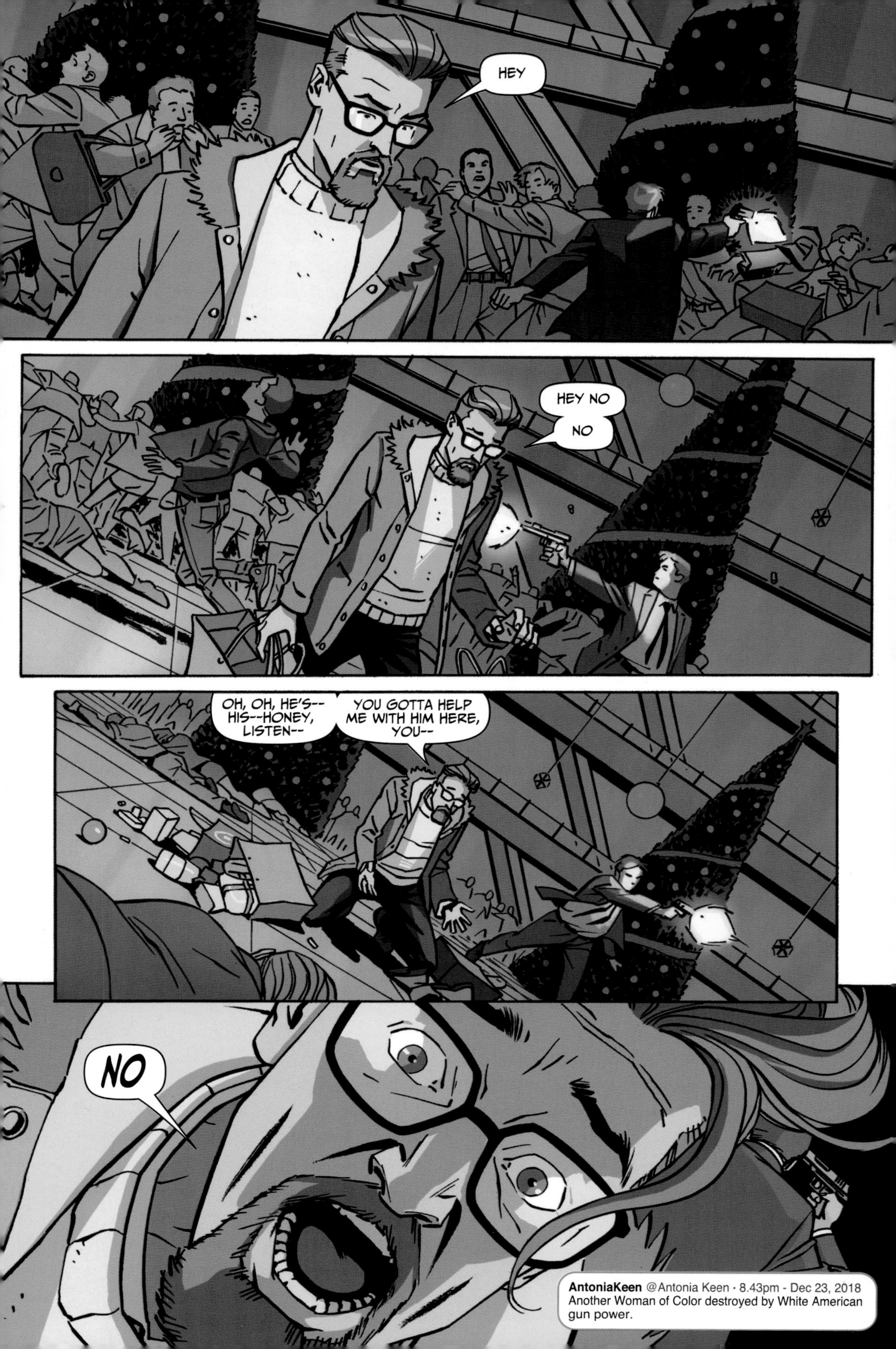
HEY
HEY NO
NO
OH, OH, HE'S--HIS--HONEY, LISTEN--
YOU GOTTA HELP ME WITH HIM HERE, YOU--
NO
AntoniaKeen @Antonia Keen · 8.43pm - Dec 23, 2018
Another Woman of Color destroyed by White American gun power.

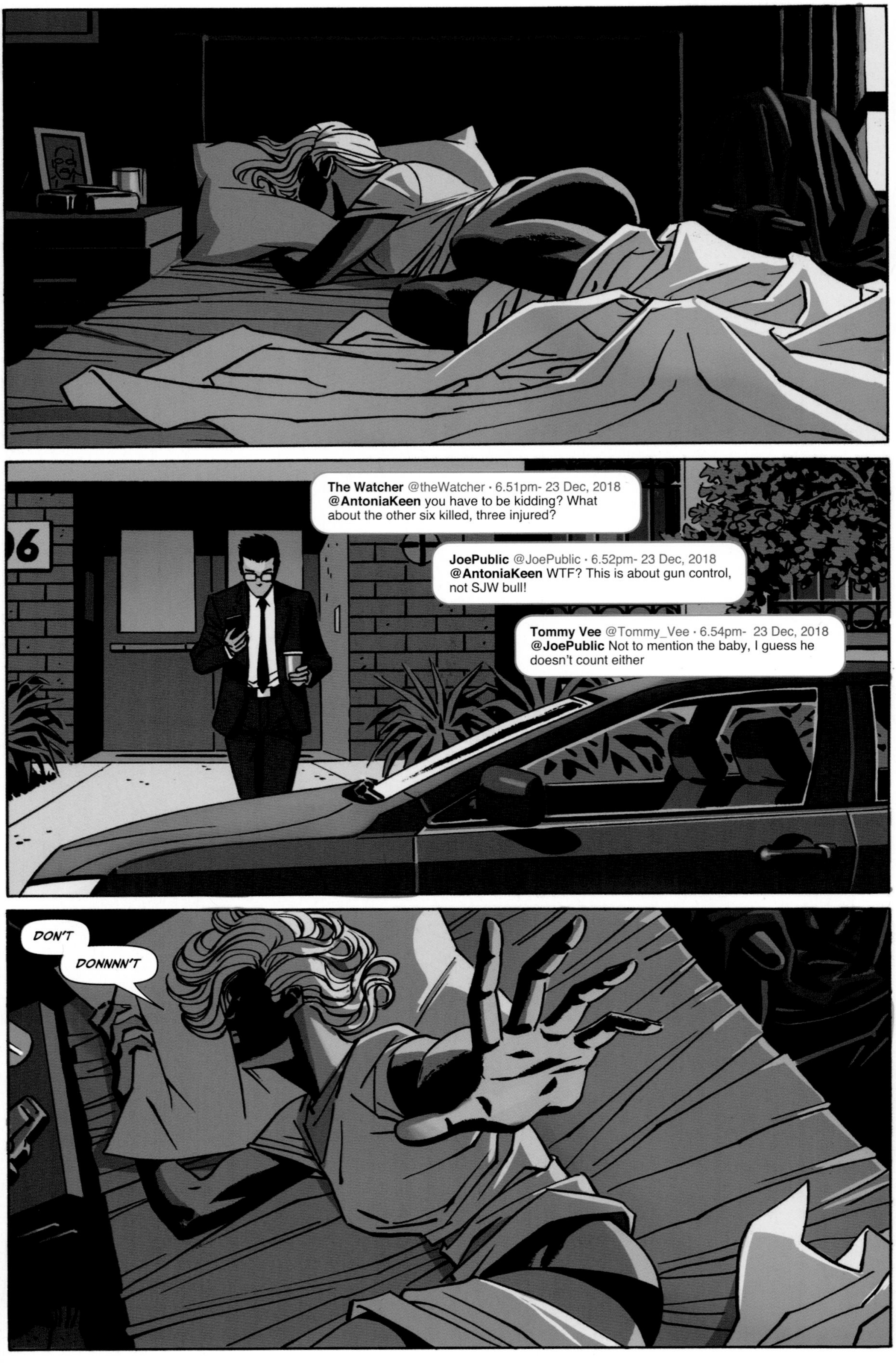
The Watcher @theWatcher · 6.51pm- 23 Dec, 2018
@AntoniaKeen you have to be kidding? What about the other six killed, three injured?
JoePublic @JoePublic · 6.52pm- 23 Dec, 2018
@AntoniaKeen WTF? This is about gun control, not SJW bull!
Tommy Vee @Tommy_Vee · 6.54pm- 23 Dec, 2018
@JoePublic Not to mention the baby, I guess he doesn't count either
DON'T
DONNNN'T

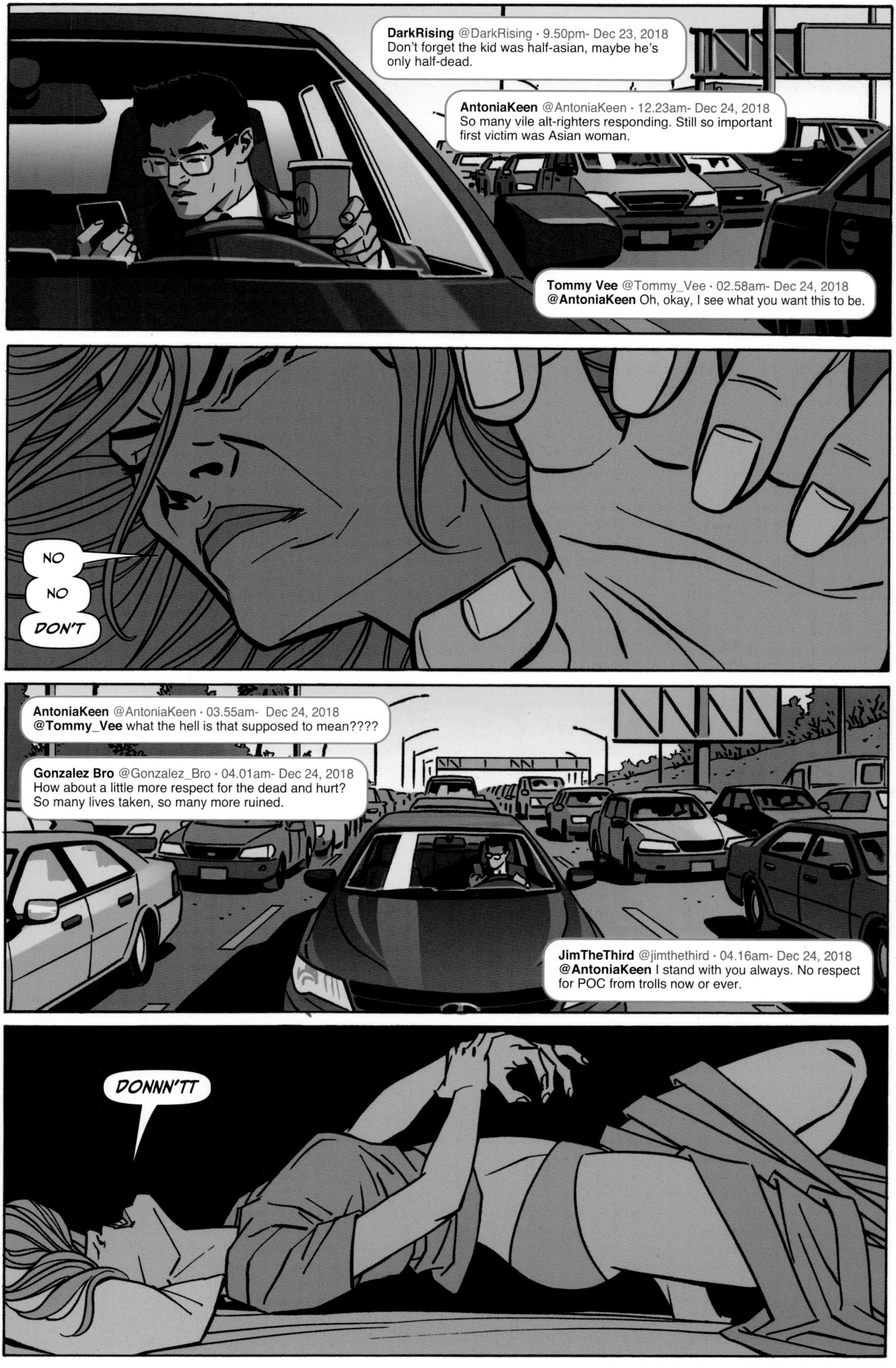
DarkRising @DarkRising · 9.50pm- Dec 23, 2018
Don't forget the kid was half-asian, maybe he's only half-dead.
AntoniaKeen @AntoniaKeen · 12.23am- Dec 24, 2018
So many vile alt-righters responding. Still so important first victim was Asian woman.
Tommy Vee @Tommy_Vee · 02.58am- Dec 24, 2018
@AntoniaKeen Oh, okay, I see what you want this to be.
NO
NO
DON'T
AntoniaKeen @AntoniaKeen · 03.55am- Dec 24, 2018
@Tommy_Vee what the hell is that supposed to mean????
Gonzalez Bro @Gonzalez_Bro · 04.01am- Dec 24, 2018
How about a little more respect for the dead and hurt? So many lives taken, so many more ruined.
JimTheThird @jimthethird · 04.16am- Dec 24, 2018
@AntoniaKeen I stand with you always. No respect for POC from trolls now or ever.
DONNN'TT

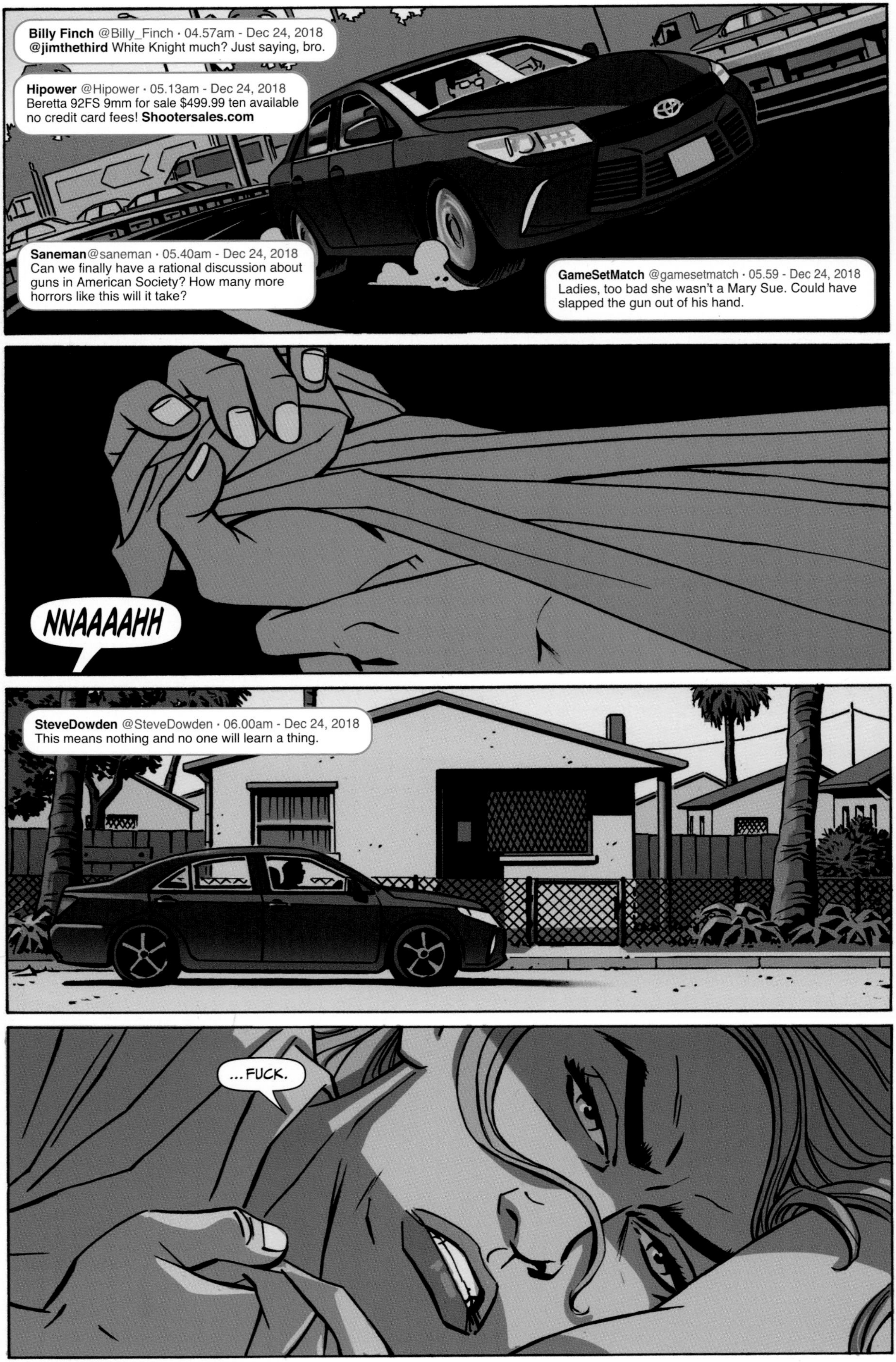
Billy Finch @Billy_Finch · 04.57am - Dec 24, 2018
@jimthethird White Knight much? Just saying, bro.
Hipower @Hipower · 05.13am - Dec 24, 2018
Beretta 92FS 9mm for sale $499.99 ten available no credit card fees! Shootersales.com
Saneman@saneman · 05.40am - Dec 24, 2018
Can we finally have a rational discussion about guns in American Society? How many more horrors like this will it take?
GameSetMatch @gamesetmatch · 05.59 - Dec 24, 2018
Ladies, too bad she wasn't a Mary Sue. Could have slapped the gun out of his hand.
NNAAAAHH
SteveDowden @SteveDowden · 06.00am - Dec 24, 2018
This means nothing and no one will learn a thing.
...FUCK.

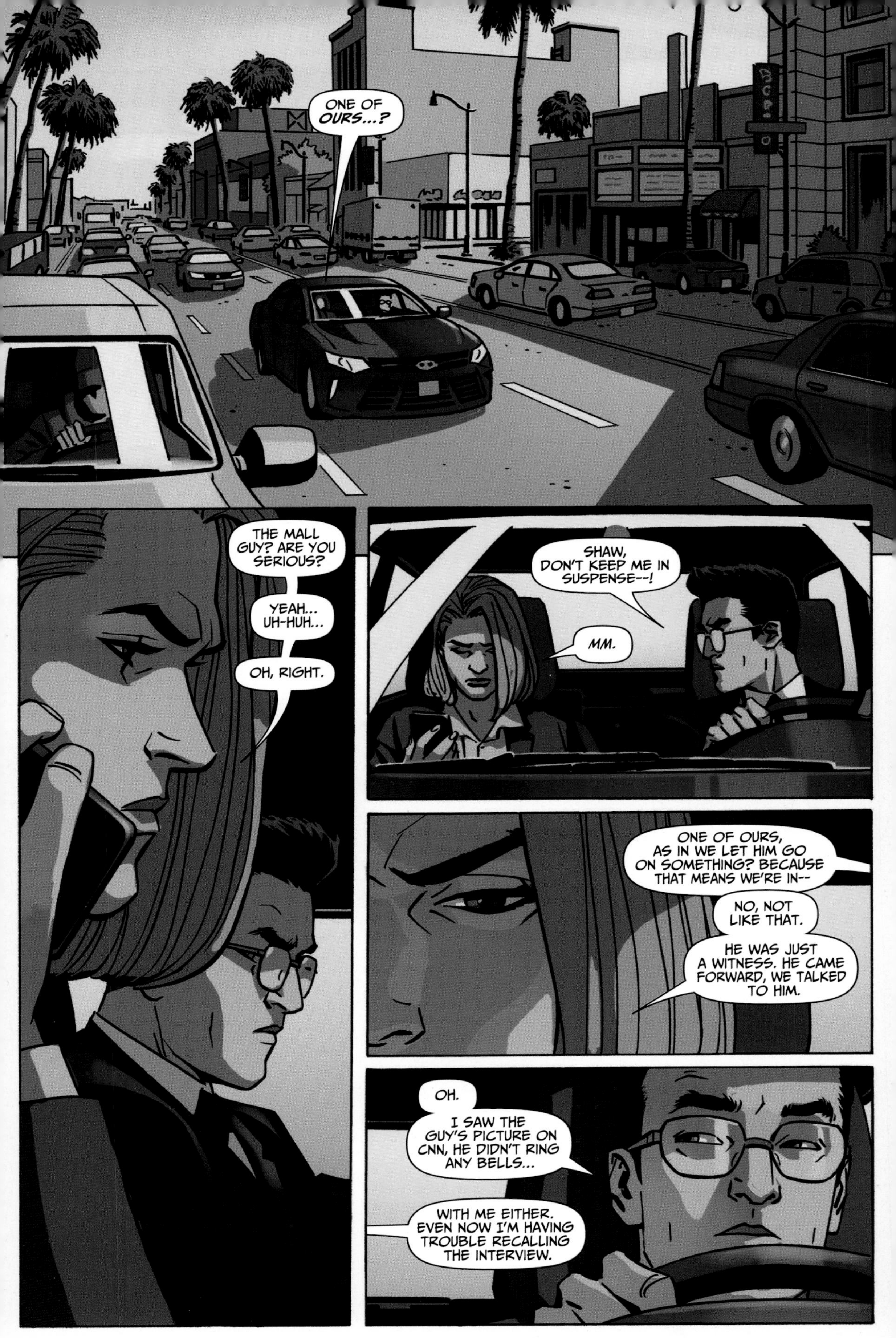
ONE OF OURS...?
THE MALL GUY? ARE YOU SERIOUS?
YEAH... UH-HUH...
OH, RIGHT.
SHAW, DON'T KEEP ME IN SUSPENSE--!
MM.
ONE OF OURS, AS IN WE LET HIM GO ON SOMETHING? BECAUSE THAT MEANS WE'RE IN--
NO, NOT LIKE THAT.
HE WAS JUST A WITNESS. HE CAME FORWARD, WE TALKED TO HIM.
OH.
I SAW THE GUY'S PICTURE ON CNN, HE DIDN'T RING ANY BELLS...
WITH ME EITHER. EVEN NOW I'M HAVING TROUBLE RECALLING THE INTERVIEW.

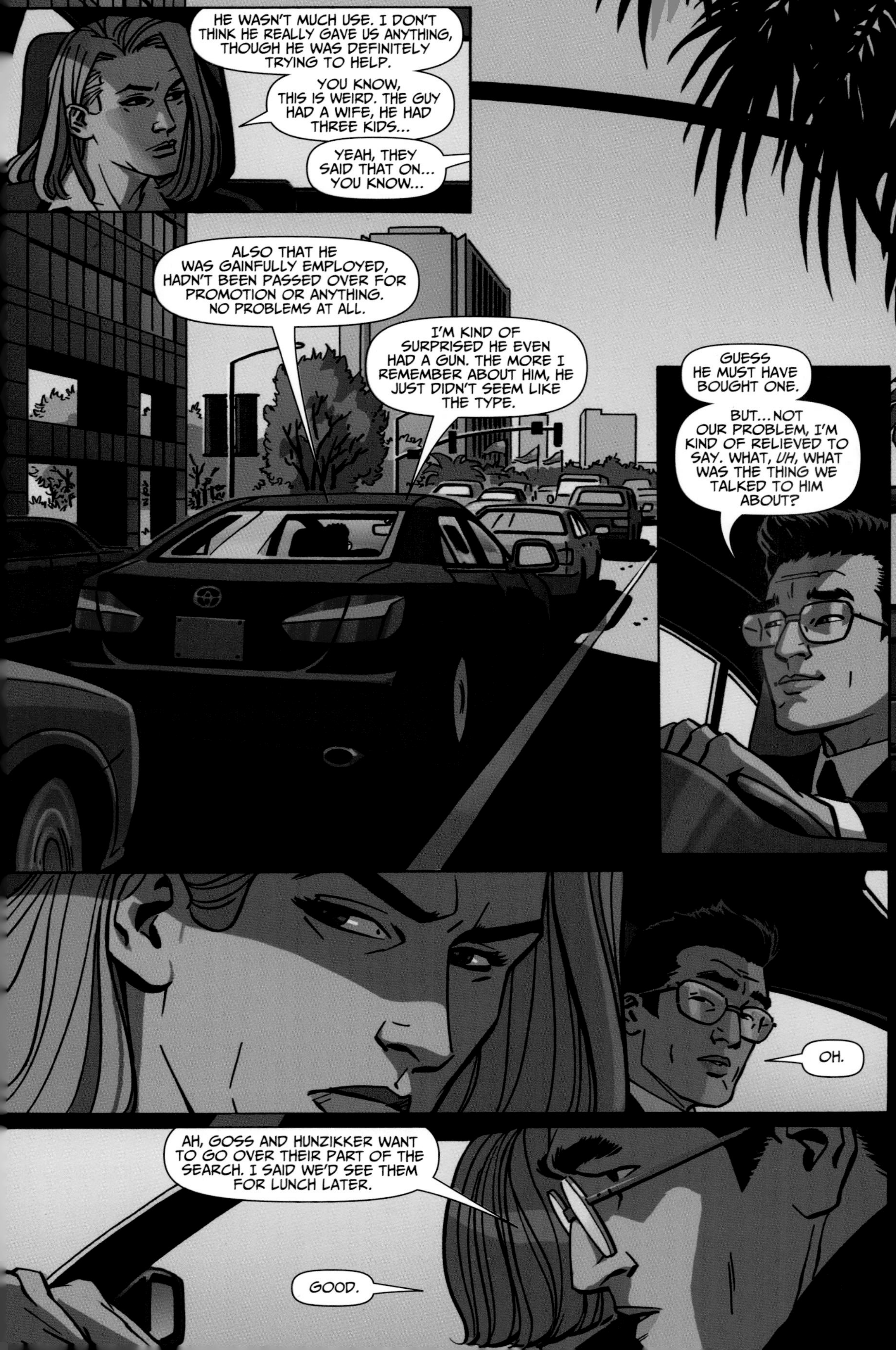
HE WASN'T MUCH USE. I DON'T THINK HE REALLY GAVE US ANYTHING, THOUGH HE WAS DEFINITELY TRYING TO HELP.
YOU KNOW, THIS IS WEIRD. THE GUY HAD A WIFE, HE HAD THREE KIDS...
YEAH, THEY SAID THAT ON... YOU KNOW...
ALSO THAT HE WAS GAINFULLY EMPLOYED, HADN'T BEEN PASSED OVER FOR PROMOTION OR ANYTHING. NO PROBLEMS AT ALL.
I'M KIND OF SURPRISED HE EVEN HAD A GUN. THE MORE I REMEMBER ABOUT HIM, HE JUST DIDN'T SEEM LIKE THE TYPE.
GUESS HE MUST HAVE BOUGHT ONE.
BUT...NOT OUR PROBLEM, I'M KIND OF RELIEVED TO SAY. WHAT, *UH*, WHAT WAS THE THING WE TALKED TO HIM ABOUT?
OH.
AH, GOSS AND HUNZIKKER WANT TO GO OVER THEIR PART OF THE SEARCH. I SAID WE'D SEE THEM FOR LUNCH LATER.
GOOD.

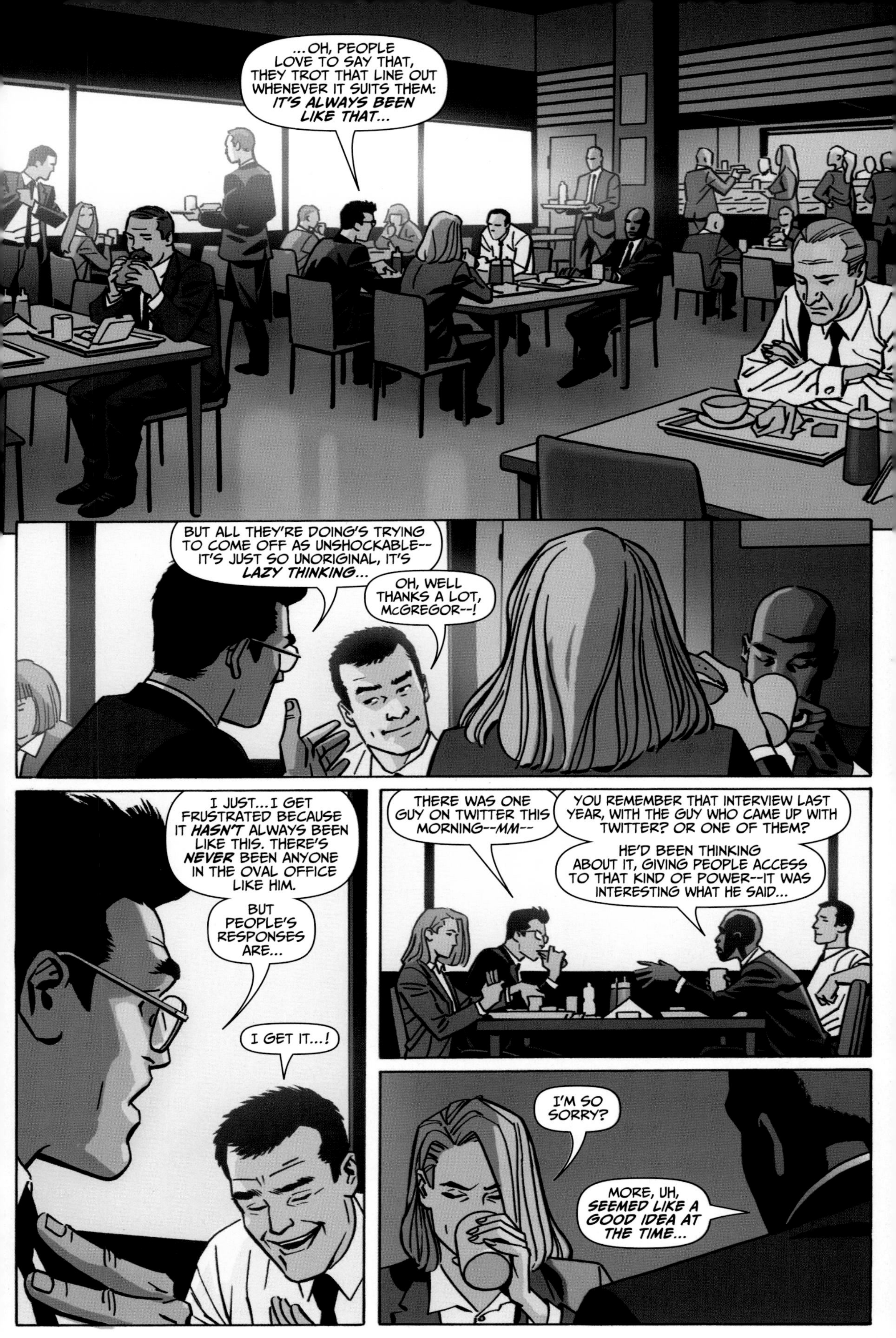
...OH, PEOPLE LOVE TO SAY THAT, THEY TROT THAT LINE OUT WHENEVER IT SUITS THEM: *IT'S ALWAYS BEEN LIKE THAT...*
BUT ALL THEY'RE DOING'S TRYING TO COME OFF AS UNSHOCKABLE-- IT'S JUST SO UNORIGINAL, IT'S *LAZY THINKING...*
OH, WELL THANKS A LOT, McGREGOR--!
I JUST...I GET FRUSTRATED BECAUSE IT *HASN'T* ALWAYS BEEN LIKE THIS. THERE'S *NEVER* BEEN ANYONE IN THE OVAL OFFICE LIKE HIM.
BUT PEOPLE'S RESPONSES ARE...
I GET IT...!
THERE WAS ONE GUY ON TWITTER THIS MORNING--*MM*--
YOU REMEMBER THAT INTERVIEW LAST YEAR, WITH THE GUY WHO CAME UP WITH TWITTER? OR ONE OF THEM?
HE'D BEEN THINKING ABOUT IT, GIVING PEOPLE ACCESS TO THAT KIND OF POWER--IT WAS INTERESTING WHAT HE SAID...
I'M SO SORRY?
MORE, UH, *SEEMED LIKE A GOOD IDEA AT THE TIME...*

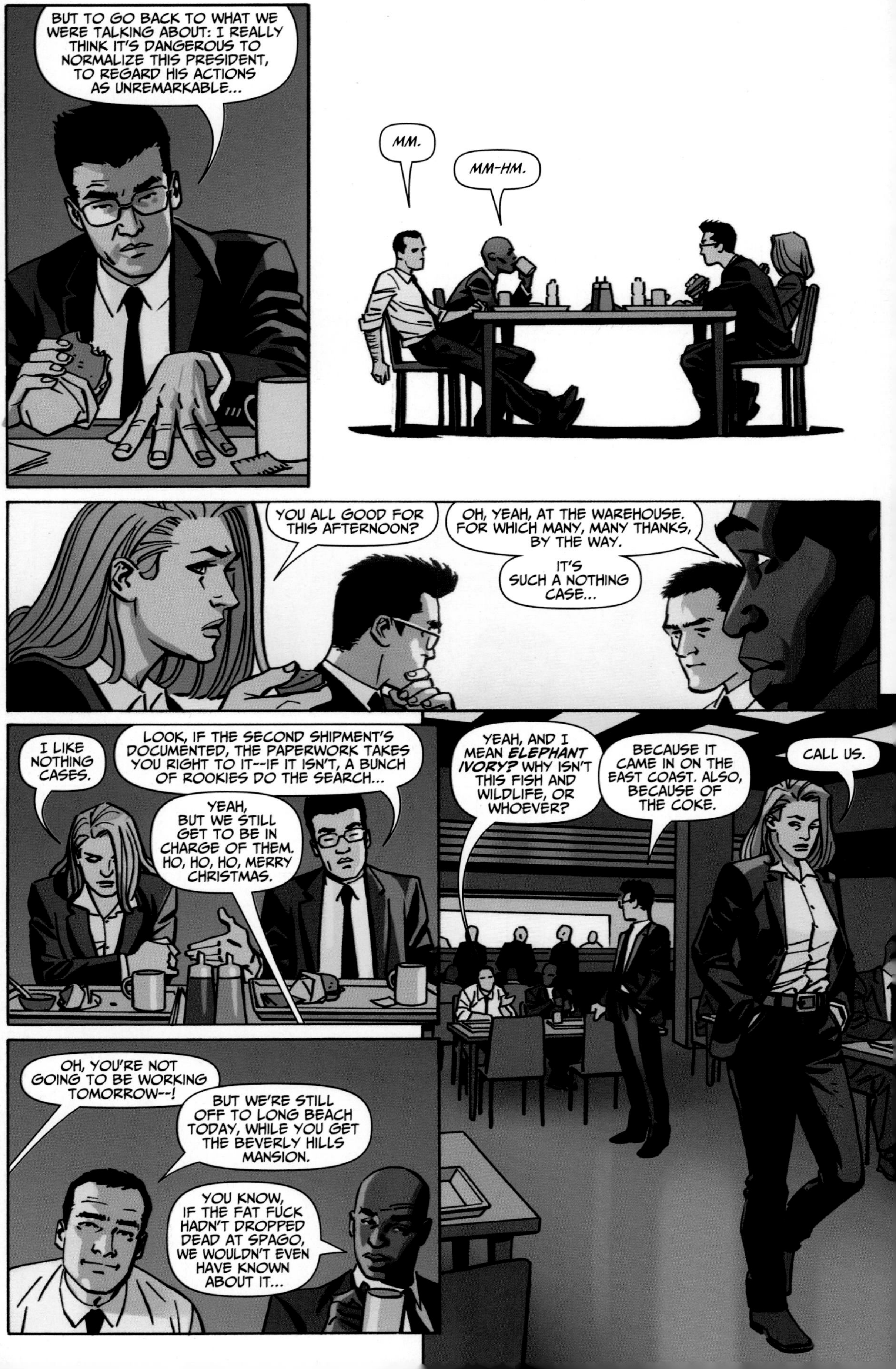
BUT TO GO BACK TO WHAT WE WERE TALKING ABOUT: I REALLY THINK IT'S DANGEROUS TO NORMALIZE THIS PRESIDENT, TO REGARD HIS ACTIONS AS UNREMARKABLE...
MM.
MM-HM.
YOU ALL GOOD FOR THIS AFTERNOON?
OH, YEAH, AT THE WAREHOUSE. FOR WHICH MANY, MANY THANKS, BY THE WAY.
IT'S SUCH A NOTHING CASE...
I LIKE NOTHING CASES.
LOOK, IF THE SECOND SHIPMENT'S DOCUMENTED, THE PAPERWORK TAKES YOU RIGHT TO IT--IF IT ISN'T, A BUNCH OF ROOKIES DO THE SEARCH...
YEAH, BUT WE STILL GET TO BE IN CHARGE OF THEM. HO, HO, HO, MERRY CHRISTMAS.
YEAH, AND I MEAN *ELEPHANT IVORY?* WHY ISN'T THIS FISH AND WILDLIFE, OR WHOEVER?
BECAUSE IT CAME IN ON THE EAST COAST. ALSO, BECAUSE OF THE COKE.
CALL US.
OH, YOU'RE NOT GOING TO BE WORKING TOMORROW--!
BUT WE'RE STILL OFF TO LONG BEACH TODAY, WHILE YOU GET THE BEVERLY HILLS MANSION.
YOU KNOW, IF THE FAT FUCK HADN'T DROPPED DEAD AT SPAGO, WE WOULDN'T EVEN HAVE KNOWN ABOUT IT...

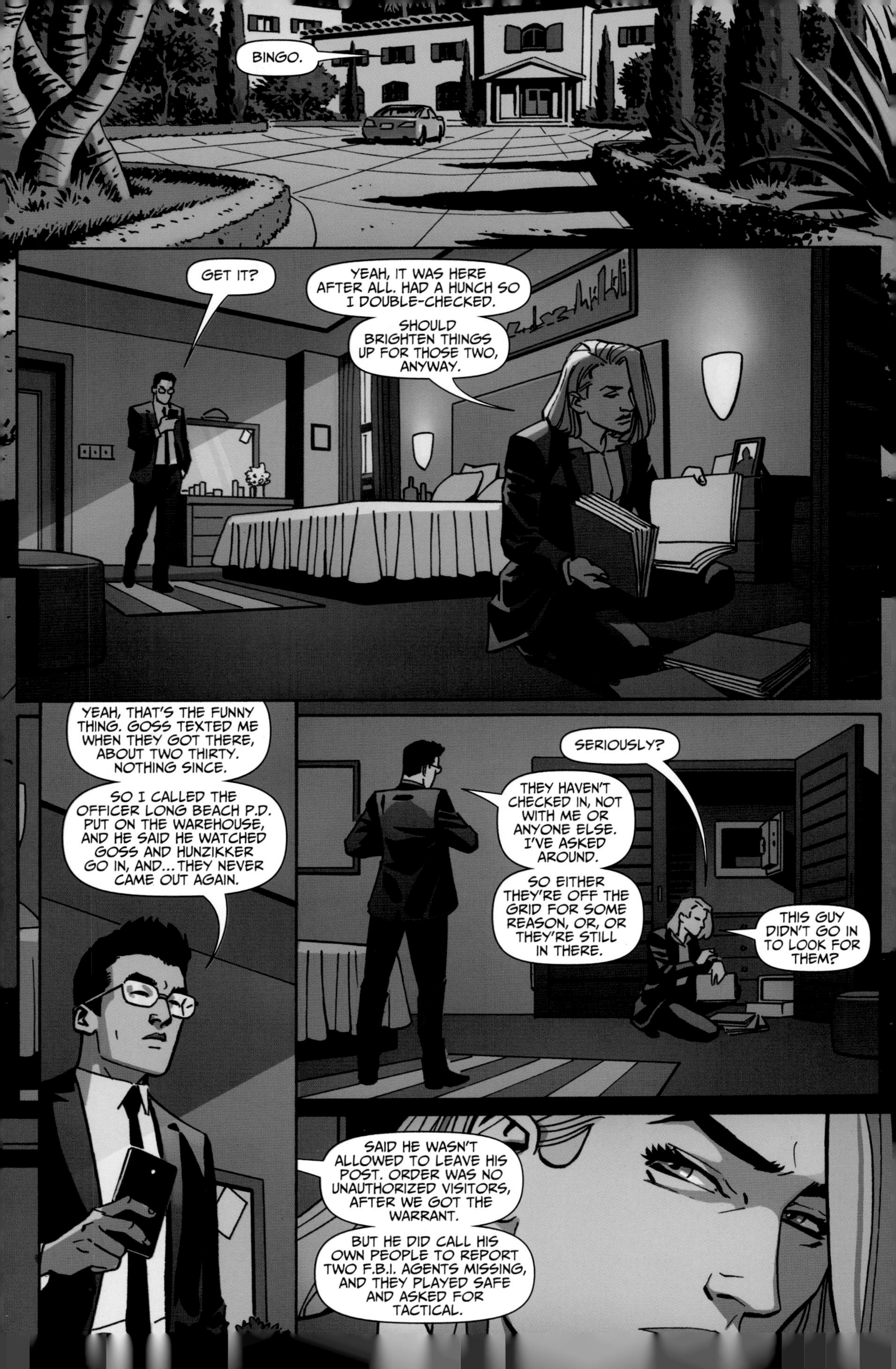
BINGO.
GET IT?
YEAH, IT WAS HERE AFTER ALL. HAD A HUNCH SO I DOUBLE-CHECKED.
SHOULD BRIGHTEN THINGS UP FOR THOSE TWO, ANYWAY.
YEAH, THAT'S THE FUNNY THING. GOSS TEXTED ME WHEN THEY GOT THERE, ABOUT TWO THIRTY. NOTHING SINCE.
SO I CALLED THE OFFICER LONG BEACH P.D. PUT ON THE WAREHOUSE, AND HE SAID HE WATCHED GOSS AND HUNZIKKER GO IN, AND... THEY NEVER CAME OUT AGAIN.
SERIOUSLY?
THEY HAVEN'T CHECKED IN, NOT WITH ME OR ANYONE ELSE. I'VE ASKED AROUND.
SO EITHER THEY'RE OFF THE GRID FOR SOME REASON, OR, OR THEY'RE STILL IN THERE.
THIS GUY DIDN'T GO IN TO LOOK FOR THEM?
SAID HE WASN'T ALLOWED TO LEAVE HIS POST. ORDER WAS NO UNAUTHORIZED VISITORS, AFTER WE GOT THE WARRANT.
BUT HE DID CALL HIS OWN PEOPLE TO REPORT TWO F.B.I. AGENTS MISSING, AND THEY PLAYED SAFE AND ASKED FOR TACTICAL.

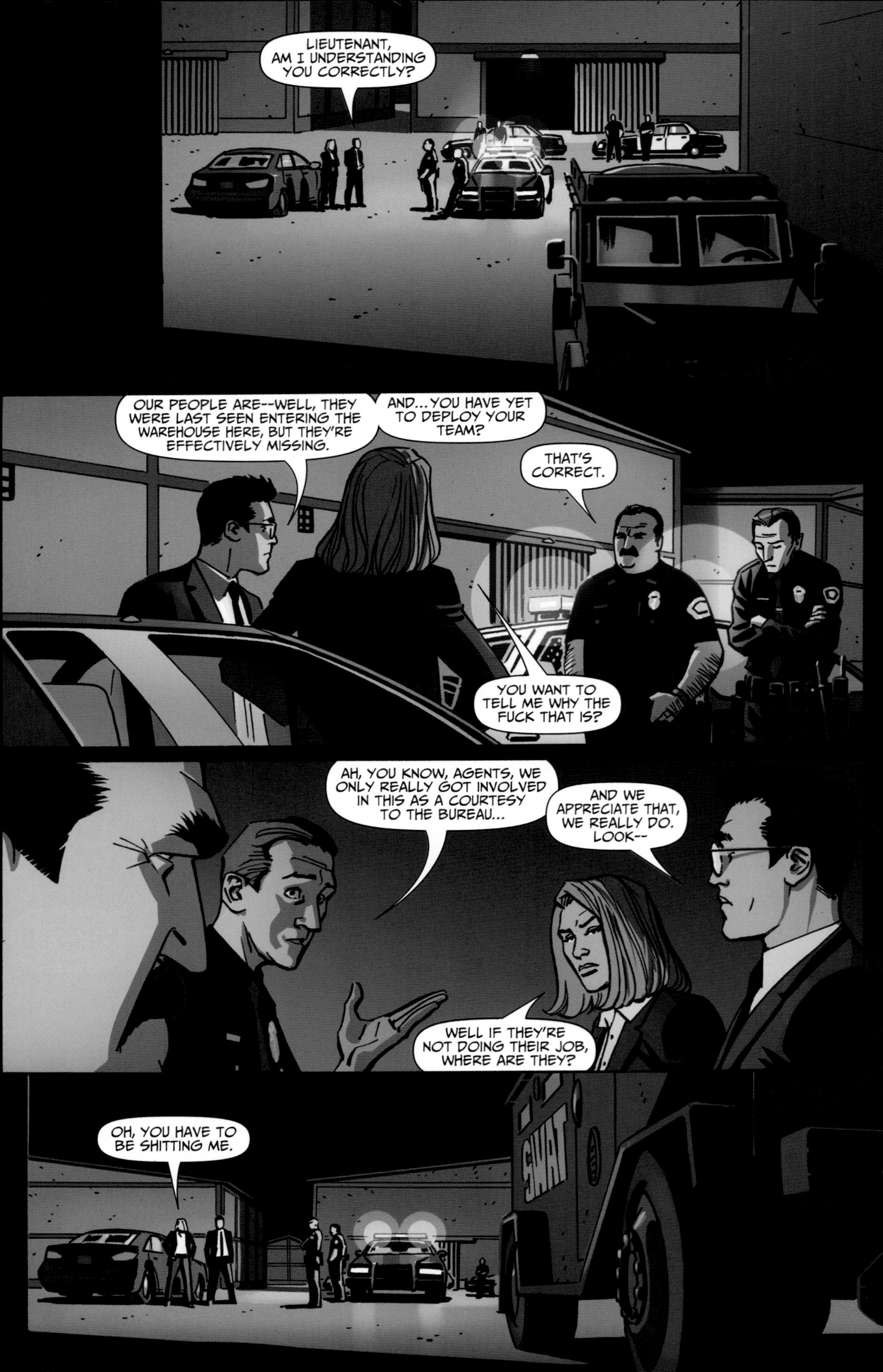
LIEUTENANT, AM I UNDERSTANDING YOU CORRECTLY?
OUR PEOPLE ARE--WELL, THEY WERE LAST SEEN ENTERING THE WAREHOUSE HERE, BUT THEY'RE EFFECTIVELY MISSING.
AND...YOU HAVE YET TO DEPLOY YOUR TEAM?
THAT'S CORRECT.
YOU WANT TO TELL ME WHY THE FUCK THAT IS?
AH, YOU KNOW, AGENTS, WE ONLY REALLY GOT INVOLVED IN THIS AS A COURTESY TO THE BUREAU...
AND WE APPRECIATE THAT, WE REALLY DO. LOOK--
WELL IF THEY'RE NOT DOING THEIR JOB, WHERE ARE THEY?
OH, YOU HAVE TO BE SHITTING ME.
SWAT

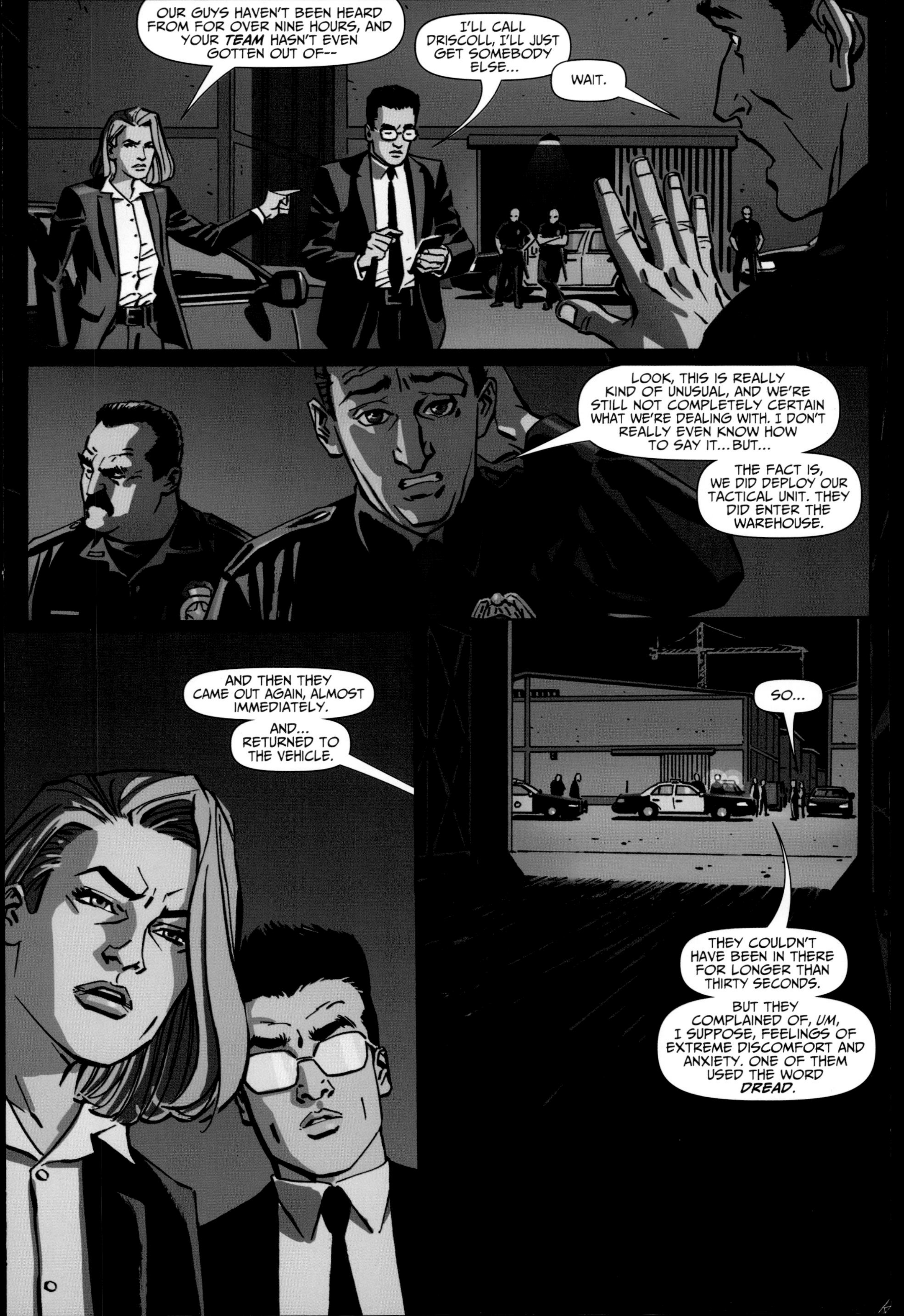
OUR GUYS HAVEN'T BEEN HEARD FROM FOR OVER NINE HOURS, AND YOUR *TEAM* HASN'T EVEN GOTTEN OUT OF--
I'LL CALL DRISCOLL, I'LL JUST GET SOMEBODY ELSE...
WAIT.
LOOK, THIS IS REALLY KIND OF UNUSUAL, AND WE'RE STILL NOT COMPLETELY CERTAIN WHAT WE'RE DEALING WITH. I DON'T REALLY EVEN KNOW HOW TO SAY IT... BUT...
THE FACT IS, WE DID DEPLOY OUR TACTICAL UNIT. THEY DID ENTER THE WAREHOUSE.
AND THEN THEY CAME OUT AGAIN, ALMOST IMMEDIATELY.
AND... RETURNED TO THE VEHICLE.
SO...
THEY COULDN'T HAVE BEEN IN THERE FOR LONGER THAN THIRTY SECONDS.
BUT THEY COMPLAINED OF, *UM*, I SUPPOSE, FEELINGS OF EXTREME DISCOMFORT AND ANXIETY. ONE OF THEM USED THE WORD ***DREAD***.

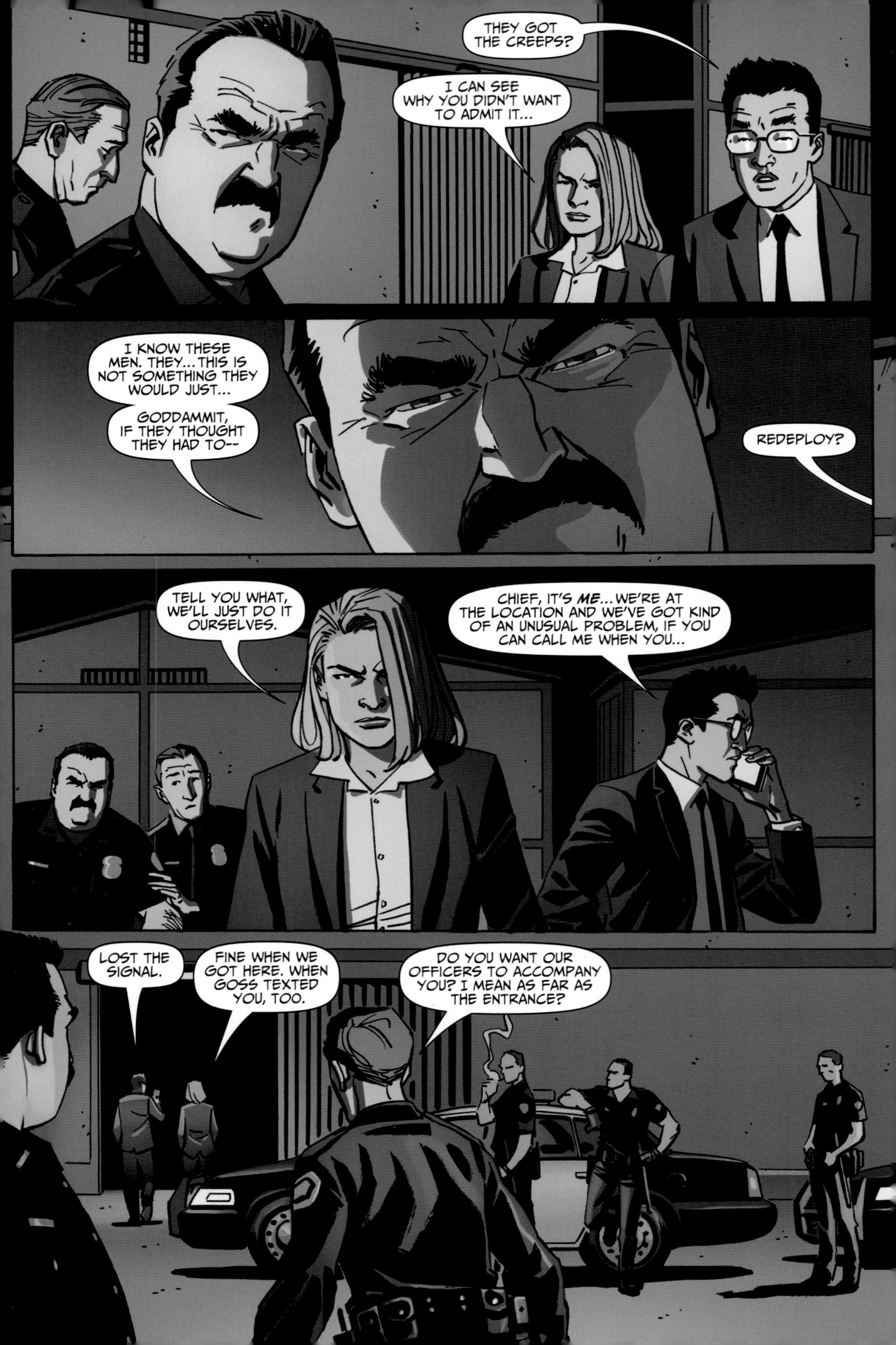
THEY GOT THE CREEPS?
I CAN SEE WHY YOU DIDN'T WANT TO ADMIT IT...
I KNOW THESE MEN. THEY... THIS IS NOT SOMETHING THEY WOULD JUST...
GODDAMMIT, IF THEY THOUGHT THEY HAD TO--
REDEPLOY?
TELL YOU WHAT, WE'LL JUST DO IT OURSELVES.
CHIEF, IT'S *ME*... WE'RE AT THE LOCATION AND WE'VE GOT KIND OF AN UNUSUAL PROBLEM, IF YOU CAN CALL ME WHEN YOU...
LOST THE SIGNAL.
FINE WHEN WE GOT HERE. WHEN GOSS TEXTED YOU, TOO.
DO YOU WANT OUR OFFICERS TO ACCOMPANY YOU? I MEAN AS FAR AS THE ENTRANCE?

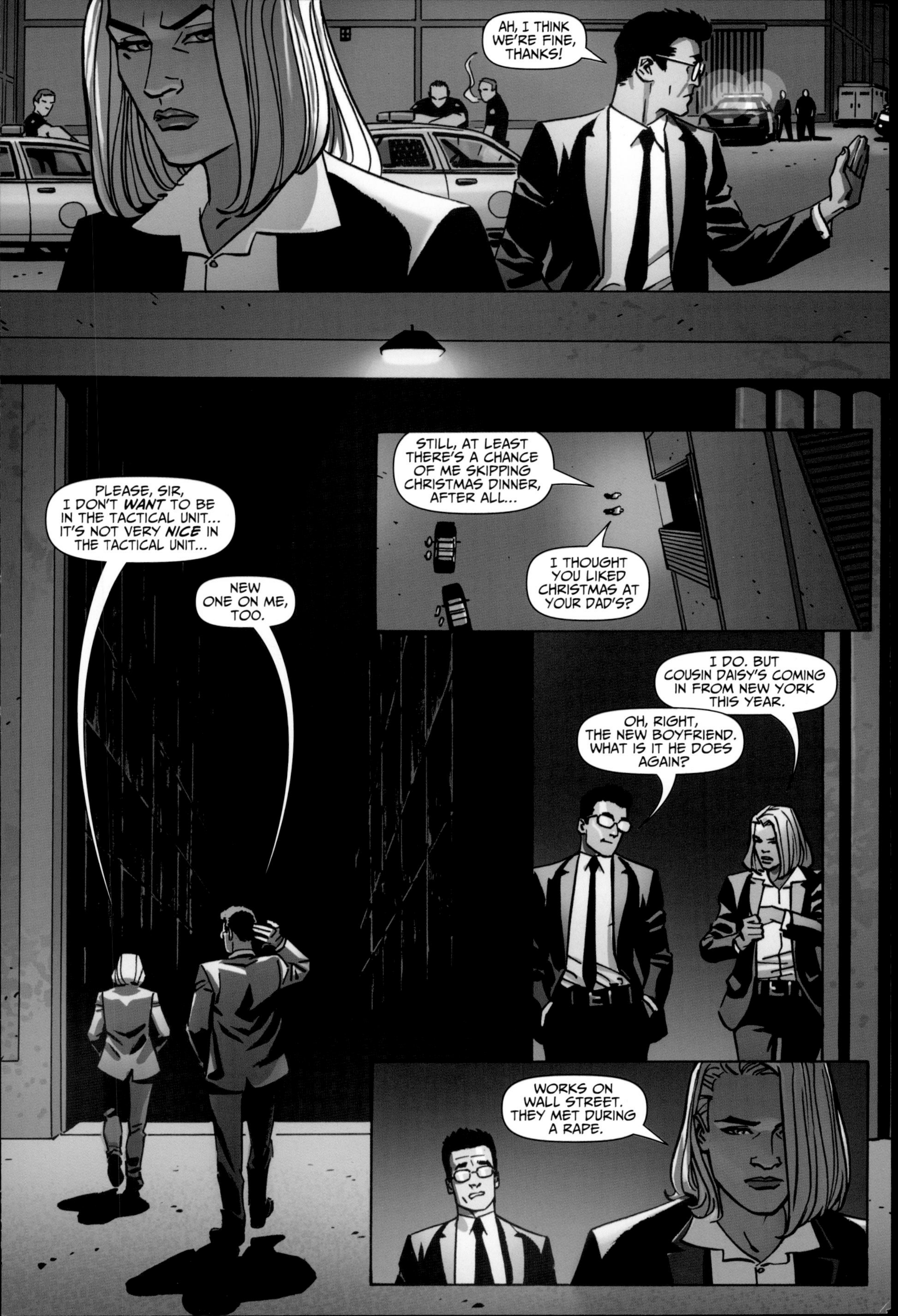
AH, I THINK WE'RE FINE, THANKS!
PLEASE, SIR, I DON'T *WANT* TO BE IN THE TACTICAL UNIT... IT'S NOT VERY *NICE* IN THE TACTICAL UNIT...
NEW ONE ON ME, TOO.
STILL, AT LEAST THERE'S A CHANCE OF ME SKIPPING CHRISTMAS DINNER, AFTER ALL...
I THOUGHT YOU LIKED CHRISTMAS AT YOUR DAD'S?
I DO. BUT COUSIN DAISY'S COMING IN FROM NEW YORK THIS YEAR.
OH, RIGHT, THE NEW BOYFRIEND. WHAT IS IT HE DOES AGAIN?
WORKS ON WALL STREET. THEY MET DURING A RAPE.

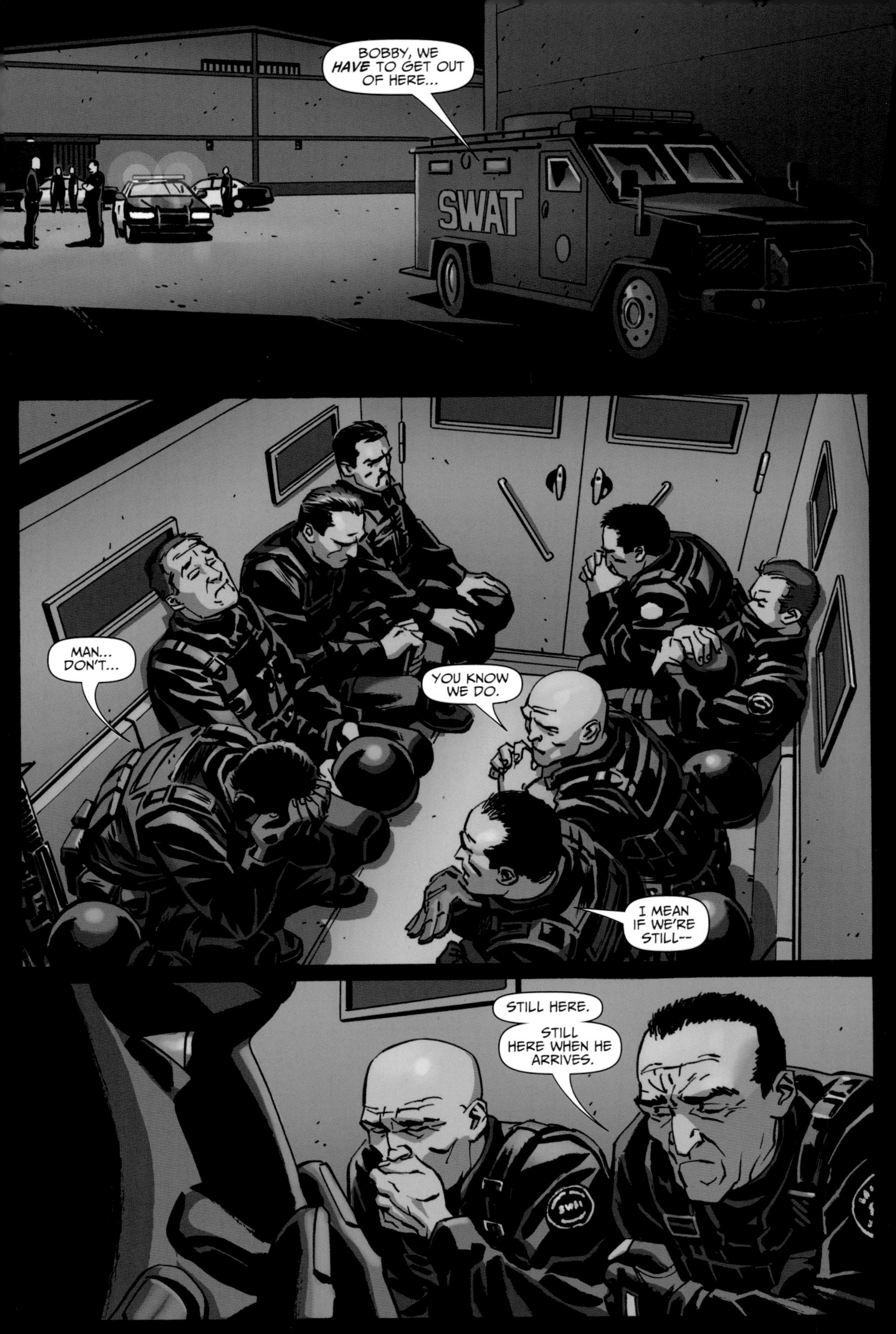
BOBBY, WE *HAVE* TO GET OUT OF HERE...
MAN... DON'T...
YOU KNOW WE DO.
I MEAN IF WE'RE STILL--
STILL HERE.
STILL HERE WHEN HE ARRIVES.
SWAT

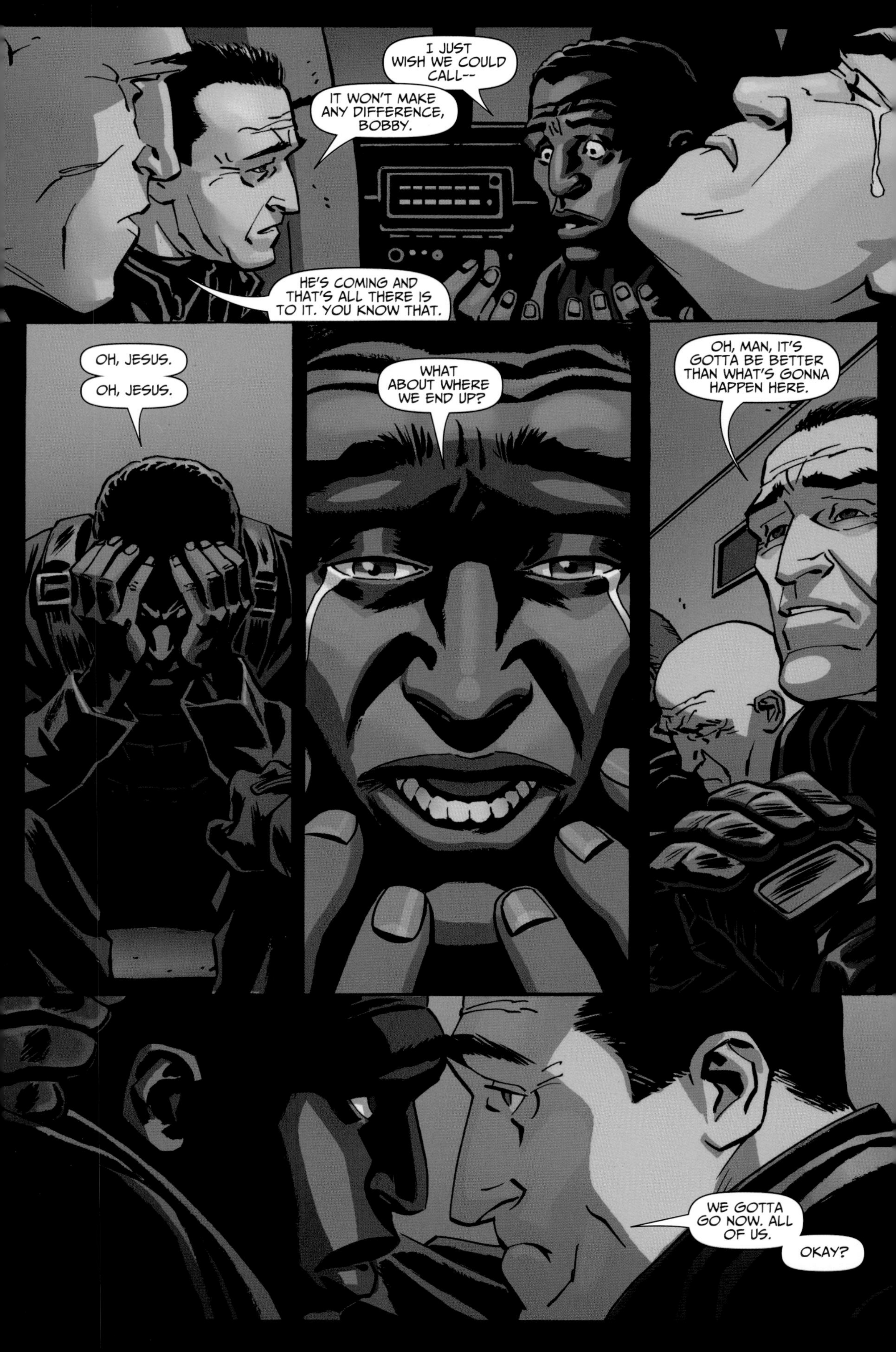
I JUST WISH WE COULD CALL--
IT WON'T MAKE ANY DIFFERENCE, BOBBY.
HE'S COMING AND THAT'S ALL THERE IS TO IT. YOU KNOW THAT.
OH, JESUS.
OH, JESUS.
WHAT ABOUT WHERE WE END UP?
OH, MAN, IT'S GOTTA BE BETTER THAN WHAT'S GONNA HAPPEN HERE.
WE GOTTA GO NOW. ALL OF US.
OKAY?

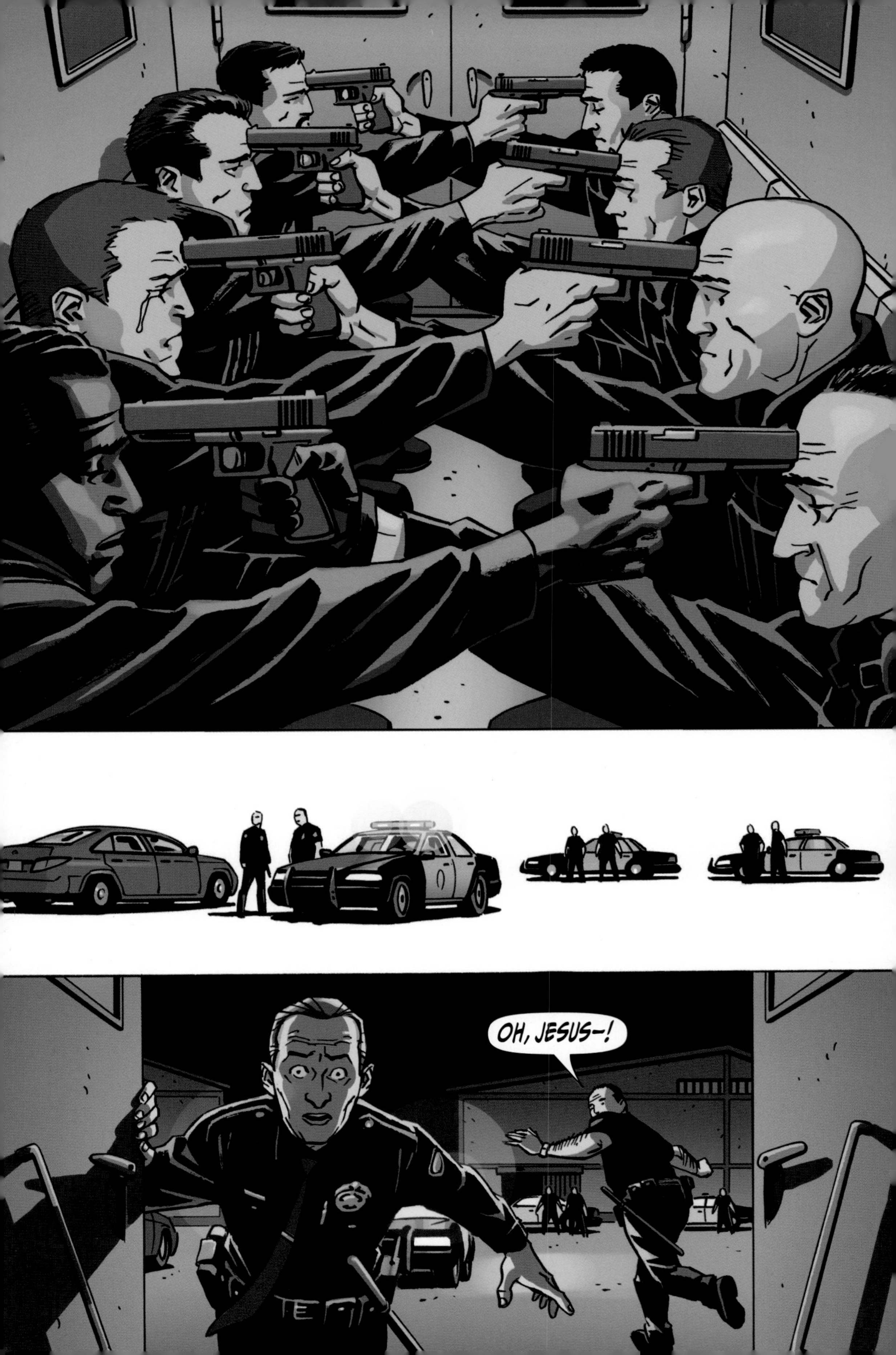
OH, JESUS--!

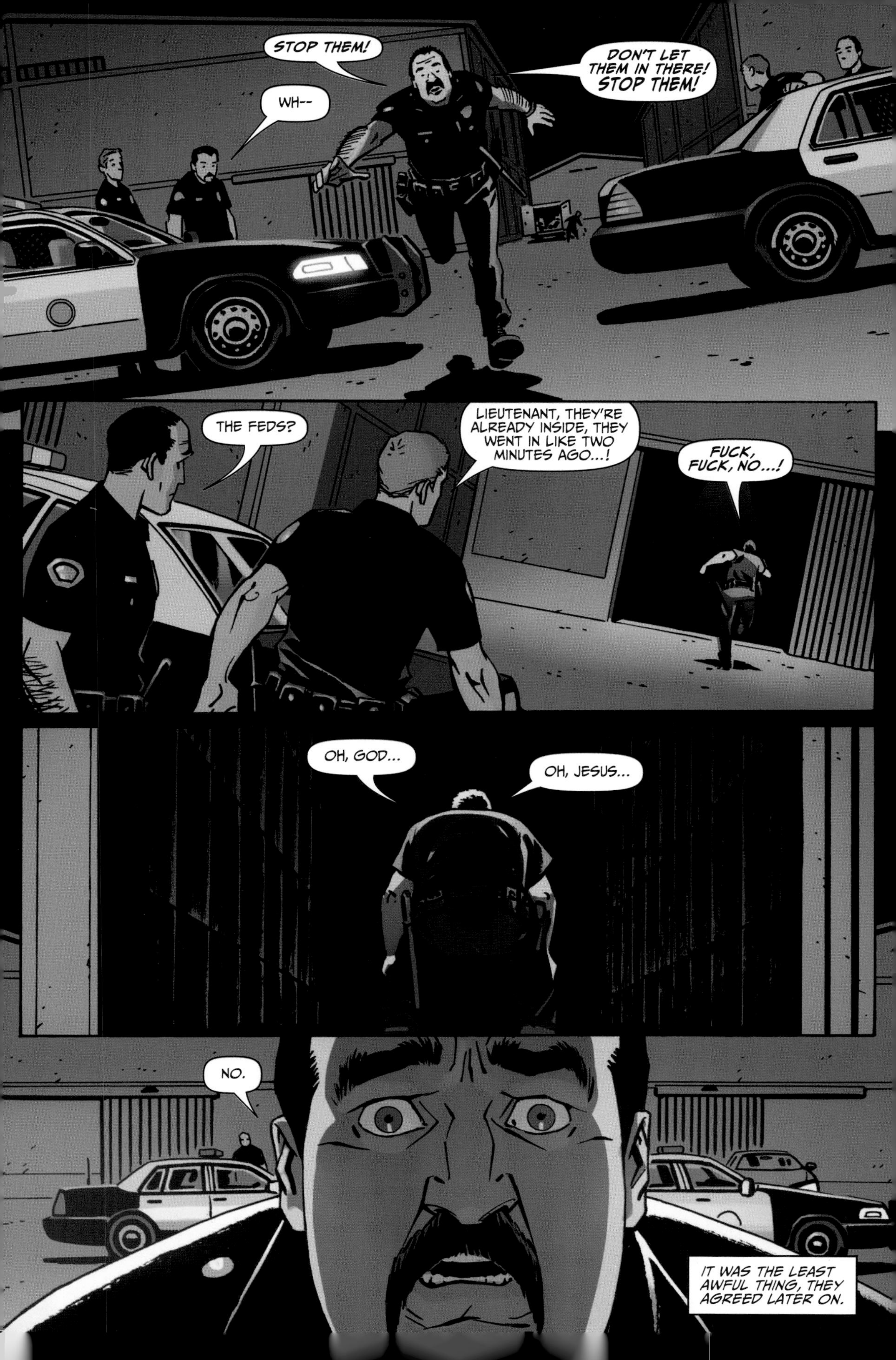
STOP THEM!
WH--
DON'T LET THEM IN THERE! STOP THEM!
THE FEDS?
LIEUTENANT, THEY'RE ALREADY INSIDE, THEY WENT IN LIKE TWO MINUTES AGO...!
FUCK, FUCK, NO...!
OH, GOD...
OH, JESUS...
NO.
IT WAS THE LEAST AWFUL THING, THEY AGREED LATER ON.

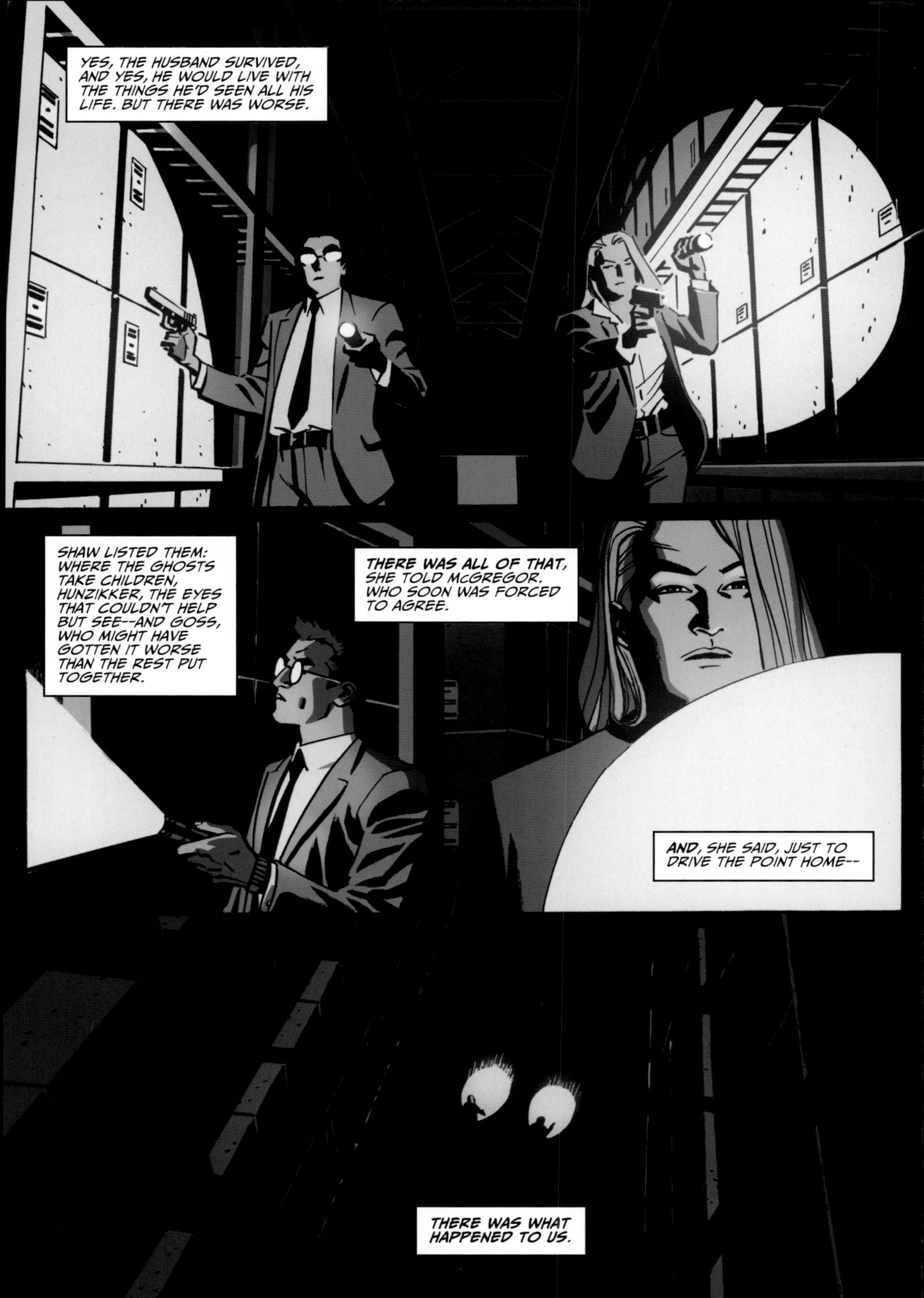
YES, THE HUSBAND SURVIVED, AND YES, HE WOULD LIVE WITH THE THINGS HE'D SEEN ALL HIS LIFE. BUT THERE WAS WORSE.
SHAW LISTED THEM: WHERE THE GHOSTS TAKE CHILDREN, HUNZIKKER, THE EYES THAT COULDN'T HELP BUT SEE--AND GOSS, WHO MIGHT HAVE GOTTEN IT WORSE THAN THE REST PUT TOGETHER.
THERE WAS ALL OF THAT, SHE TOLD McGREGOR. WHO SOON WAS FORCED TO AGREE.
AND, SHE SAID, JUST TO DRIVE THE POINT HOME--
THERE WAS WHAT HAPPENED TO US.

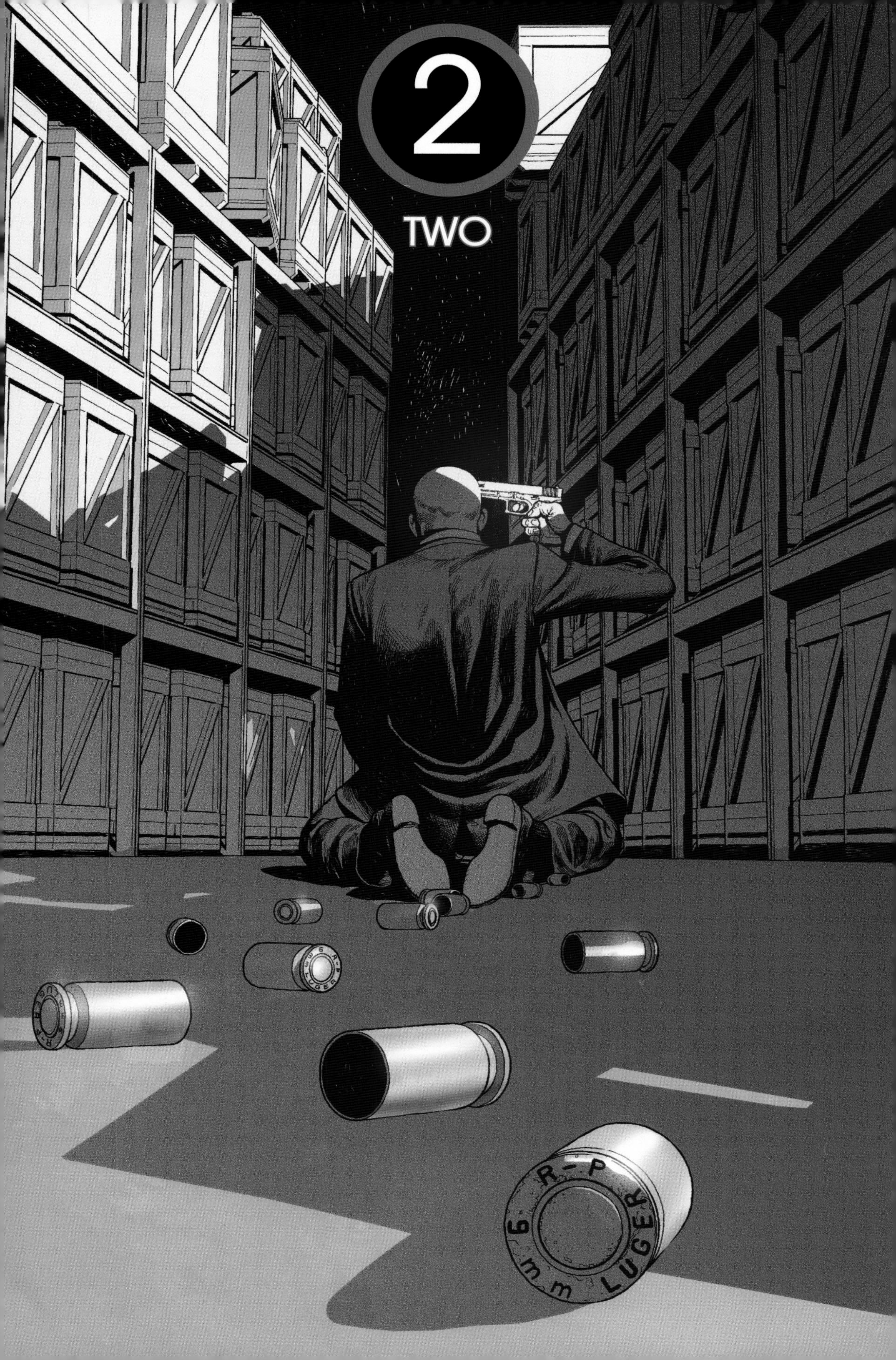
2
TWO
R-P
9 mm LUGER

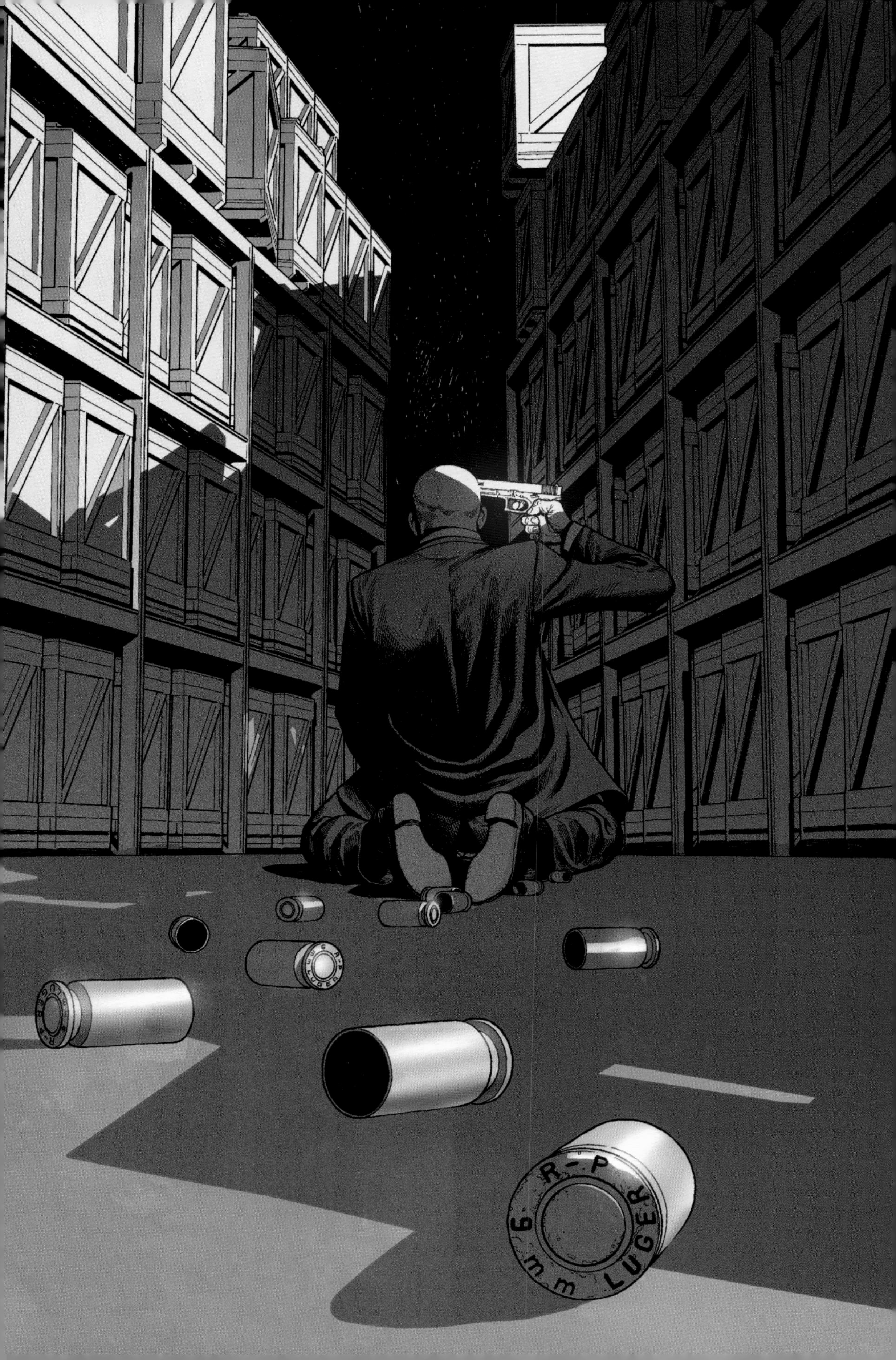
R-P
9mm LUGER

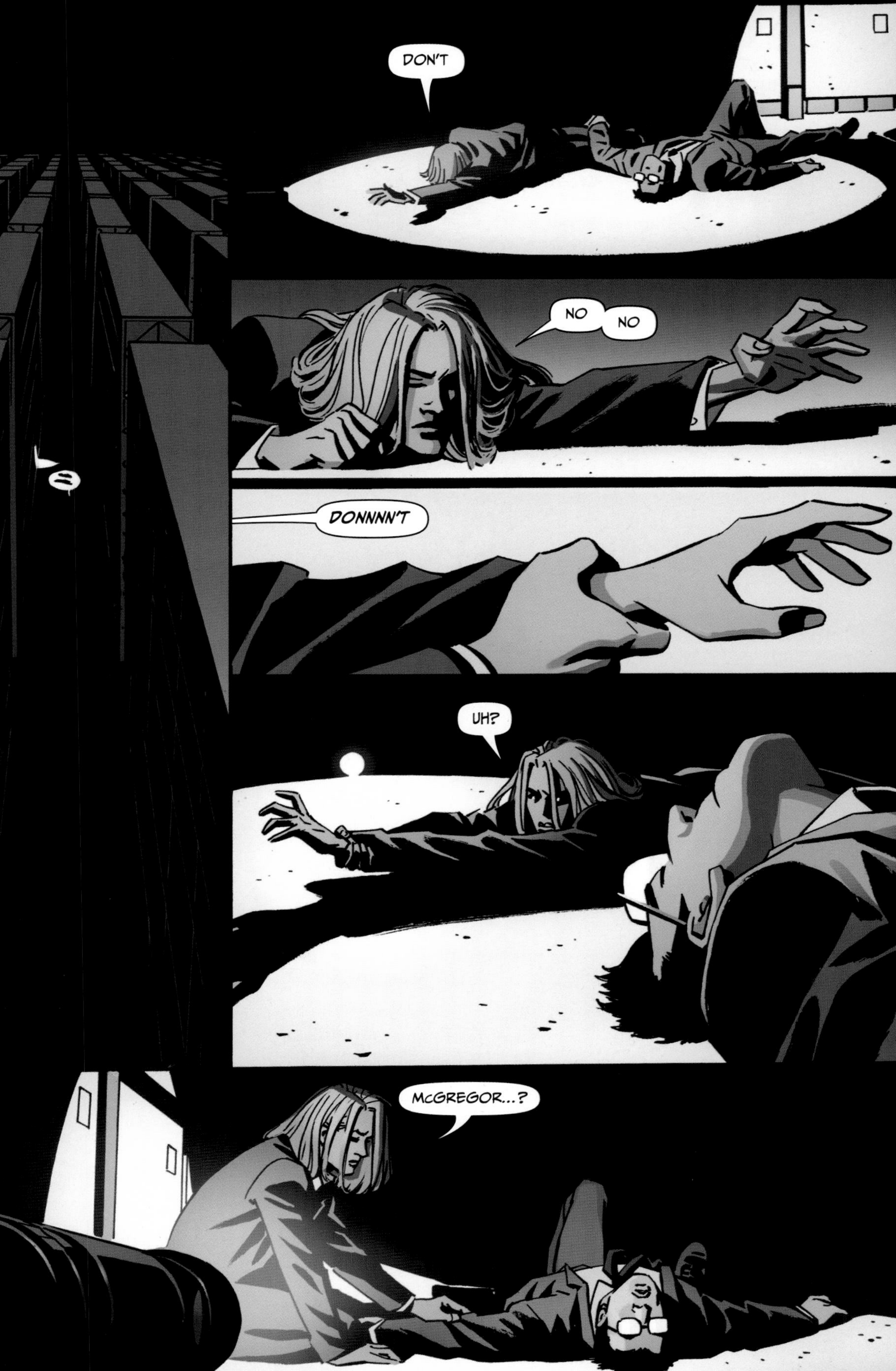
DON'T
NO
NO
DONNNN'T
UH?
McGREGOR...?

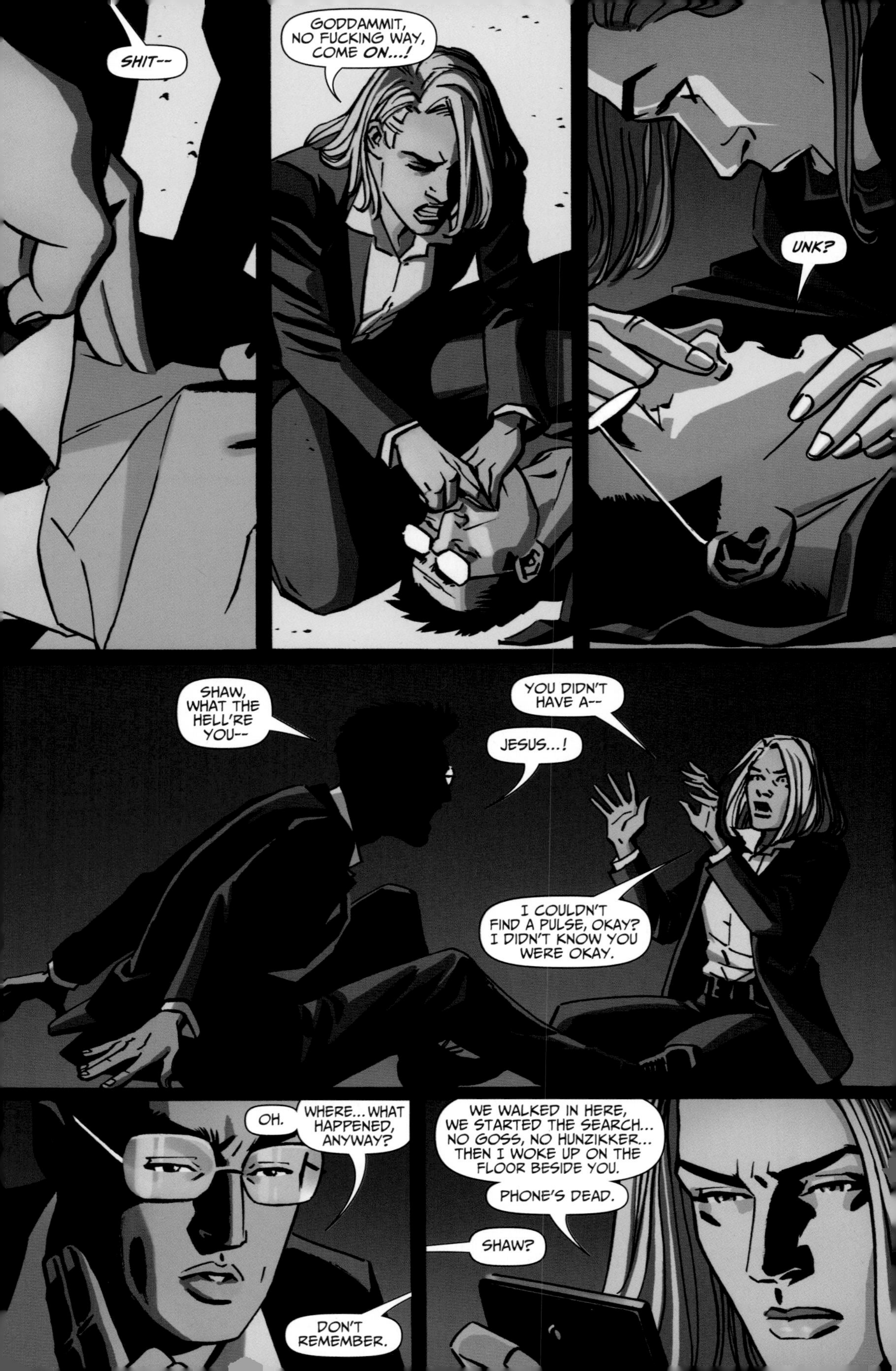
SHIT--
GODDAMMIT, NO FUCKING WAY, COME ON...!
UNK?
SHAW, WHAT THE HELL'RE YOU--
YOU DIDN'T HAVE A--
JESUS...!
I COULDN'T FIND A PULSE, OKAY? I DIDN'T KNOW YOU WERE OKAY.
OH.
WHERE...WHAT HAPPENED, ANYWAY?
DON'T REMEMBER.
WE WALKED IN HERE, WE STARTED THE SEARCH... NO GOSS, NO HUNZIKKER... THEN I WOKE UP ON THE FLOOR BESIDE YOU.
PHONE'S DEAD.
SHAW?

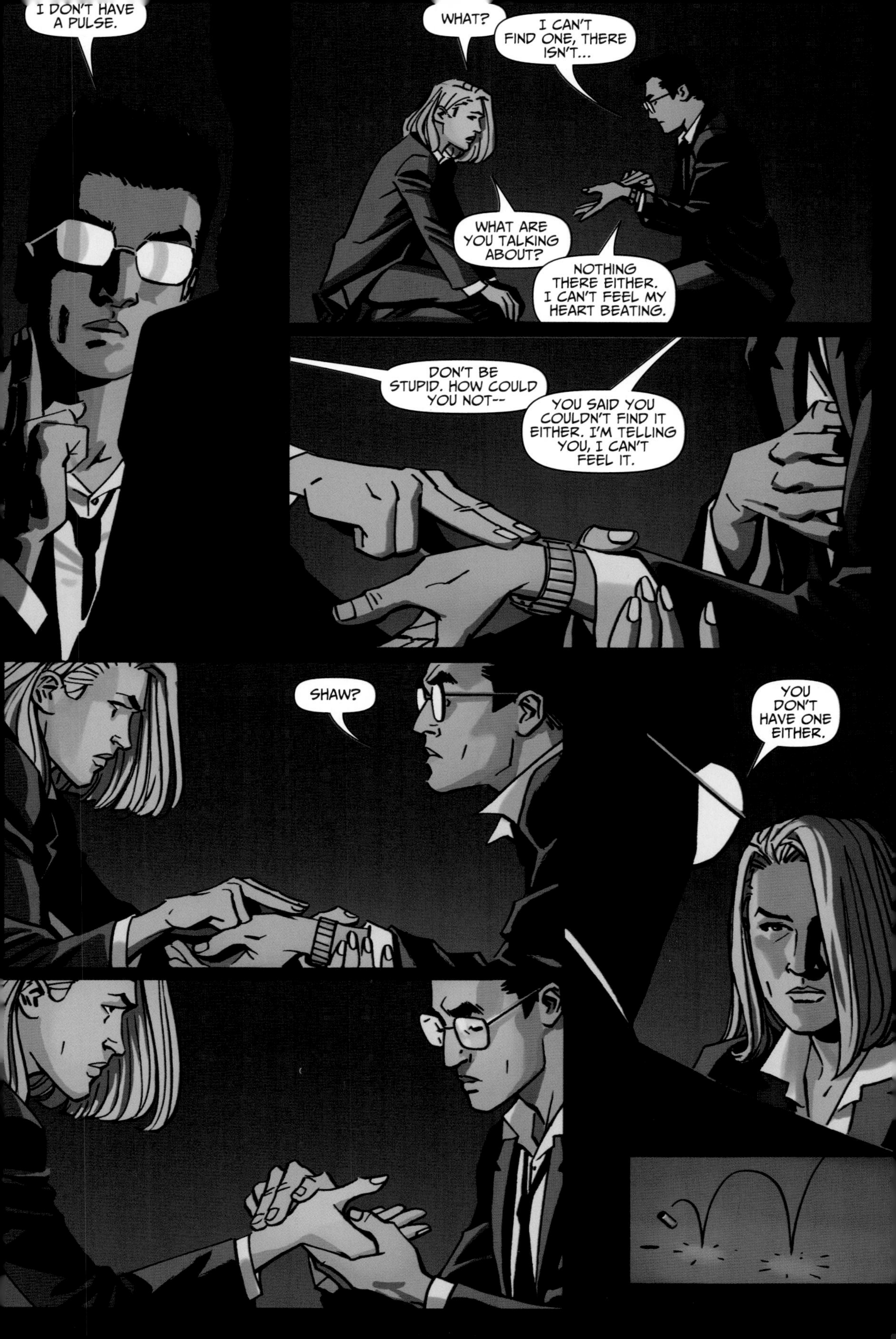
I DON'T HAVE A PULSE.
WHAT?
I CAN'T FIND ONE, THERE ISN'T...
WHAT ARE YOU TALKING ABOUT?
NOTHING THERE EITHER. I CAN'T FEEL MY HEART BEATING.
DON'T BE STUPID. HOW COULD YOU NOT--
YOU SAID YOU COULDN'T FIND IT EITHER. I'M TELLING YOU, I CAN'T FEEL IT.
SHAW?
YOU DON'T HAVE ONE EITHER.

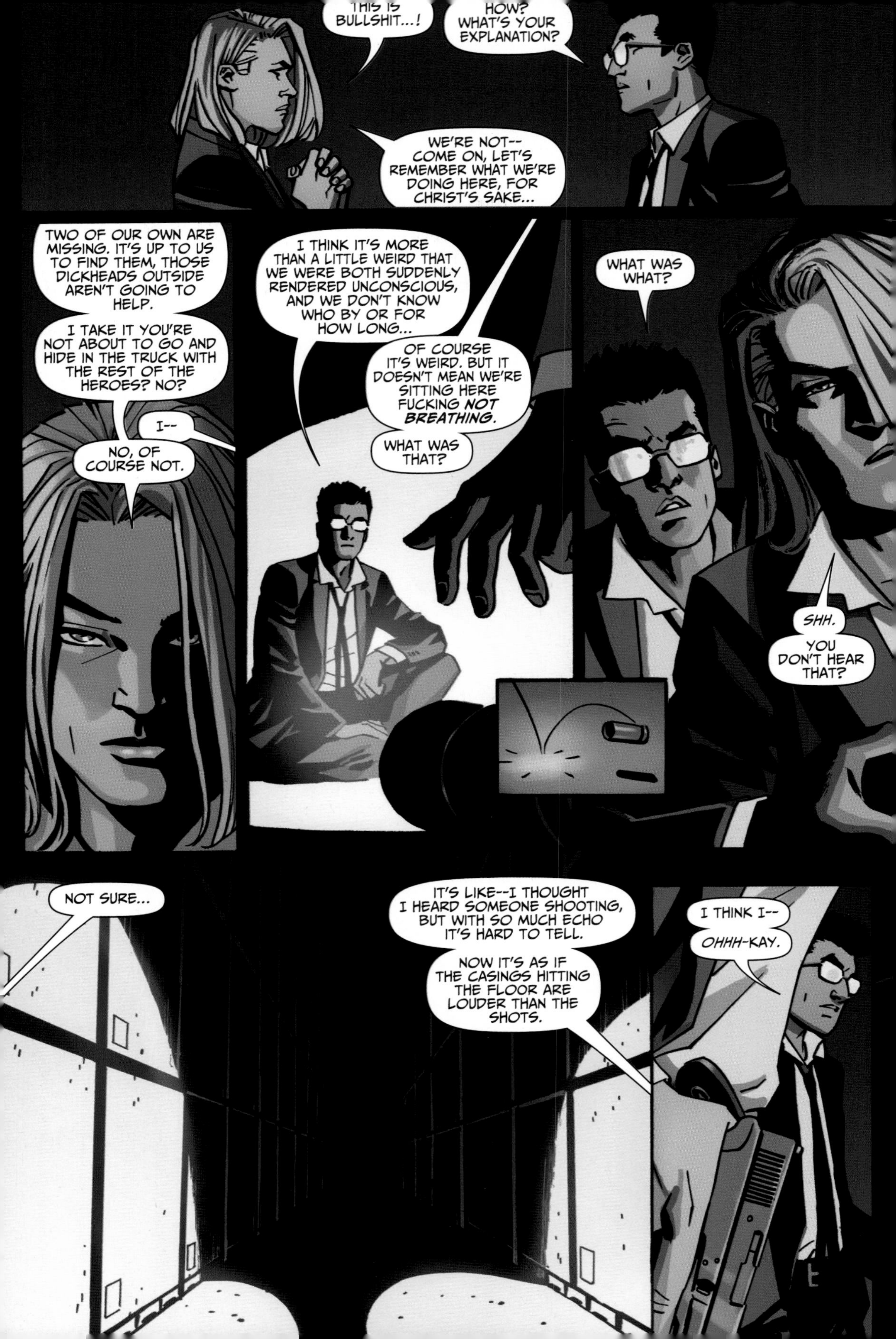
THIS IS BULLSHIT...!
HOW? WHAT'S YOUR EXPLANATION?
WE'RE NOT-- COME ON, LET'S REMEMBER WHAT WE'RE DOING HERE, FOR CHRIST'S SAKE...
TWO OF OUR OWN ARE MISSING. IT'S UP TO US TO FIND THEM, THOSE DICKHEADS OUTSIDE AREN'T GOING TO HELP.
I TAKE IT YOU'RE NOT ABOUT TO GO AND HIDE IN THE TRUCK WITH THE REST OF THE HEROES? NO?
I--
NO, OF COURSE NOT.
I THINK IT'S MORE THAN A LITTLE WEIRD THAT WE WERE BOTH SUDDENLY RENDERED UNCONSCIOUS, AND WE DON'T KNOW WHO BY OR FOR HOW LONG...
OF COURSE IT'S WEIRD. BUT IT DOESN'T MEAN WE'RE SITTING HERE FUCKING NOT BREATHING.
WHAT WAS THAT?
WHAT WAS WHAT?
SHH.
YOU DON'T HEAR THAT?
NOT SURE...
IT'S LIKE--I THOUGHT I HEARD SOMEONE SHOOTING, BUT WITH SO MUCH ECHO IT'S HARD TO TELL.
NOW IT'S AS IF THE CASINGS HITTING THE FLOOR ARE LOUDER THAN THE SHOTS.
I THINK I--
OHHH-KAY.

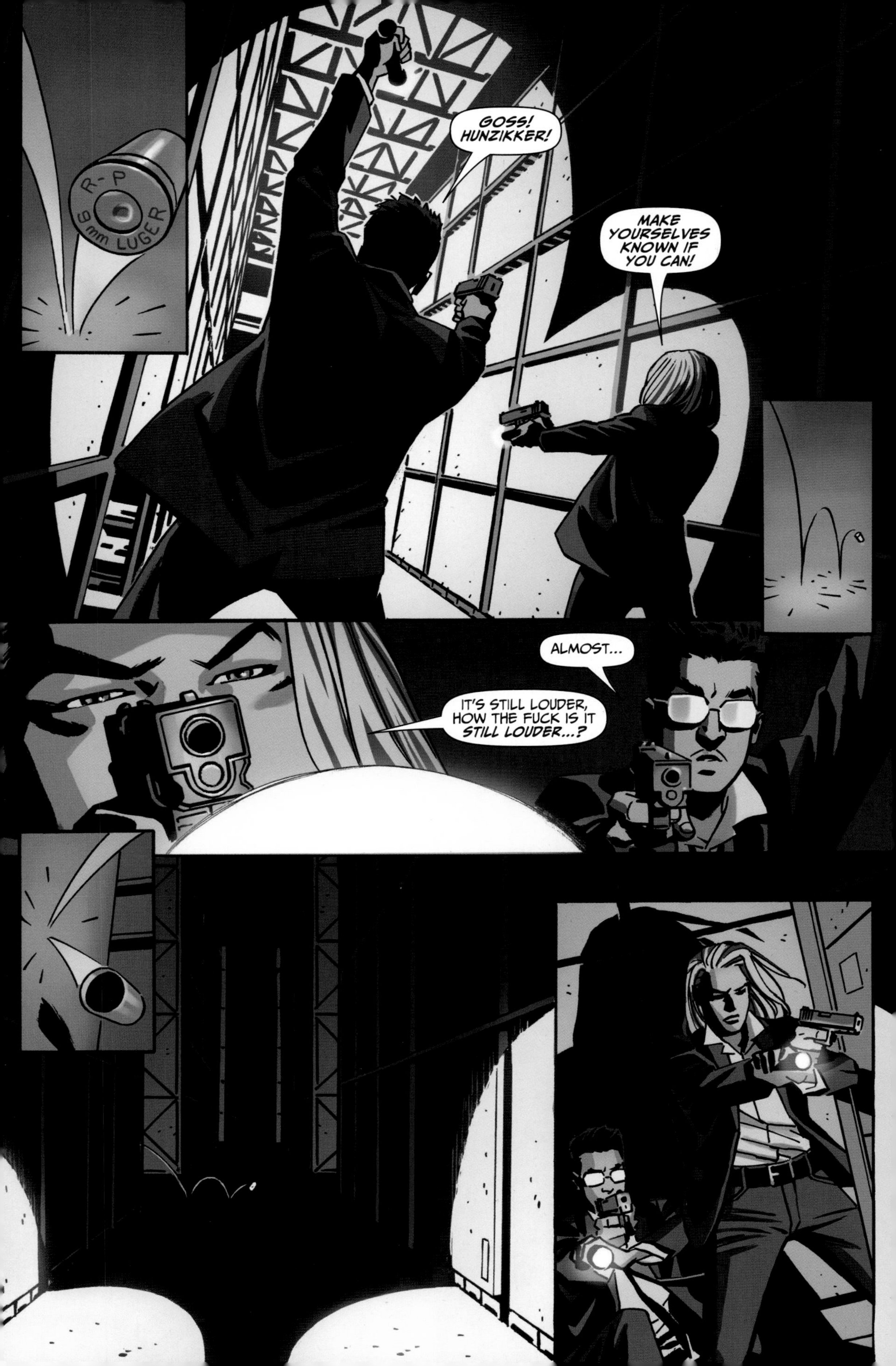
R-P
9 mm LUGER
GOSS! HUNZIKKER!
MAKE YOURSELVES KNOWN IF YOU CAN!
ALMOST...
IT'S STILL LOUDER, HOW THE FUCK IS IT STILL LOUDER...?

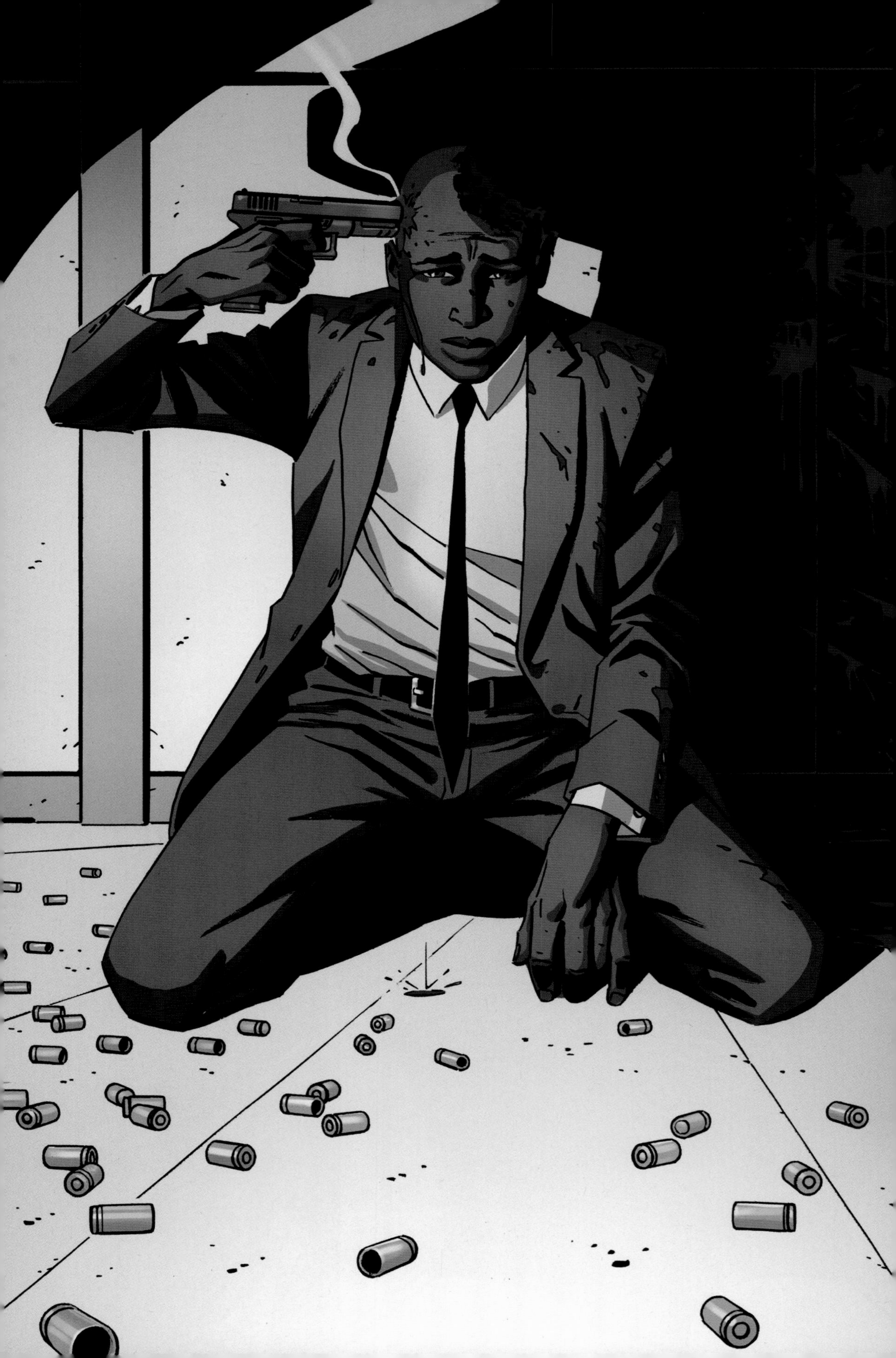

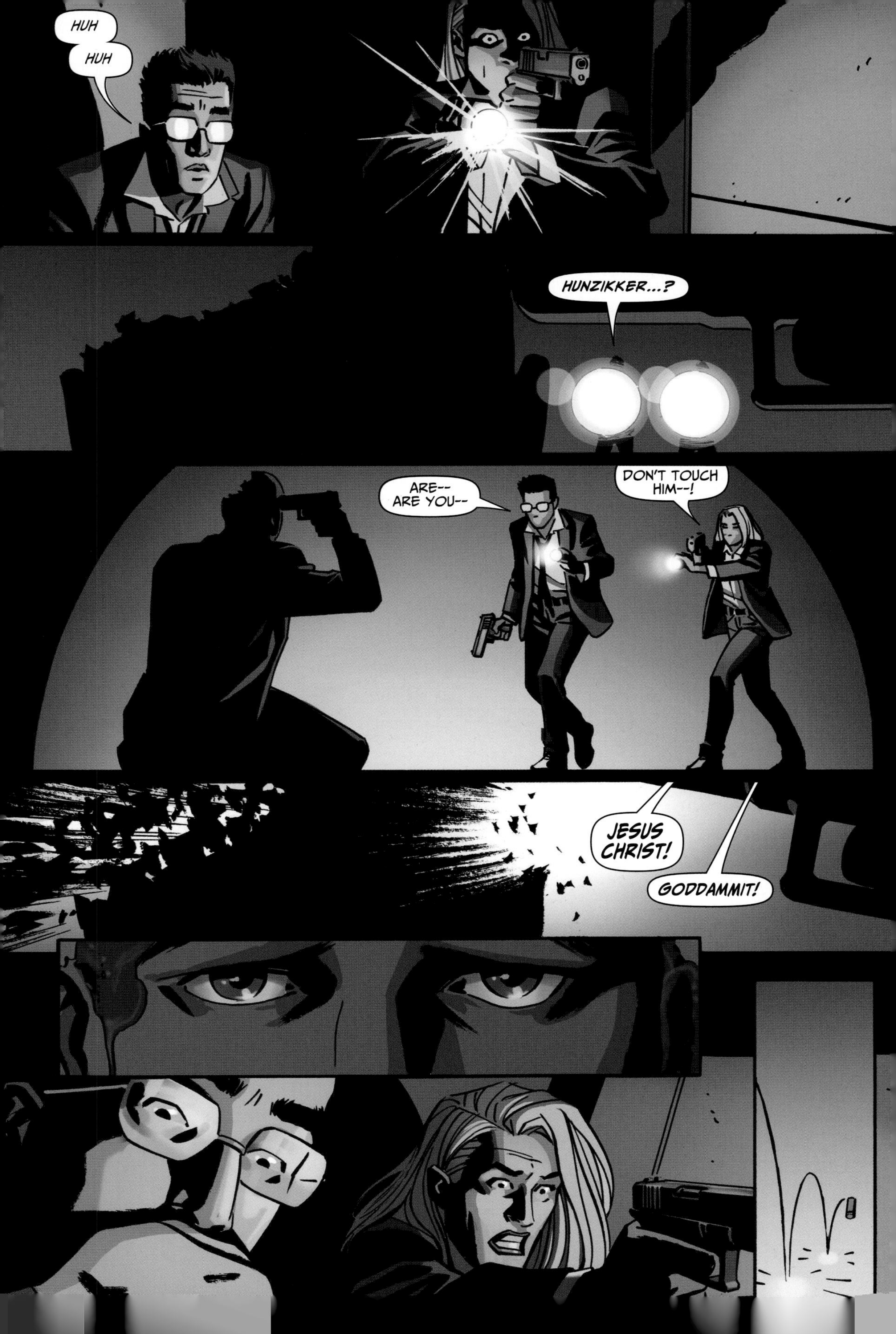
HUH
HUH
HUNZIKKER...?
ARE--
ARE YOU--
DON'T TOUCH HIM--!
JESUS CHRIST!
GODDAMMIT!

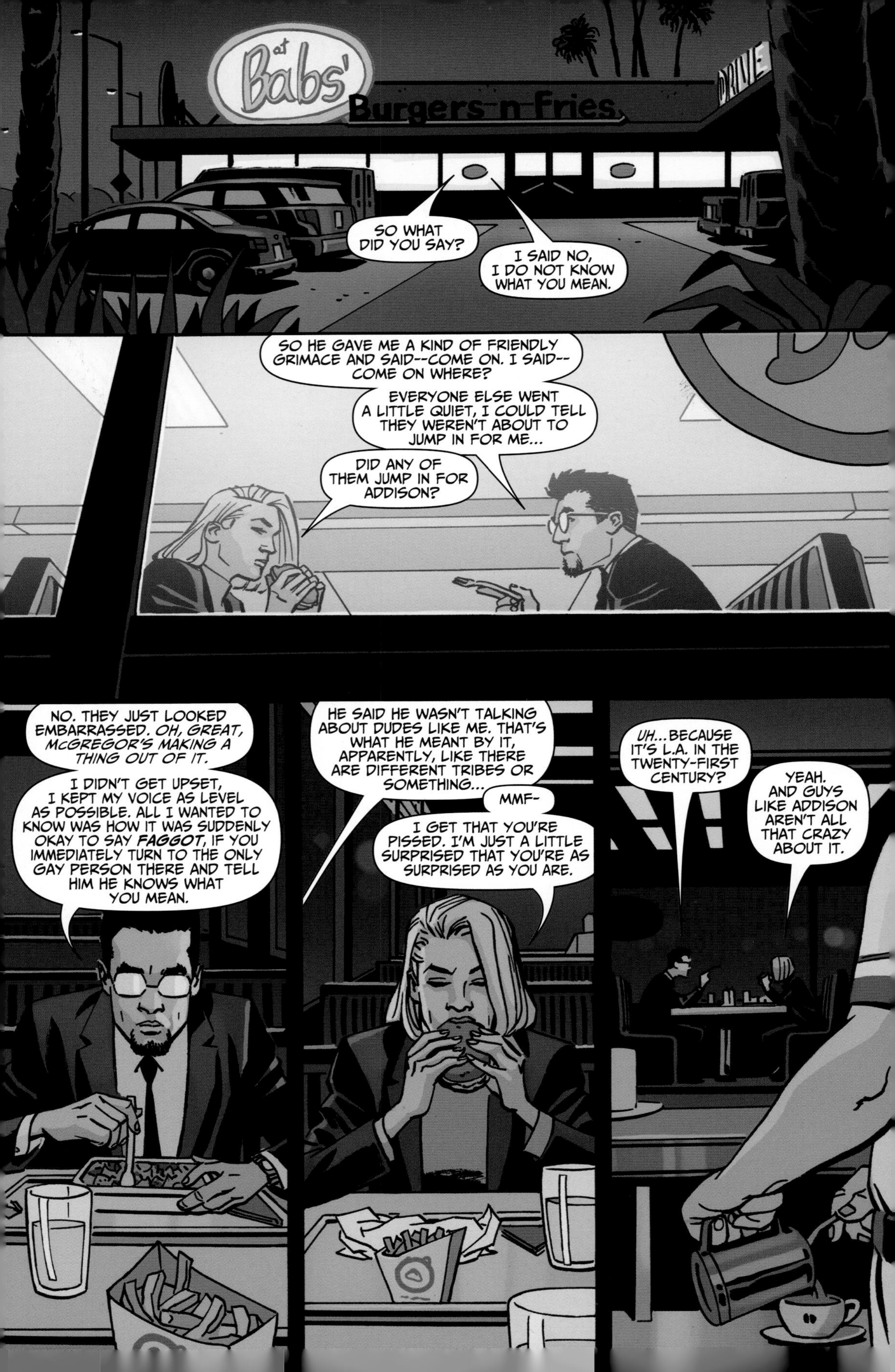
at Babs'
Burgers-n-Fries
DRIVE
SO WHAT DID YOU SAY?
I SAID NO, I DO NOT KNOW WHAT YOU MEAN.
SO HE GAVE ME A KIND OF FRIENDLY GRIMACE AND SAID--COME ON. I SAID--COME ON WHERE?
EVERYONE ELSE WENT A LITTLE QUIET, I COULD TELL THEY WEREN'T ABOUT TO JUMP IN FOR ME...
DID ANY OF THEM JUMP IN FOR ADDISON?
NO. THEY JUST LOOKED EMBARRASSED. *OH, GREAT, McGREGOR'S MAKING A THING OUT OF IT.*
I DIDN'T GET UPSET, I KEPT MY VOICE AS LEVEL AS POSSIBLE. ALL I WANTED TO KNOW WAS HOW IT WAS SUDDENLY OKAY TO SAY ***FAGGOT***, IF YOU IMMEDIATELY TURN TO THE ONLY GAY PERSON THERE AND TELL HIM HE KNOWS WHAT YOU MEAN.
HE SAID HE WASN'T TALKING ABOUT DUDES LIKE ME. THAT'S WHAT HE MEANT BY IT, APPARENTLY, LIKE THERE ARE DIFFERENT TRIBES OR SOMETHING...
MMF-
I GET THAT YOU'RE PISSED. I'M JUST A LITTLE SURPRISED THAT YOU'RE AS SURPRISED AS YOU ARE.
UH...BECAUSE IT'S L.A. IN THE TWENTY-FIRST CENTURY?
YEAH. AND GUYS LIKE ADDISON AREN'T ALL THAT CRAZY ABOUT IT.

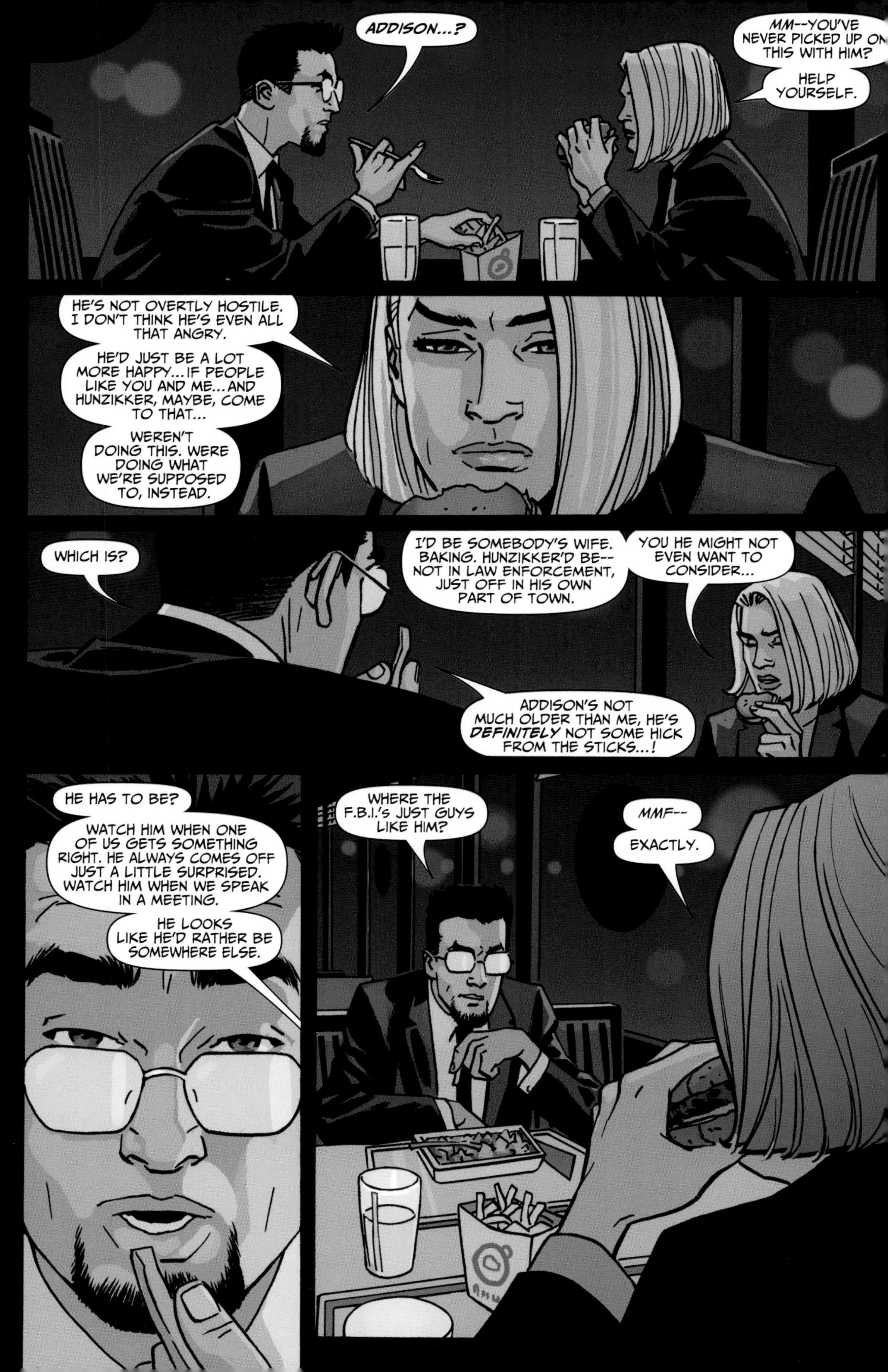
ADDISON...?
MM--YOU'VE NEVER PICKED UP ON THIS WITH HIM?
HELP YOURSELF.
HE'S NOT OVERTLY HOSTILE. I DON'T THINK HE'S EVEN ALL THAT ANGRY.
HE'D JUST BE A LOT MORE HAPPY...IF PEOPLE LIKE YOU AND ME...AND HUNZIKKER, MAYBE, COME TO THAT...
WEREN'T DOING THIS. WERE DOING WHAT WE'RE SUPPOSED TO, INSTEAD.
WHICH IS?
I'D BE SOMEBODY'S WIFE. BAKING. HUNZIKKER'D BE--NOT IN LAW ENFORCEMENT, JUST OFF IN HIS OWN PART OF TOWN.
YOU HE MIGHT NOT EVEN WANT TO CONSIDER...
ADDISON'S NOT MUCH OLDER THAN ME, HE'S *DEFINITELY* NOT SOME HICK FROM THE STICKS...!
HE HAS TO BE?
WATCH HIM WHEN ONE OF US GETS SOMETHING RIGHT. HE ALWAYS COMES OFF JUST A LITTLE SURPRISED. WATCH HIM WHEN WE SPEAK IN A MEETING.
HE LOOKS LIKE HE'D RATHER BE SOMEWHERE ELSE.
WHERE THE F.B.I.'S JUST GUYS LIKE HIM?
MMF--
EXACTLY.

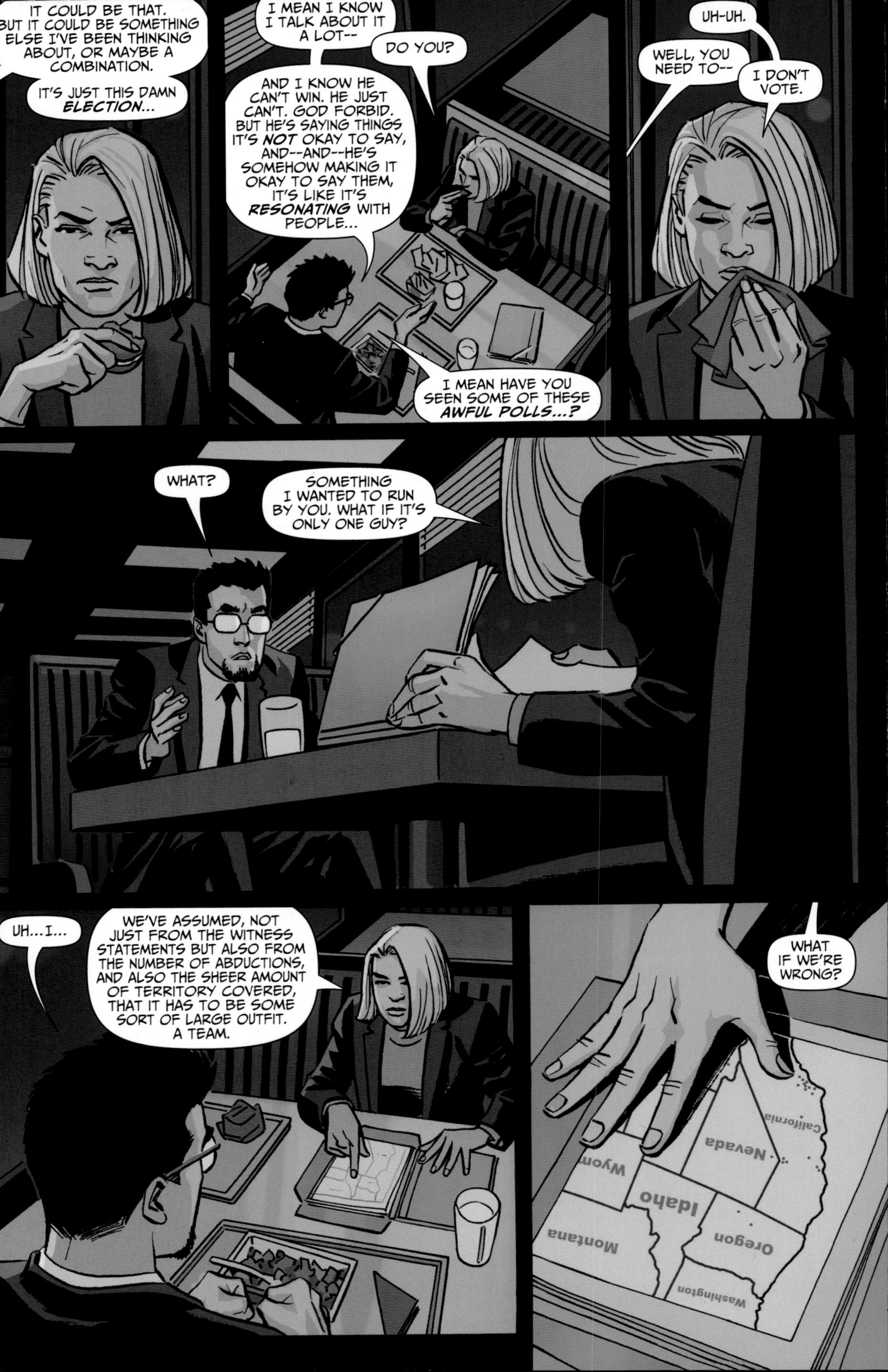
IT COULD BE THAT. BUT IT COULD BE SOMETHING ELSE I'VE BEEN THINKING ABOUT, OR MAYBE A COMBINATION.
IT'S JUST THIS DAMN ELECTION...
I MEAN I KNOW I TALK ABOUT IT A LOT--
DO YOU?
AND I KNOW HE CAN'T WIN. HE JUST CAN'T. GOD FORBID. BUT HE'S SAYING THINGS IT'S NOT OKAY TO SAY, AND--AND--HE'S SOMEHOW MAKING IT OKAY TO SAY THEM, IT'S LIKE IT'S RESONATING WITH PEOPLE...
I MEAN HAVE YOU SEEN SOME OF THESE AWFUL POLLS...?
UH-UH.
WELL, YOU NEED TO--
I DON'T VOTE.
WHAT?
SOMETHING I WANTED TO RUN BY YOU. WHAT IF IT'S ONLY ONE GUY?
UH...I...
WE'VE ASSUMED, NOT JUST FROM THE WITNESS STATEMENTS BUT ALSO FROM THE NUMBER OF ABDUCTIONS, AND ALSO THE SHEER AMOUNT OF TERRITORY COVERED, THAT IT HAS TO BE SOME SORT OF LARGE OUTFIT. A TEAM.
WHAT IF WE'RE WRONG?
California
Nevada
Wyom
Idaho
Montana
Oregon
Washington

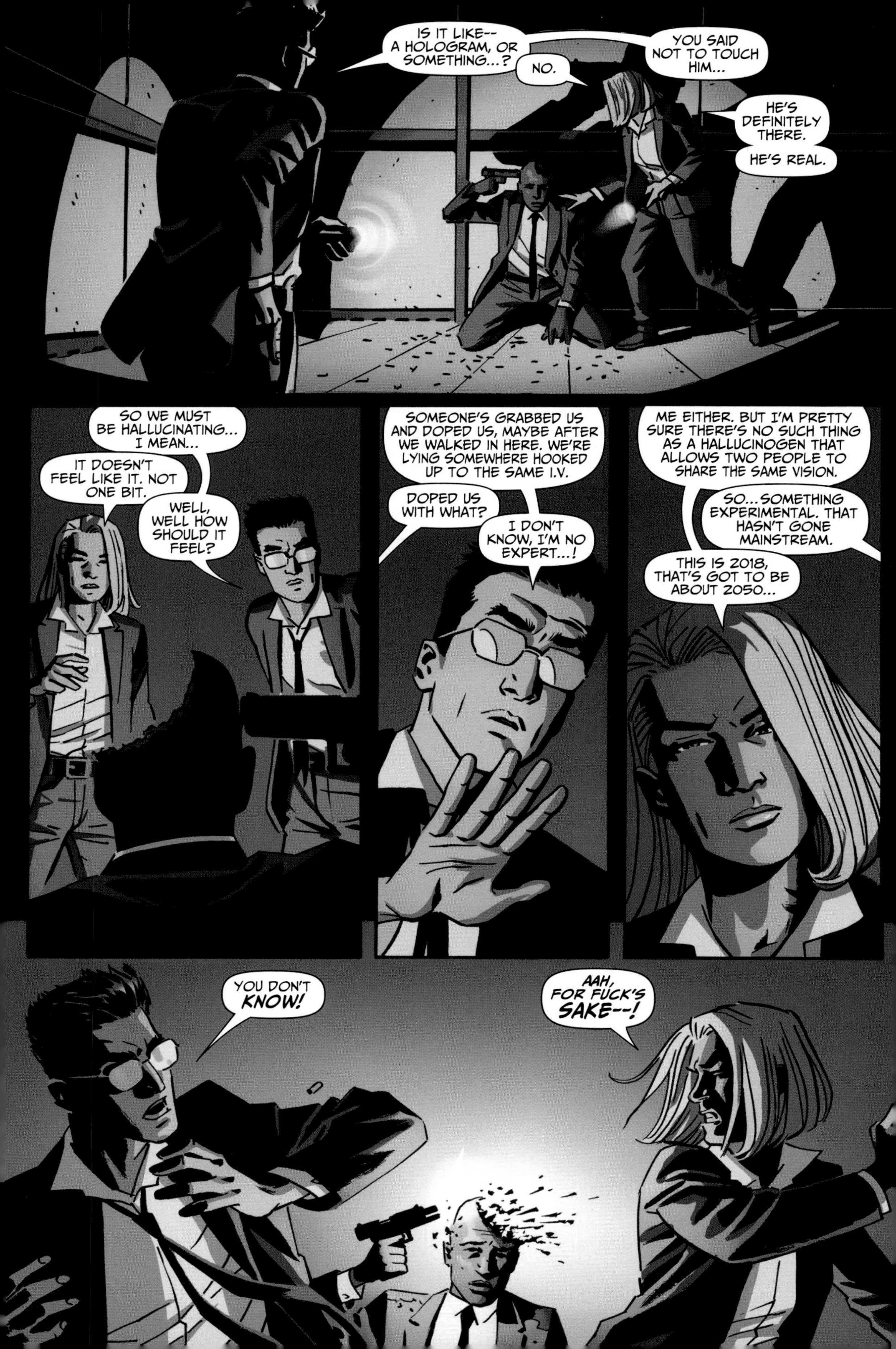
IS IT LIKE-- A HOLOGRAM, OR SOMETHING...?
NO.
YOU SAID NOT TO TOUCH HIM...
HE'S DEFINITELY THERE.
HE'S REAL.
SO WE MUST BE HALLUCINATING... I MEAN...
IT DOESN'T FEEL LIKE IT. NOT ONE BIT.
WELL, WELL HOW SHOULD IT FEEL?
SOMEONE'S GRABBED US AND DOPED US, MAYBE AFTER WE WALKED IN HERE. WE'RE LYING SOMEWHERE HOOKED UP TO THE SAME I.V.
DOPED US WITH WHAT?
I DON'T KNOW, I'M NO EXPERT...!
ME EITHER. BUT I'M PRETTY SURE THERE'S NO SUCH THING AS A HALLUCINOGEN THAT ALLOWS TWO PEOPLE TO SHARE THE SAME VISION.
SO...SOMETHING EXPERIMENTAL. THAT HASN'T GONE MAINSTREAM.
THIS IS 2018, THAT'S GOT TO BE ABOUT 2050...
YOU DON'T KNOW!
AAH, FOR FUCK'S SAKE--!

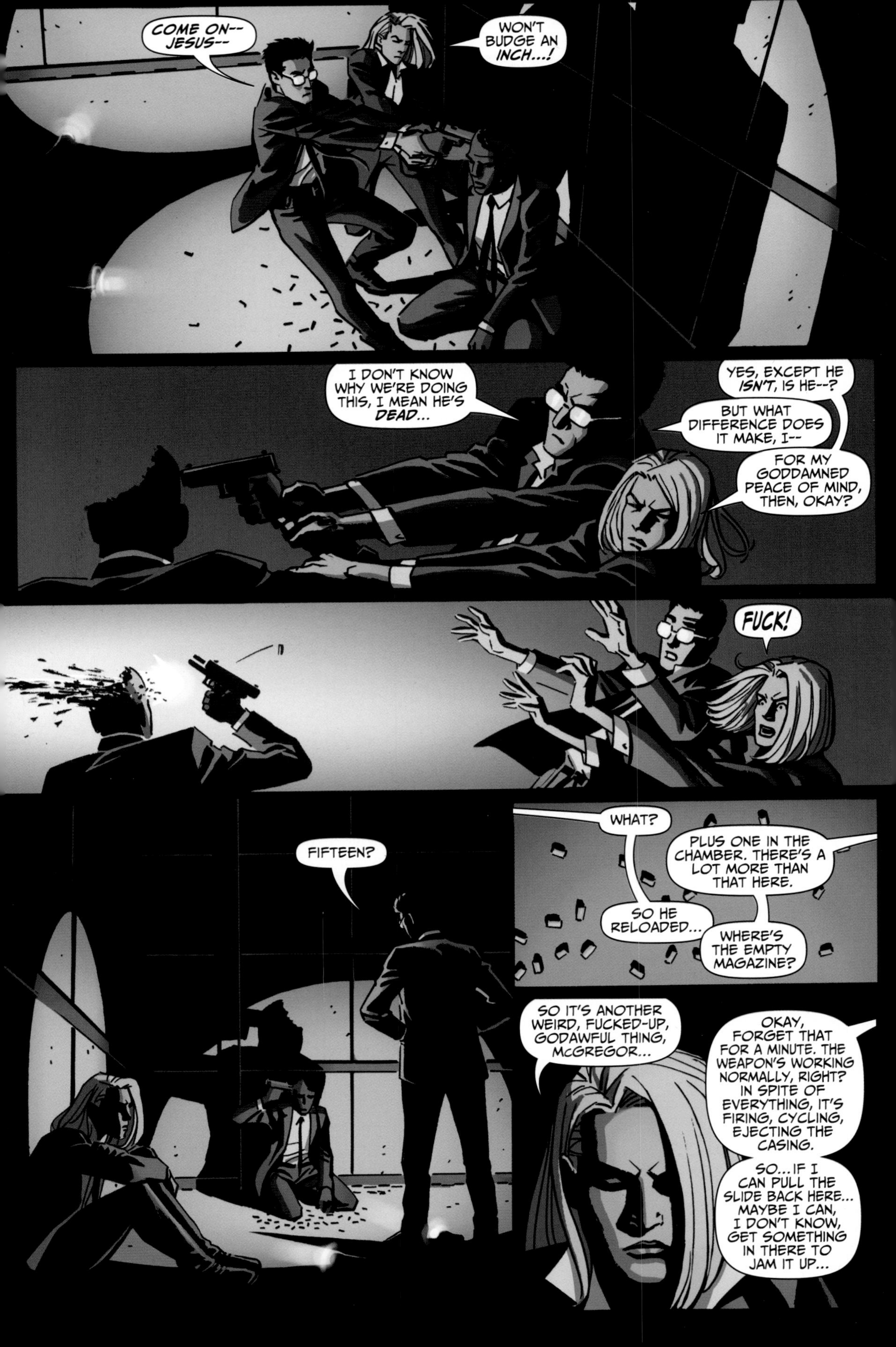
COME ON-- JESUS--
WON'T BUDGE AN *INCH*...!
I DON'T KNOW WHY WE'RE DOING THIS, I MEAN HE'S *DEAD*...
YES, EXCEPT HE *ISN'T*, IS HE--?
BUT WHAT DIFFERENCE DOES IT MAKE, I--
FOR MY GODDAMNED PEACE OF MIND, THEN, OKAY?
FUCK!
FIFTEEN?
WHAT?
PLUS ONE IN THE CHAMBER. THERE'S A LOT MORE THAN THAT HERE.
SO HE RELOADED...
WHERE'S THE EMPTY MAGAZINE?
SO IT'S ANOTHER WEIRD, FUCKED-UP, GODAWFUL THING, McGREGOR...
OKAY, FORGET THAT FOR A MINUTE. THE WEAPON'S WORKING NORMALLY, RIGHT? IN SPITE OF EVERYTHING, IT'S FIRING, CYCLING, EJECTING THE CASING.
SO...IF I CAN PULL THE SLIDE BACK HERE... MAYBE I CAN, I DON'T KNOW, GET SOMETHING IN THERE TO JAM IT UP...

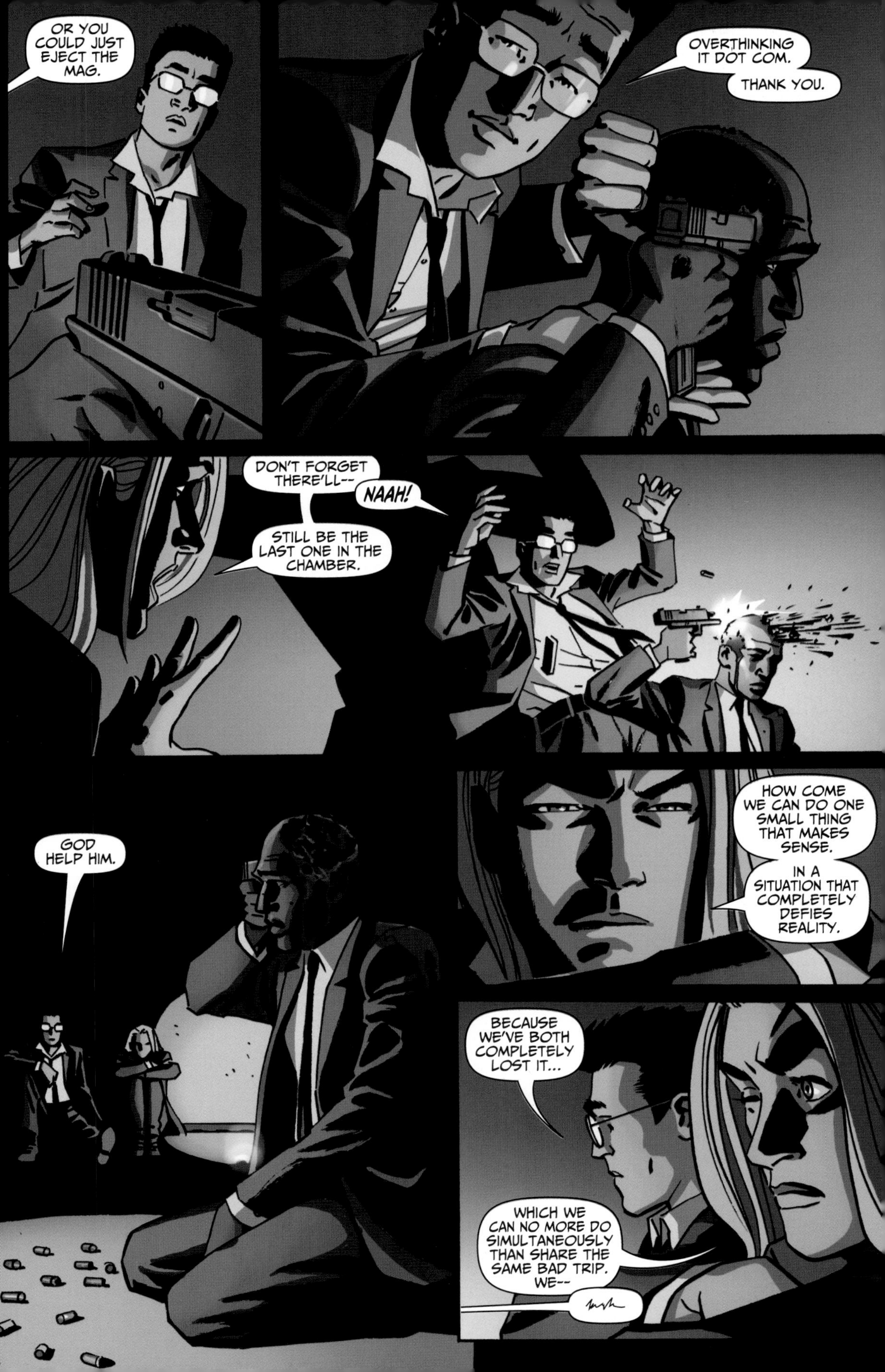
OR YOU COULD JUST EJECT THE MAG.
OVERTHINKING IT DOT COM.
THANK YOU.
DON'T FORGET THERE'LL--
NAAH!
STILL BE THE LAST ONE IN THE CHAMBER.
HOW COME WE CAN DO ONE SMALL THING THAT MAKES SENSE.
IN A SITUATION THAT COMPLETELY DEFIES REALITY.
GOD HELP HIM.
BECAUSE WE'VE BOTH COMPLETELY LOST IT...
WHICH WE CAN NO MORE DO SIMULTANEOUSLY THAN SHARE THE SAME BAD TRIP. WE--

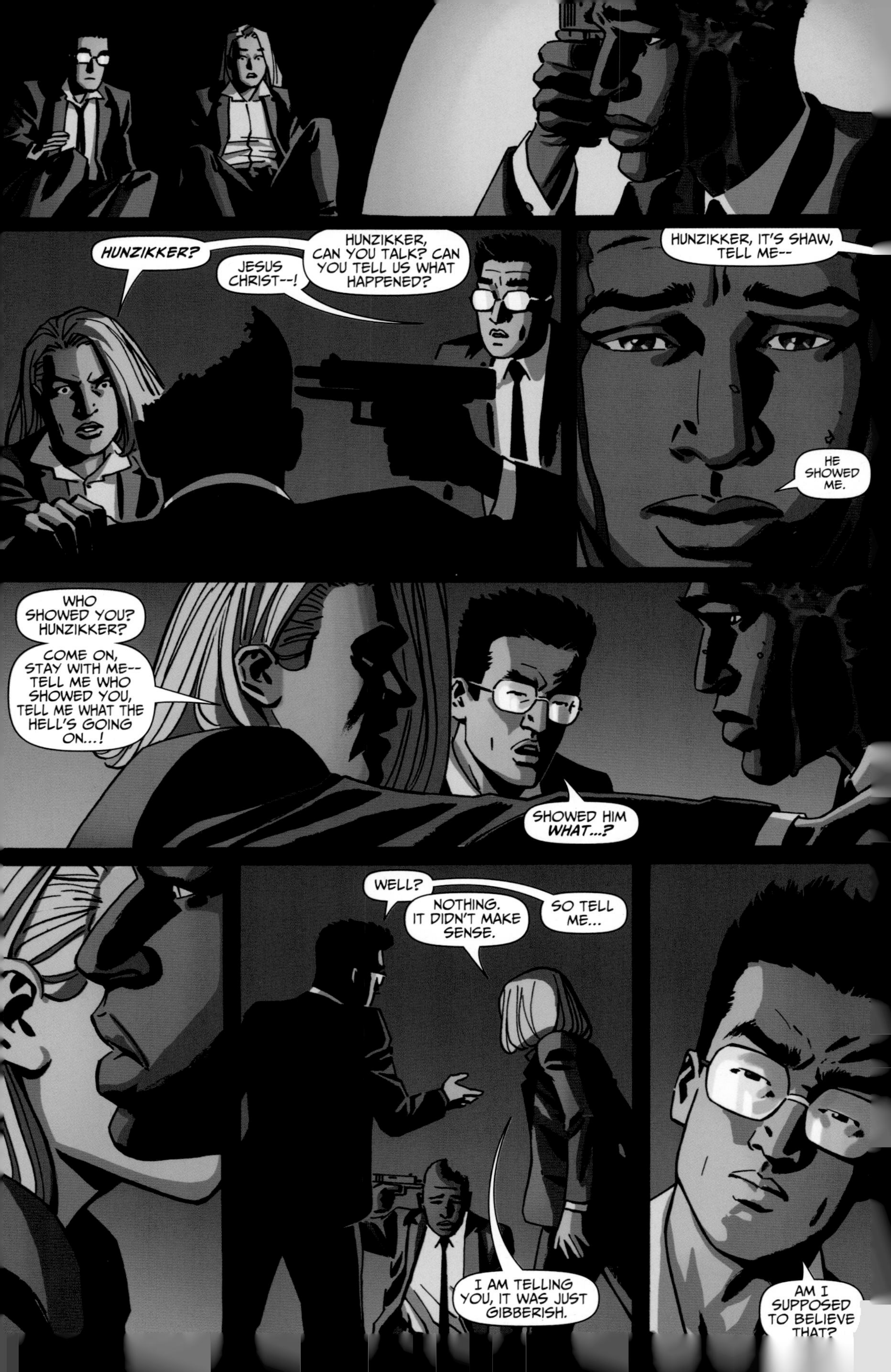
HUNZIKKER?
JESUS CHRIST--!
HUNZIKKER, CAN YOU TALK? CAN YOU TELL US WHAT HAPPENED?
HUNZIKKER, IT'S SHAW, TELL ME--
HE SHOWED ME.
WHO SHOWED YOU? HUNZIKKER?
COME ON, STAY WITH ME-- TELL ME WHO SHOWED YOU, TELL ME WHAT THE HELL'S GOING ON...!
SHOWED HIM *WHAT...?*
WELL?
NOTHING. IT DIDN'T MAKE SENSE.
SO TELL ME...
I AM TELLING YOU, IT WAS JUST GIBBERISH.
AM I SUPPOSED TO BELIEVE THAT?

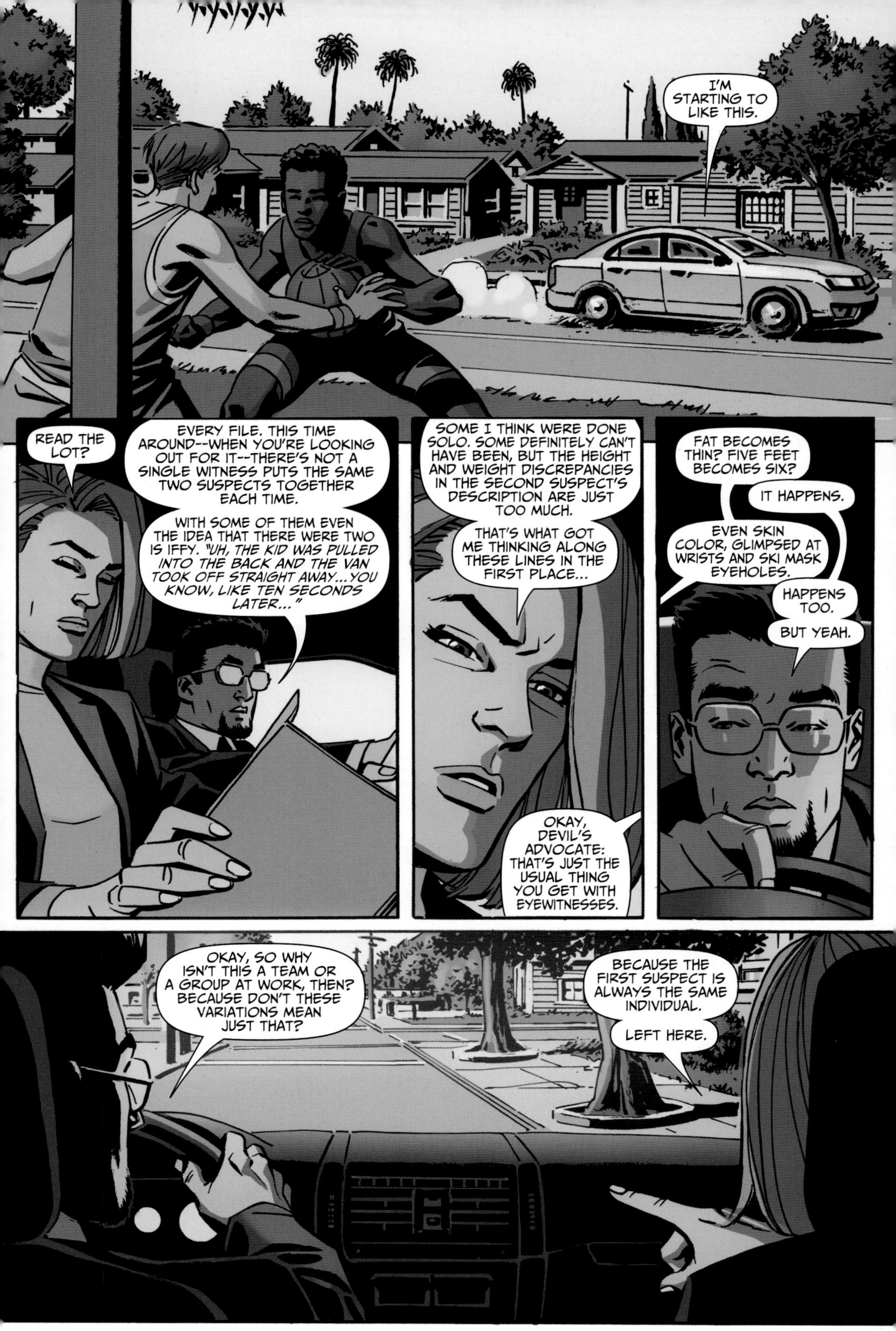
I'M STARTING TO LIKE THIS.
READ THE LOT?
EVERY FILE. THIS TIME AROUND--WHEN YOU'RE LOOKING OUT FOR IT--THERE'S NOT A SINGLE WITNESS PUTS THE SAME TWO SUSPECTS TOGETHER EACH TIME.
WITH SOME OF THEM EVEN THE IDEA THAT THERE WERE TWO IS IFFY. *"UH, THE KID WAS PULLED INTO THE BACK AND THE VAN TOOK OFF STRAIGHT AWAY...YOU KNOW, LIKE TEN SECONDS LATER..."*
SOME I THINK WERE DONE SOLO. SOME DEFINITELY CAN'T HAVE BEEN, BUT THE HEIGHT AND WEIGHT DISCREPANCIES IN THE SECOND SUSPECT'S DESCRIPTION ARE JUST TOO MUCH.
THAT'S WHAT GOT ME THINKING ALONG THESE LINES IN THE FIRST PLACE...
OKAY, DEVIL'S ADVOCATE: THAT'S JUST THE USUAL THING YOU GET WITH EYEWITNESSES.
FAT BECOMES THIN? FIVE FEET BECOMES SIX?
IT HAPPENS.
EVEN SKIN COLOR, GLIMPSED AT WRISTS AND SKI MASK EYEHOLES.
HAPPENS TOO.
BUT YEAH.
OKAY, SO WHY ISN'T THIS A TEAM OR A GROUP AT WORK, THEN? BECAUSE DON'T THESE VARIATIONS MEAN JUST THAT?
BECAUSE THE FIRST SUSPECT IS ALWAYS THE SAME INDIVIDUAL.
LEFT HERE.

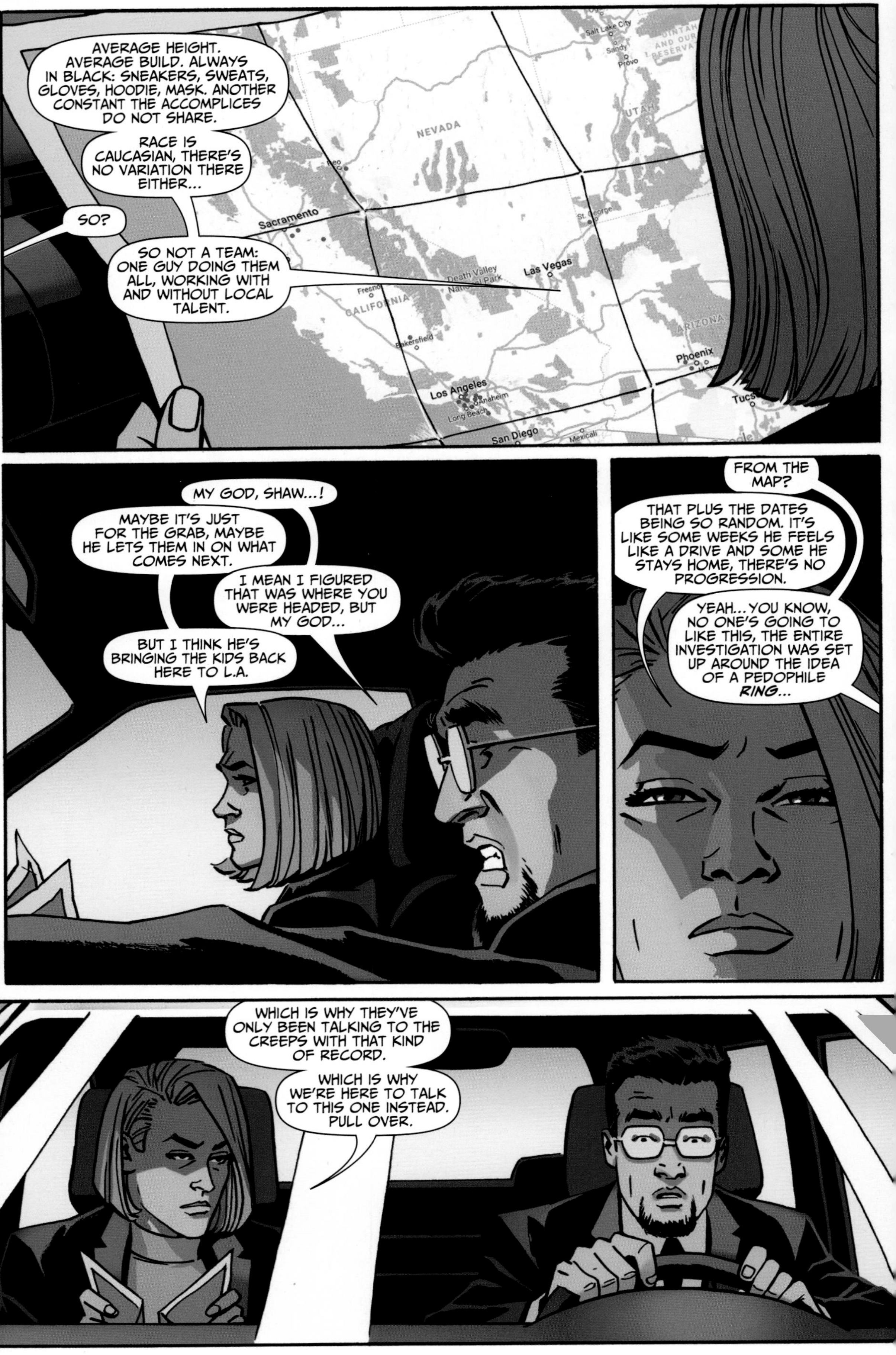

AVERAGE HEIGHT. AVERAGE BUILD. ALWAYS IN BLACK: SNEAKERS, SWEATS, GLOVES, HOODIE, MASK. ANOTHER CONSTANT THE ACCOMPLICES DO NOT SHARE.
RACE IS CAUCASIAN, THERE'S NO VARIATION THERE EITHER...
SO?
SO NOT A TEAM: ONE GUY DOING THEM ALL, WORKING WITH AND WITHOUT LOCAL TALENT.
Salt Lake City
Sandy
Provo
NEVADA
UTAH
Sacramento
St. George
Las Vegas
Death Valley National Park
Fresno
CALIFORNIA
ARIZONA
Bakersfield
Phoenix
Los Angeles
Anaheim
Long Beach
San Diego
Mexicali
MY GOD, SHAW...!
MAYBE IT'S JUST FOR THE GRAB, MAYBE HE LETS THEM IN ON WHAT COMES NEXT.
I MEAN I FIGURED THAT WAS WHERE YOU WERE HEADED, BUT MY GOD...
BUT I THINK HE'S BRINGING THE KIDS BACK HERE TO L.A.
FROM THE MAP?
THAT PLUS THE DATES BEING SO RANDOM. IT'S LIKE SOME WEEKS HE FEELS LIKE A DRIVE AND SOME HE STAYS HOME, THERE'S NO PROGRESSION.
YEAH... YOU KNOW, NO ONE'S GOING TO LIKE THIS, THE ENTIRE INVESTIGATION WAS SET UP AROUND THE IDEA OF A PEDOPHILE *RING*...
WHICH IS WHY THEY'VE ONLY BEEN TALKING TO THE CREEPS WITH THAT KIND OF RECORD.
WHICH IS WHY WE'RE HERE TO TALK TO THIS ONE INSTEAD. PULL OVER.

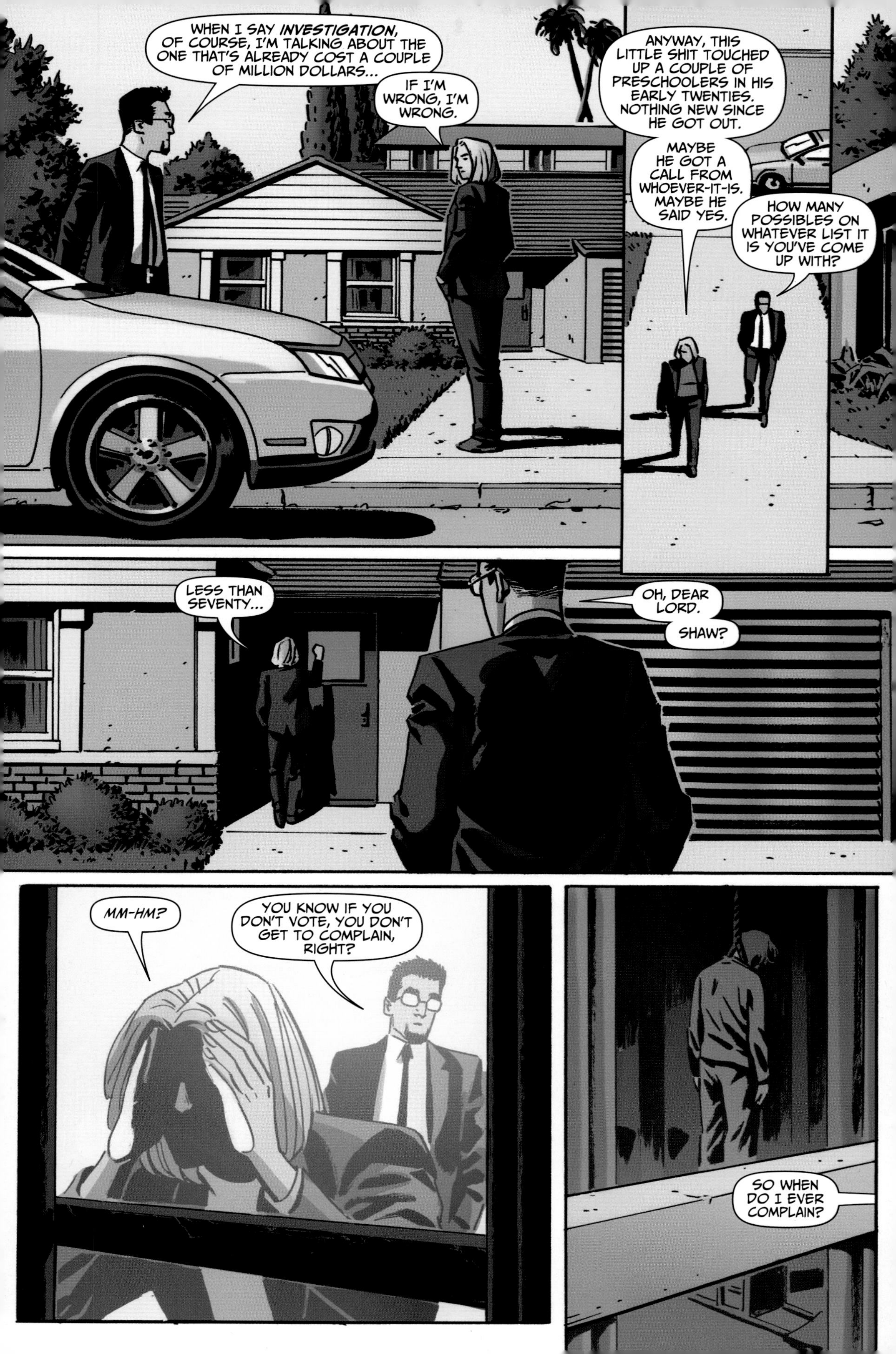
WHEN I SAY *INVESTIGATION*, OF COURSE, I'M TALKING ABOUT THE ONE THAT'S ALREADY COST A COUPLE OF MILLION DOLLARS...
IF I'M WRONG, I'M WRONG.
ANYWAY, THIS LITTLE SHIT TOUCHED UP A COUPLE OF PRESCHOOLERS IN HIS EARLY TWENTIES. NOTHING NEW SINCE HE GOT OUT.
MAYBE HE GOT A CALL FROM WHOEVER-IT-IS. MAYBE HE SAID YES.
HOW MANY POSSIBLES ON WHATEVER LIST IT IS YOU'VE COME UP WITH?
LESS THAN SEVENTY...
OH, DEAR LORD.
SHAW?
MM-HM?
YOU KNOW IF YOU DON'T VOTE, YOU DON'T GET TO COMPLAIN, RIGHT?
SO WHEN DO I EVER COMPLAIN?

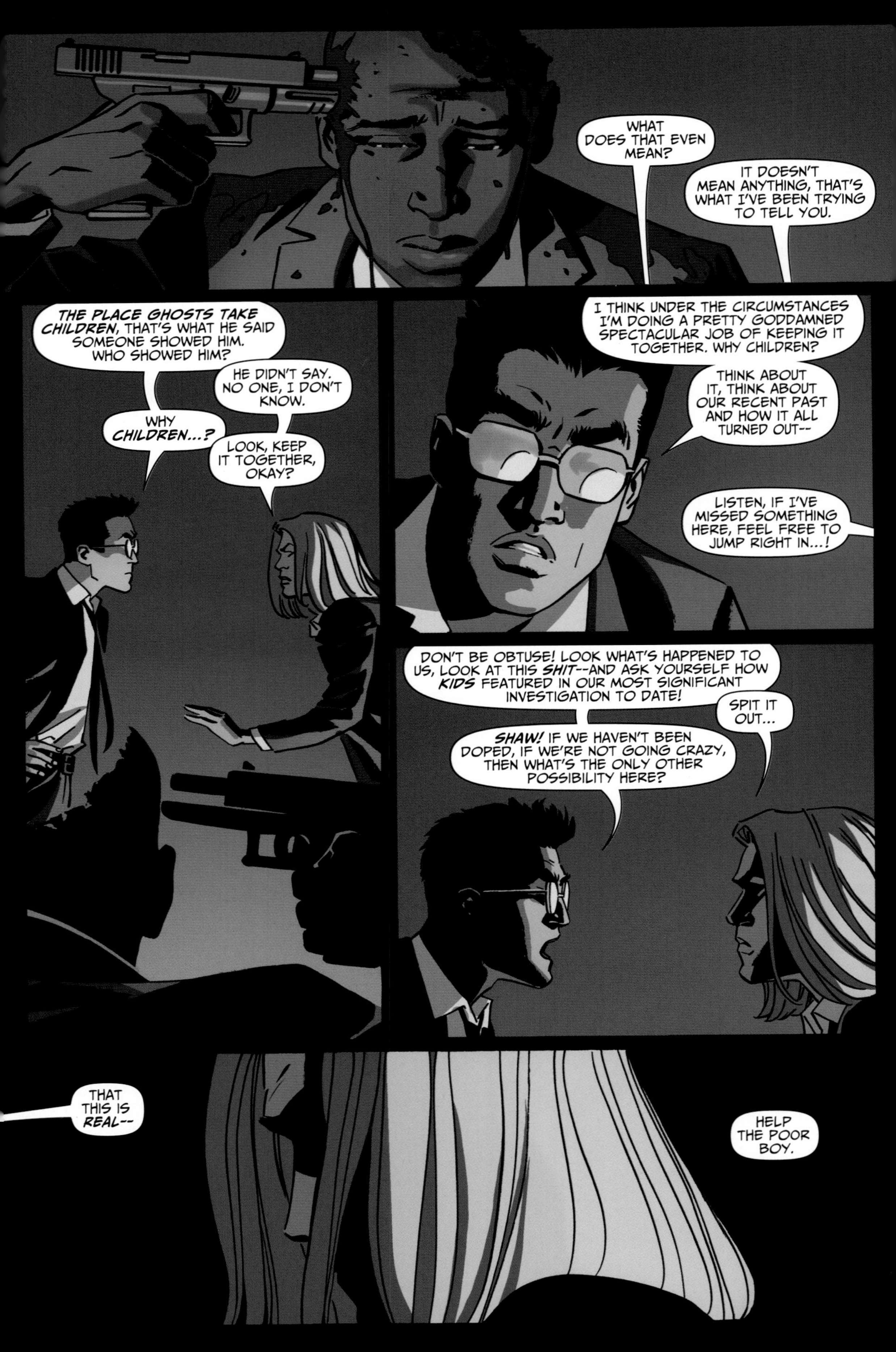
WHAT DOES THAT EVEN MEAN?
IT DOESN'T MEAN ANYTHING, THAT'S WHAT I'VE BEEN TRYING TO TELL YOU.
THE PLACE GHOSTS TAKE CHILDREN, THAT'S WHAT HE SAID SOMEONE SHOWED HIM. WHO SHOWED HIM?
HE DIDN'T SAY. NO ONE, I DON'T KNOW.
WHY CHILDREN...?
LOOK, KEEP IT TOGETHER, OKAY?
I THINK UNDER THE CIRCUMSTANCES I'M DOING A PRETTY GODDAMNED SPECTACULAR JOB OF KEEPING IT TOGETHER. WHY CHILDREN?
THINK ABOUT IT, THINK ABOUT OUR RECENT PAST AND HOW IT ALL TURNED OUT--
LISTEN, IF I'VE MISSED SOMETHING HERE, FEEL FREE TO JUMP RIGHT IN...!
DON'T BE OBTUSE! LOOK WHAT'S HAPPENED TO US, LOOK AT THIS SHIT--AND ASK YOURSELF HOW KIDS FEATURED IN OUR MOST SIGNIFICANT INVESTIGATION TO DATE!
SPIT IT OUT...
SHAW! IF WE HAVEN'T BEEN DOPED, IF WE'RE NOT GOING CRAZY, THEN WHAT'S THE ONLY OTHER POSSIBILITY HERE?
THAT THIS IS REAL--
HELP THE POOR BOY.

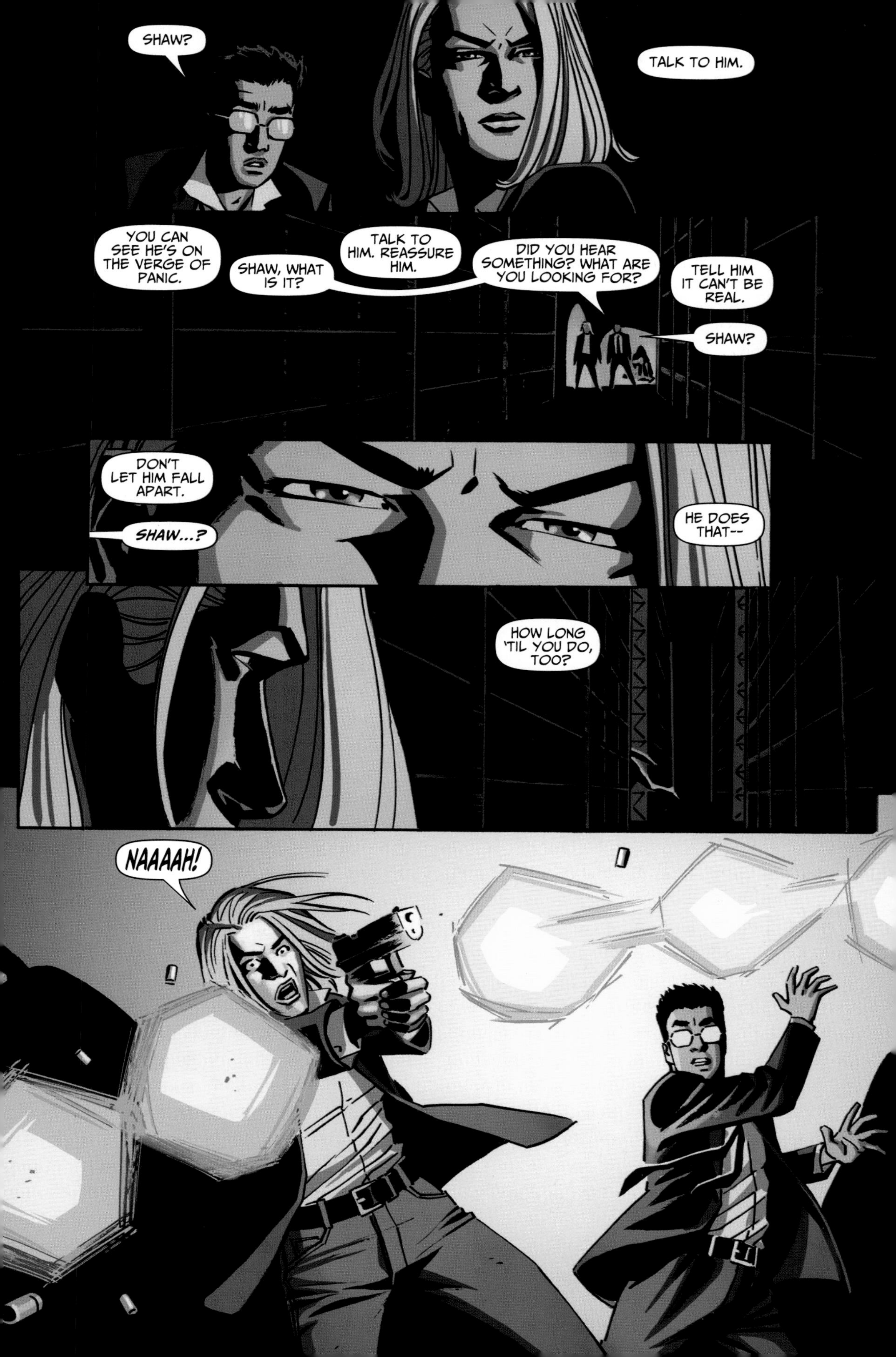
SHAW?
TALK TO HIM.
YOU CAN SEE HE'S ON THE VERGE OF PANIC.
SHAW, WHAT IS IT?
TALK TO HIM. REASSURE HIM.
DID YOU HEAR SOMETHING? WHAT ARE YOU LOOKING FOR?
TELL HIM IT CAN'T BE REAL.
SHAW?
DON'T LET HIM FALL APART.
SHAW...?
HE DOES THAT--
HOW LONG 'TIL YOU DO, TOO?
NAAAAH!

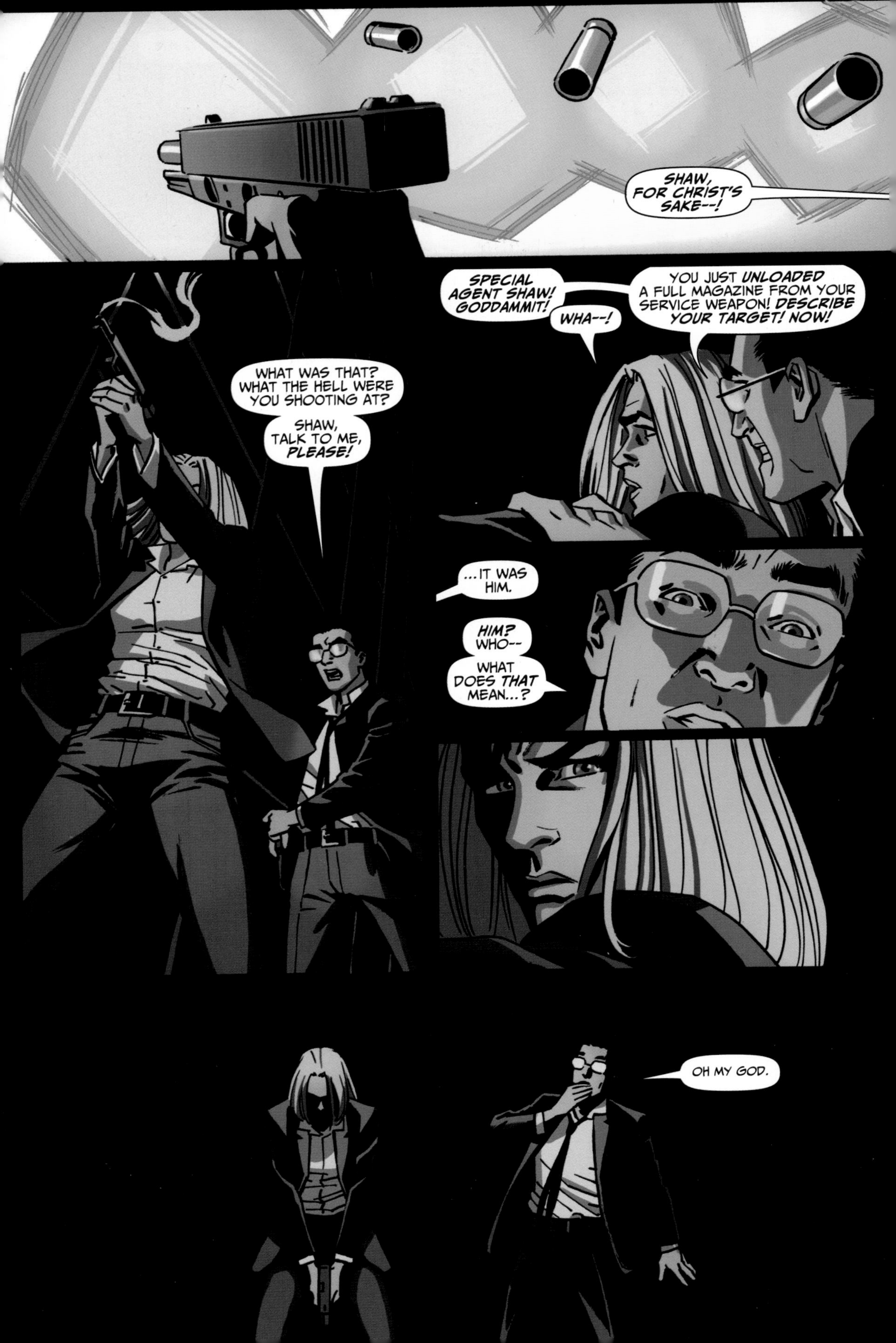
SHAW, FOR CHRIST'S SAKE--!
WHAT WAS THAT? WHAT THE HELL WERE YOU SHOOTING AT?
SHAW, TALK TO ME, PLEASE!
SPECIAL AGENT SHAW! GODDAMMIT!
WHA--!
YOU JUST UNLOADED A FULL MAGAZINE FROM YOUR SERVICE WEAPON! DESCRIBE YOUR TARGET! NOW!
...IT WAS HIM.
HIM? WHO--
WHAT DOES THAT MEAN...?
OH MY GOD.

3

THREE

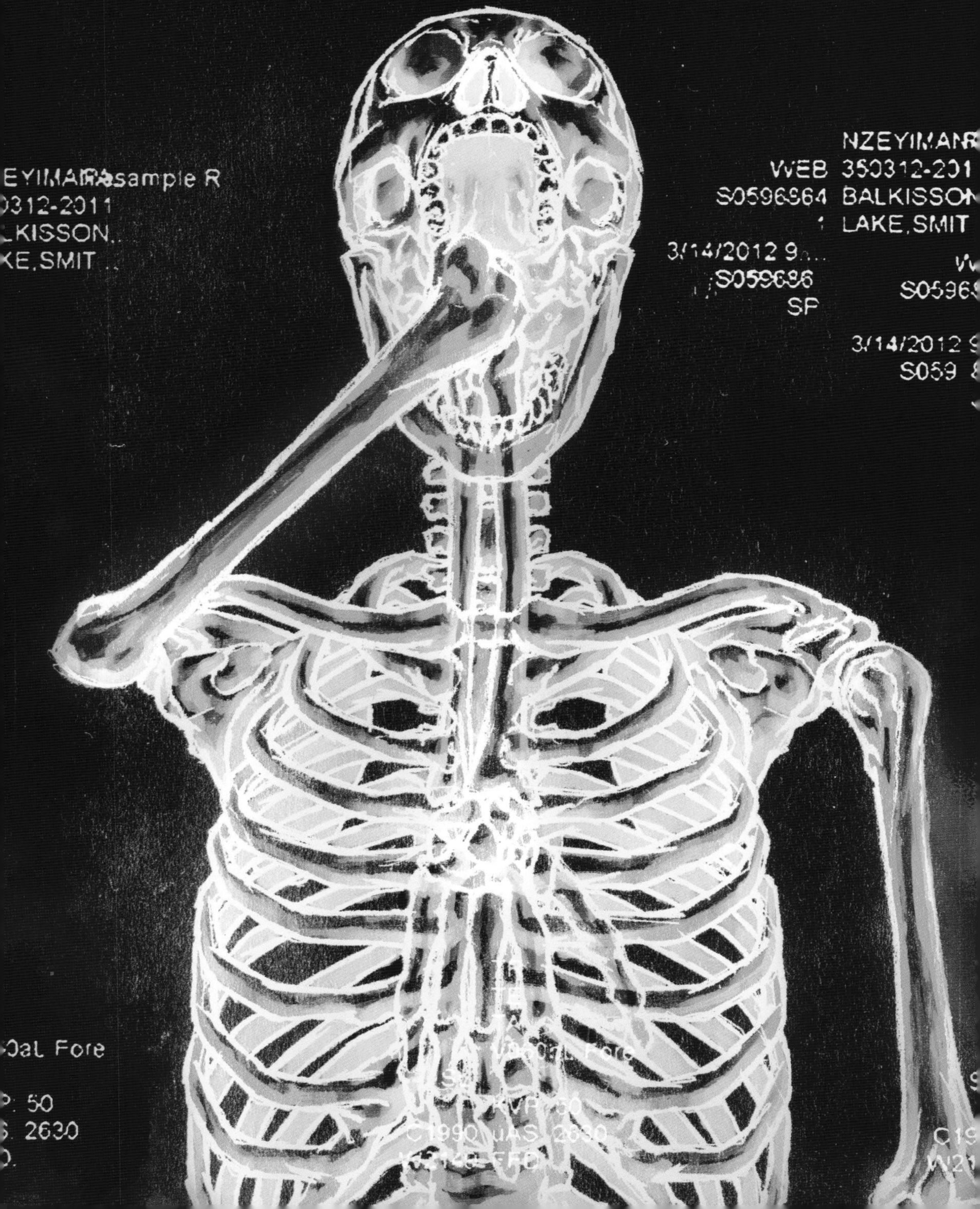
EYIMANasample R
0312-2011
LKISSON..
KE,SMIT ..
NZEYIMANI
WEB 350312-201
S0596864 BALKISSON
1 LAKE,SMIT
3/14/2012 9...
S059686
SP
S0596
3/14/2012
S059
Oal Fore
: 50
. 2630

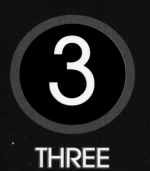

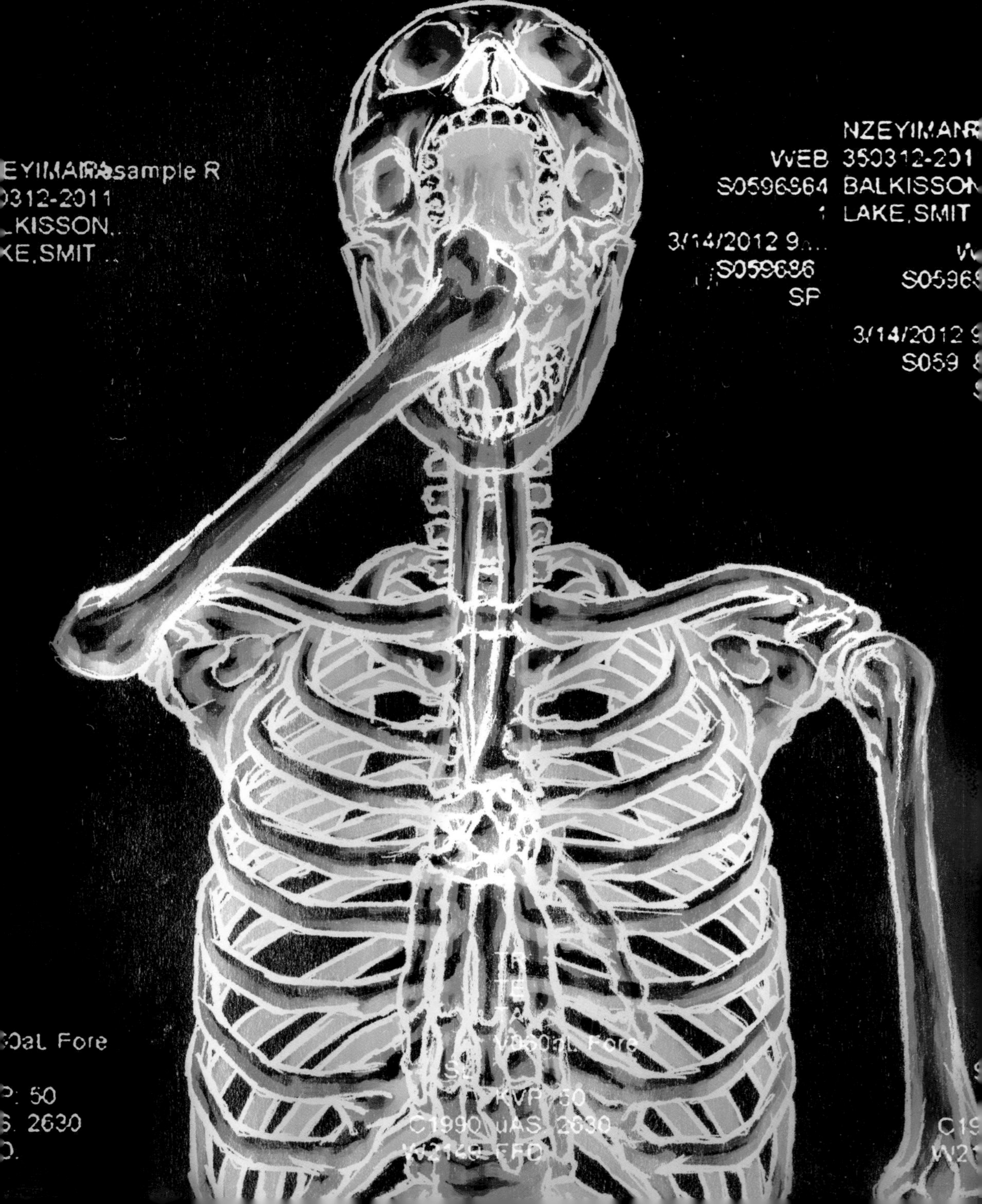
NZEYIMANR
WEB 350312-201
S0596964 BALKISSON
1 LAKE,SMIT
3/14/2012 9
S059686
SP
3/14/2012 9
S059
KVP 50
mAS 2630

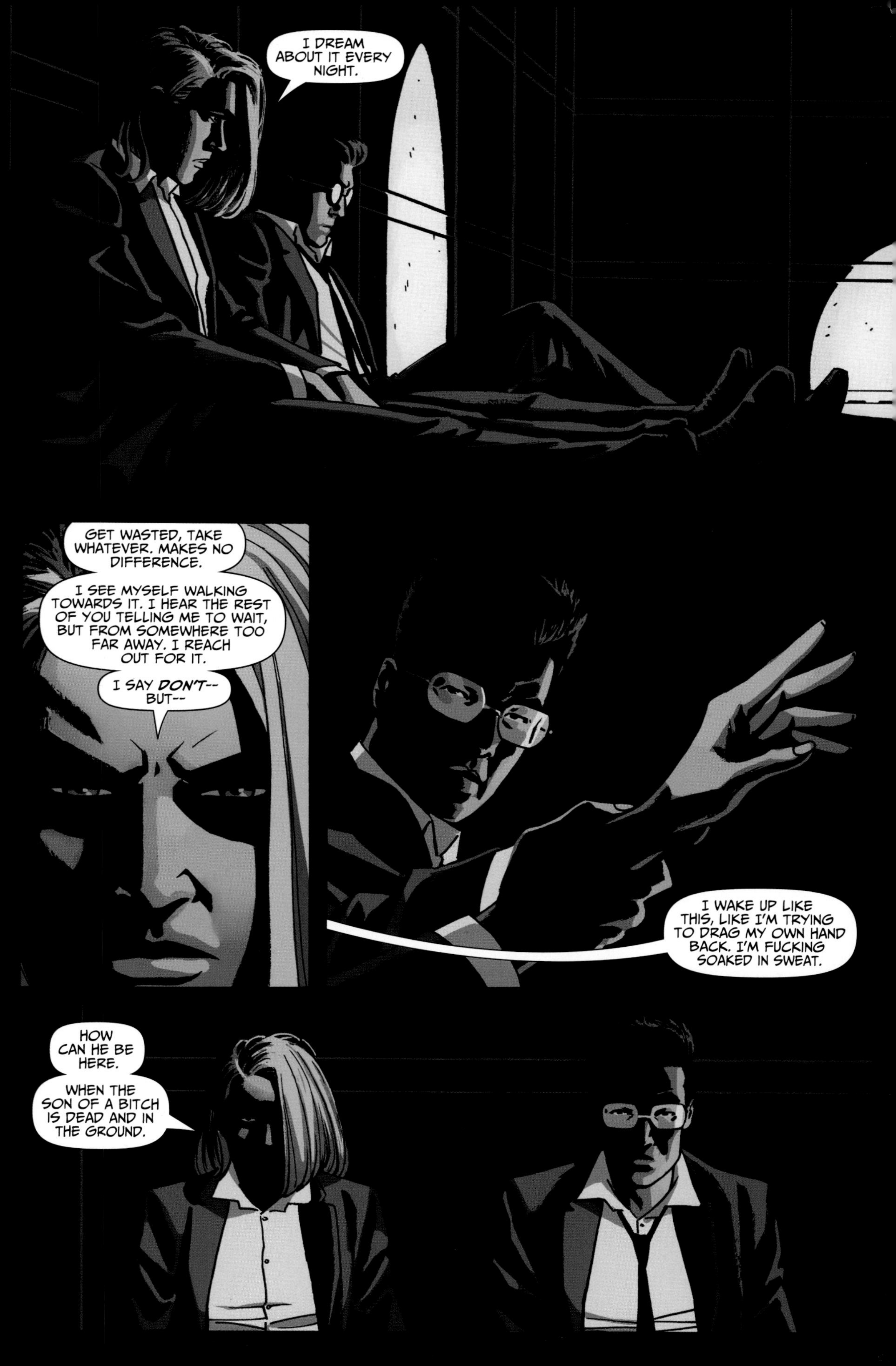
I DREAM ABOUT IT EVERY NIGHT.
GET WASTED, TAKE WHATEVER. MAKES NO DIFFERENCE.
I SEE MYSELF WALKING TOWARDS IT. I HEAR THE REST OF YOU TELLING ME TO WAIT, BUT FROM SOMEWHERE TOO FAR AWAY. I REACH OUT FOR IT.
I SAY *DON'T*-- BUT--
I WAKE UP LIKE THIS, LIKE I'M TRYING TO DRAG MY OWN HAND BACK. I'M FUCKING SOAKED IN SWEAT.
HOW CAN HE BE HERE.
WHEN THE SON OF A BITCH IS DEAD AND IN THE GROUND.

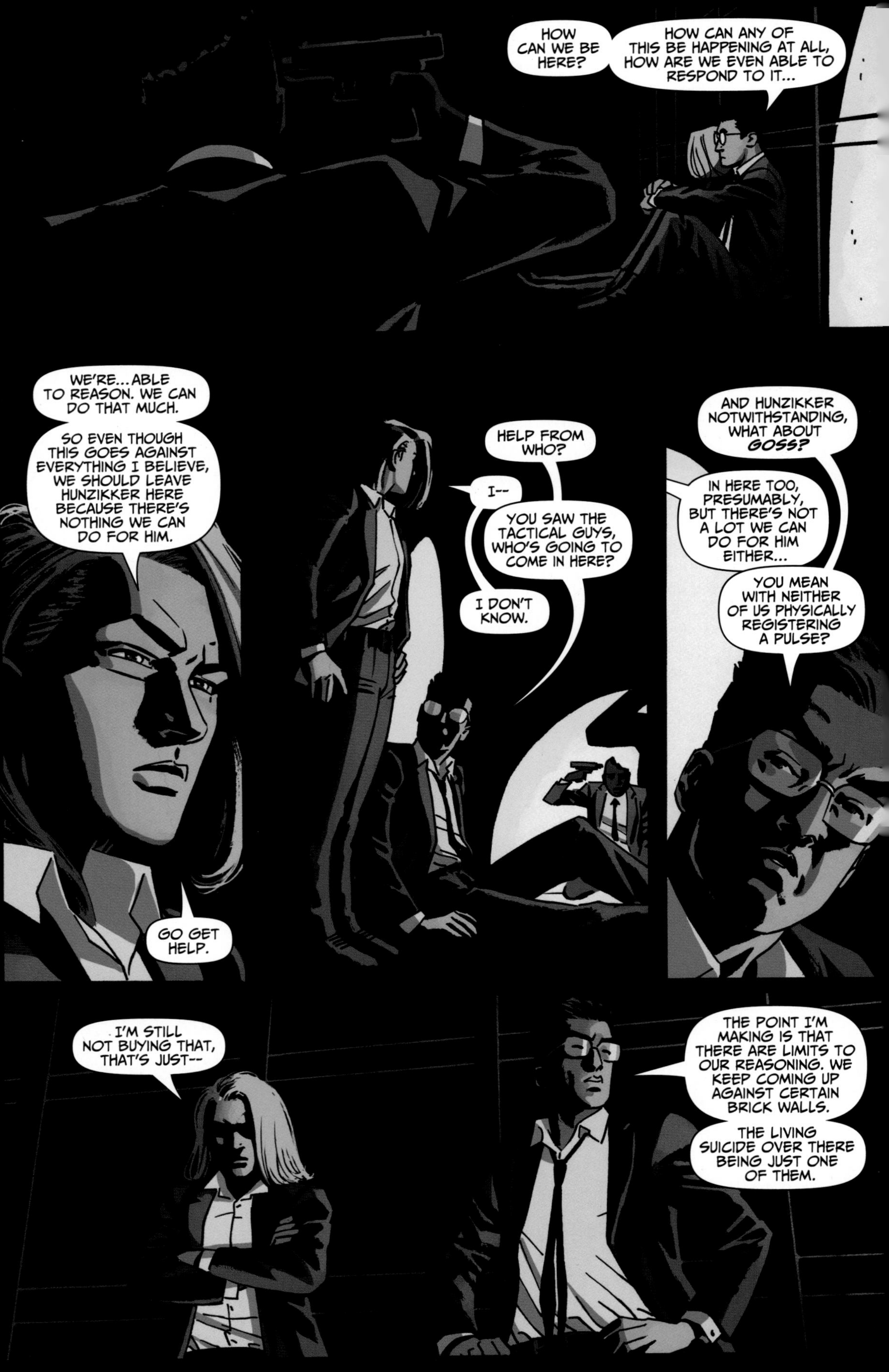
HOW CAN WE BE HERE?
HOW CAN ANY OF THIS BE HAPPENING AT ALL, HOW ARE WE EVEN ABLE TO RESPOND TO IT...
WE'RE... ABLE TO REASON. WE CAN DO THAT MUCH.
SO EVEN THOUGH THIS GOES AGAINST EVERYTHING I BELIEVE, WE SHOULD LEAVE HUNZIKKER HERE BECAUSE THERE'S NOTHING WE CAN DO FOR HIM.
GO GET HELP.
HELP FROM WHO?
I--
YOU SAW THE TACTICAL GUYS, WHO'S GOING TO COME IN HERE?
I DON'T KNOW.
AND HUNZIKKER NOTWITHSTANDING, WHAT ABOUT GOSS?
IN HERE TOO, PRESUMABLY, BUT THERE'S NOT A LOT WE CAN DO FOR HIM EITHER...
YOU MEAN WITH NEITHER OF US PHYSICALLY REGISTERING A PULSE?
I'M STILL NOT BUYING THAT, THAT'S JUST--
THE POINT I'M MAKING IS THAT THERE ARE LIMITS TO OUR REASONING. WE KEEP COMING UP AGAINST CERTAIN BRICK WALLS.
THE LIVING SUICIDE OVER THERE BEING JUST ONE OF THEM.

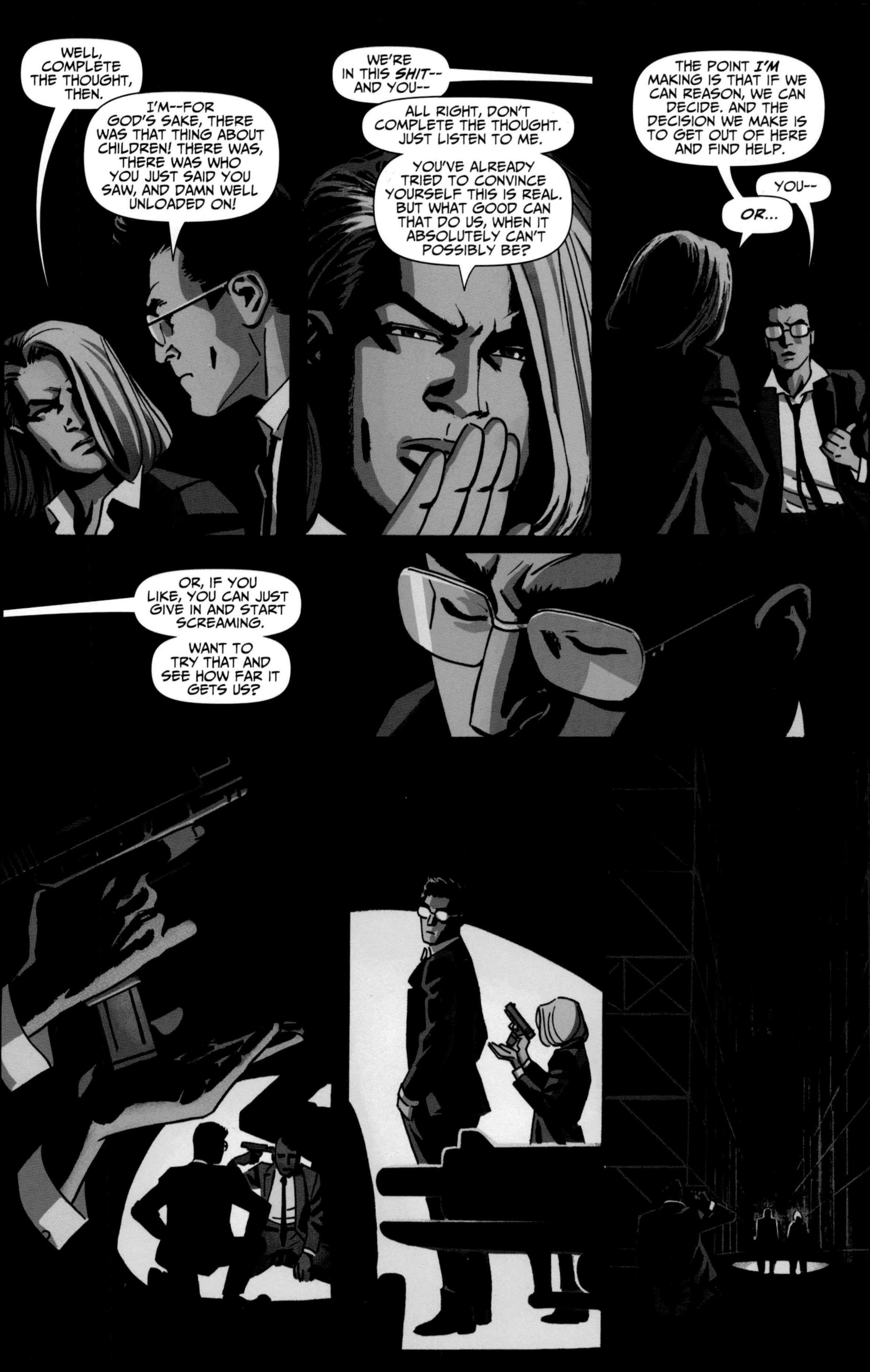
WELL, COMPLETE THE THOUGHT, THEN.
I'M--FOR GOD'S SAKE, THERE WAS THAT THING ABOUT CHILDREN! THERE WAS, THERE WAS WHO YOU JUST SAID YOU SAW, AND DAMN WELL UNLOADED ON!
WE'RE IN THIS SHIT-- AND YOU--
ALL RIGHT, DON'T COMPLETE THE THOUGHT. JUST LISTEN TO ME.
YOU'VE ALREADY TRIED TO CONVINCE YOURSELF THIS IS REAL. BUT WHAT GOOD CAN THAT DO US, WHEN IT ABSOLUTELY CAN'T POSSIBLY BE?
THE POINT I'M MAKING IS THAT IF WE CAN REASON, WE CAN DECIDE. AND THE DECISION WE MAKE IS TO GET OUT OF HERE AND FIND HELP.
OR...
YOU--
OR, IF YOU LIKE, YOU CAN JUST GIVE IN AND START SCREAMING.
WANT TO TRY THAT AND SEE HOW FAR IT GETS US?

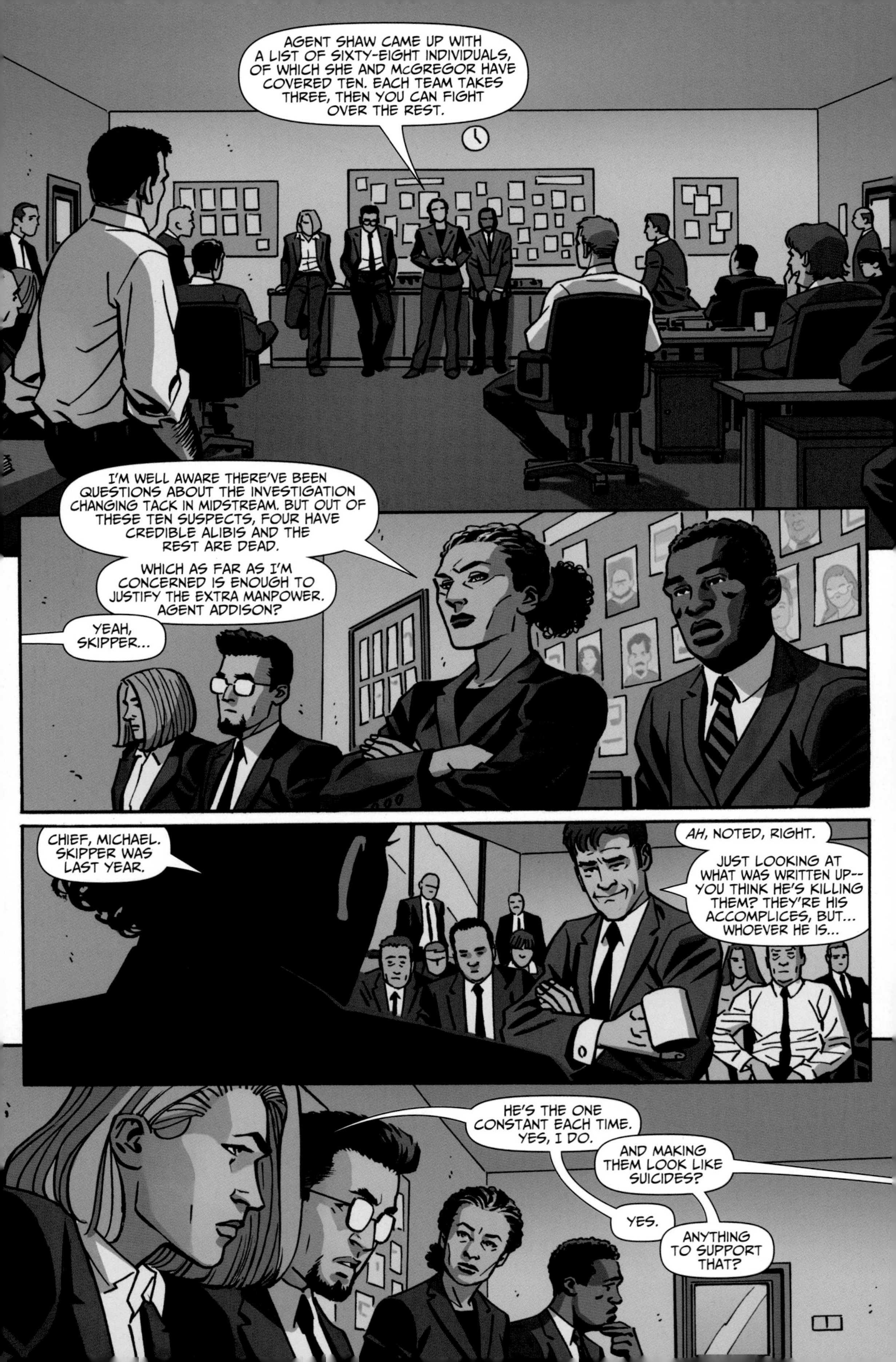
AGENT SHAW CAME UP WITH A LIST OF SIXTY-EIGHT INDIVIDUALS, OF WHICH SHE AND McGREGOR HAVE COVERED TEN. EACH TEAM TAKES THREE, THEN YOU CAN FIGHT OVER THE REST.
I'M WELL AWARE THERE'VE BEEN QUESTIONS ABOUT THE INVESTIGATION CHANGING TACK IN MIDSTREAM. BUT OUT OF THESE TEN SUSPECTS, FOUR HAVE CREDIBLE ALIBIS AND THE REST ARE DEAD.
WHICH AS FAR AS I'M CONCERNED IS ENOUGH TO JUSTIFY THE EXTRA MANPOWER. AGENT ADDISON?
YEAH, SKIPPER...
CHIEF, MICHAEL. SKIPPER WAS LAST YEAR.
AH, NOTED, RIGHT.
JUST LOOKING AT WHAT WAS WRITTEN UP-- YOU THINK HE'S KILLING THEM? THEY'RE HIS ACCOMPLICES, BUT... WHOEVER HE IS...
HE'S THE ONE CONSTANT EACH TIME. YES, I DO.
AND MAKING THEM LOOK LIKE SUICIDES?
YES.
ANYTHING TO SUPPORT THAT?

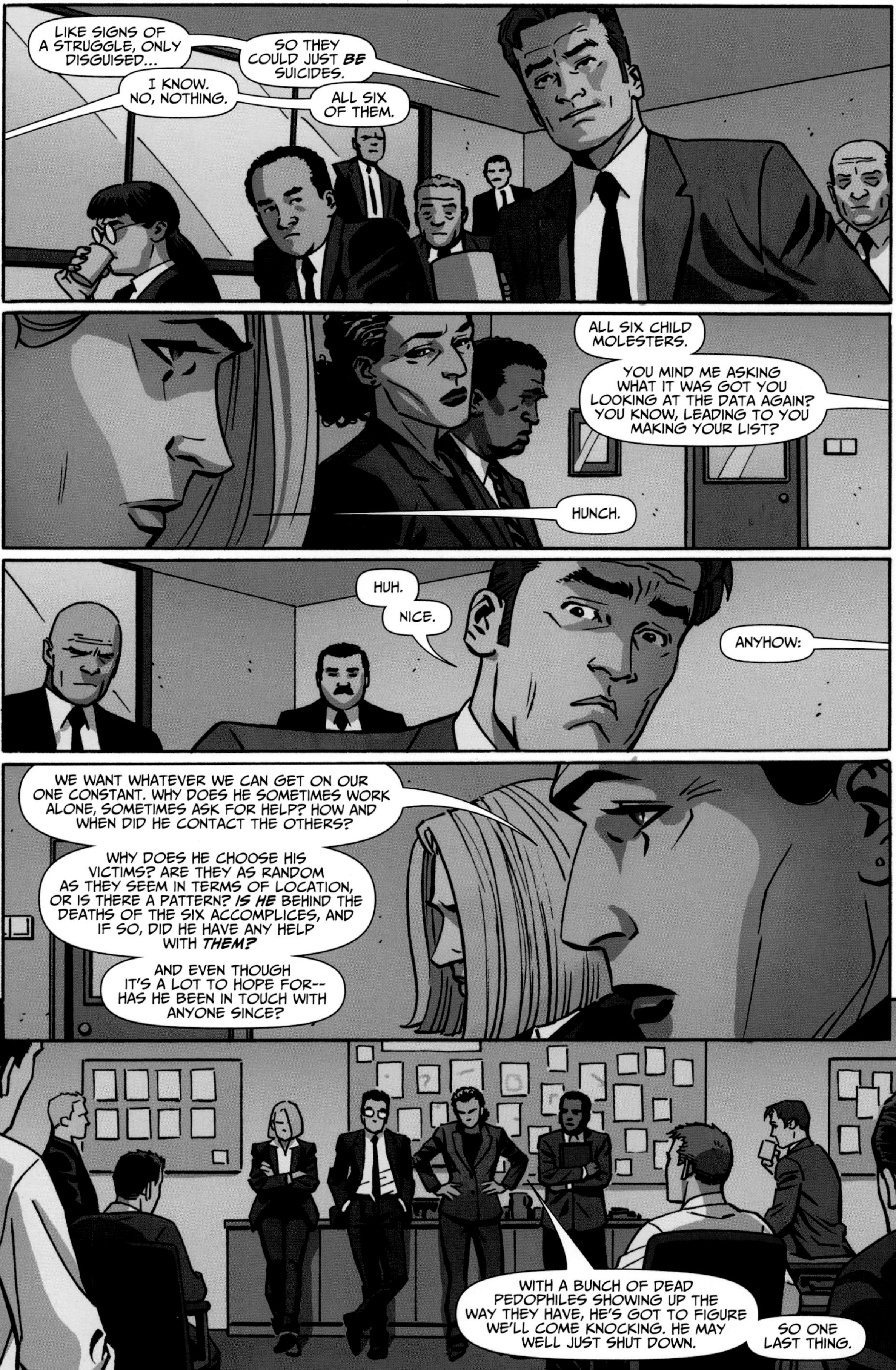
LIKE SIGNS OF A STRUGGLE, ONLY DISGUISED...
SO THEY COULD JUST *BE* SUICIDES.
I KNOW. NO, NOTHING.
ALL SIX OF THEM.
ALL SIX CHILD MOLESTERS.
YOU MIND ME ASKING WHAT IT WAS GOT YOU LOOKING AT THE DATA AGAIN? YOU KNOW, LEADING TO YOU MAKING YOUR LIST?
HUNCH.
HUH.
NICE.
ANYHOW:
WE WANT WHATEVER WE CAN GET ON OUR ONE CONSTANT. WHY DOES HE SOMETIMES WORK ALONE, SOMETIMES ASK FOR HELP? HOW AND WHEN DID HE CONTACT THE OTHERS?
WHY DOES HE CHOOSE HIS VICTIMS? ARE THEY AS RANDOM AS THEY SEEM IN TERMS OF LOCATION, OR IS THERE A PATTERN? *IS HE* BEHIND THE DEATHS OF THE SIX ACCOMPLICES, AND IF SO, DID HE HAVE ANY HELP WITH *THEM?*
AND EVEN THOUGH IT'S A LOT TO HOPE FOR-- HAS HE BEEN IN TOUCH WITH ANYONE SINCE?
WITH A BUNCH OF DEAD PEDOPHILES SHOWING UP THE WAY THEY HAVE, HE'S GOT TO FIGURE WE'LL COME KNOCKING. HE MAY WELL JUST SHUT DOWN.
SO ONE LAST THING.

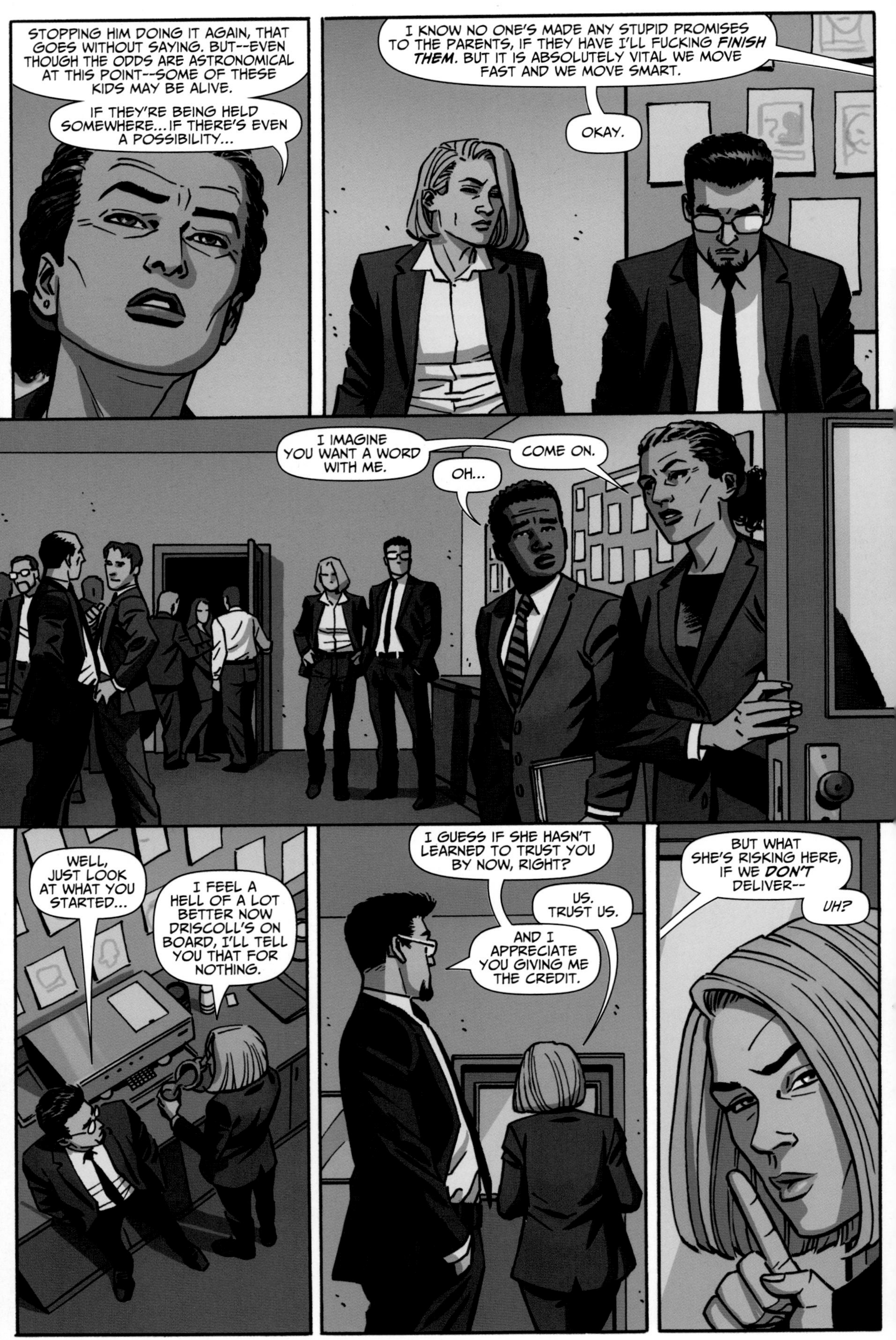
STOPPING HIM DOING IT AGAIN, THAT GOES WITHOUT SAYING. BUT--EVEN THOUGH THE ODDS ARE ASTRONOMICAL AT THIS POINT--SOME OF THESE KIDS MAY BE ALIVE.
IF THEY'RE BEING HELD SOMEWHERE... IF THERE'S EVEN A POSSIBILITY...
I KNOW NO ONE'S MADE ANY STUPID PROMISES TO THE PARENTS, IF THEY HAVE I'LL FUCKING *FINISH THEM.* BUT IT IS ABSOLUTELY VITAL WE MOVE FAST AND WE MOVE SMART.
OKAY.
I IMAGINE YOU WANT A WORD WITH ME.
COME ON.
OH...
WELL, JUST LOOK AT WHAT YOU STARTED...
I FEEL A HELL OF A LOT BETTER NOW DRISCOLL'S ON BOARD, I'LL TELL YOU THAT FOR NOTHING.
I GUESS IF SHE HASN'T LEARNED TO TRUST YOU BY NOW, RIGHT?
US. TRUST US.
AND I APPRECIATE YOU GIVING ME THE CREDIT.
BUT WHAT SHE'S RISKING HERE, IF WE *DON'T* DELIVER--
UH?

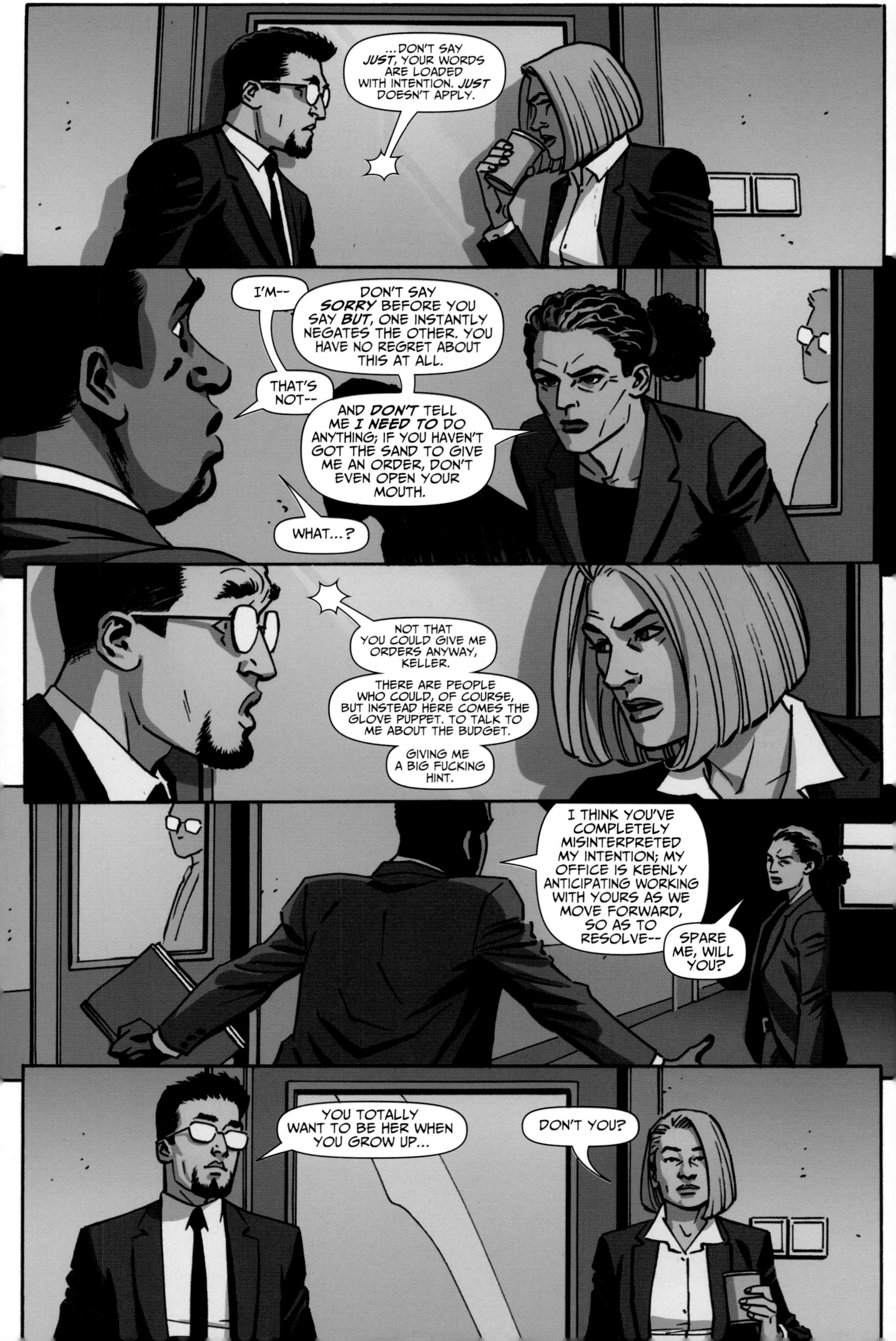
...DON'T SAY JUST, YOUR WORDS ARE LOADED WITH INTENTION. JUST DOESN'T APPLY.
I'M--
DON'T SAY SORRY BEFORE YOU SAY BUT, ONE INSTANTLY NEGATES THE OTHER. YOU HAVE NO REGRET ABOUT THIS AT ALL.
THAT'S NOT--
AND DON'T TELL ME I NEED TO DO ANYTHING; IF YOU HAVEN'T GOT THE SAND TO GIVE ME AN ORDER, DON'T EVEN OPEN YOUR MOUTH.
WHAT...?
NOT THAT YOU COULD GIVE ME ORDERS ANYWAY, KELLER.
THERE ARE PEOPLE WHO COULD, OF COURSE, BUT INSTEAD HERE COMES THE GLOVE PUPPET. TO TALK TO ME ABOUT THE BUDGET.
GIVING ME A BIG FUCKING HINT.
I THINK YOU'VE COMPLETELY MISINTERPRETED MY INTENTION; MY OFFICE IS KEENLY ANTICIPATING WORKING WITH YOURS AS WE MOVE FORWARD, SO AS TO RESOLVE--
SPARE ME, WILL YOU?
YOU TOTALLY WANT TO BE HER WHEN YOU GROW UP...
DON'T YOU?

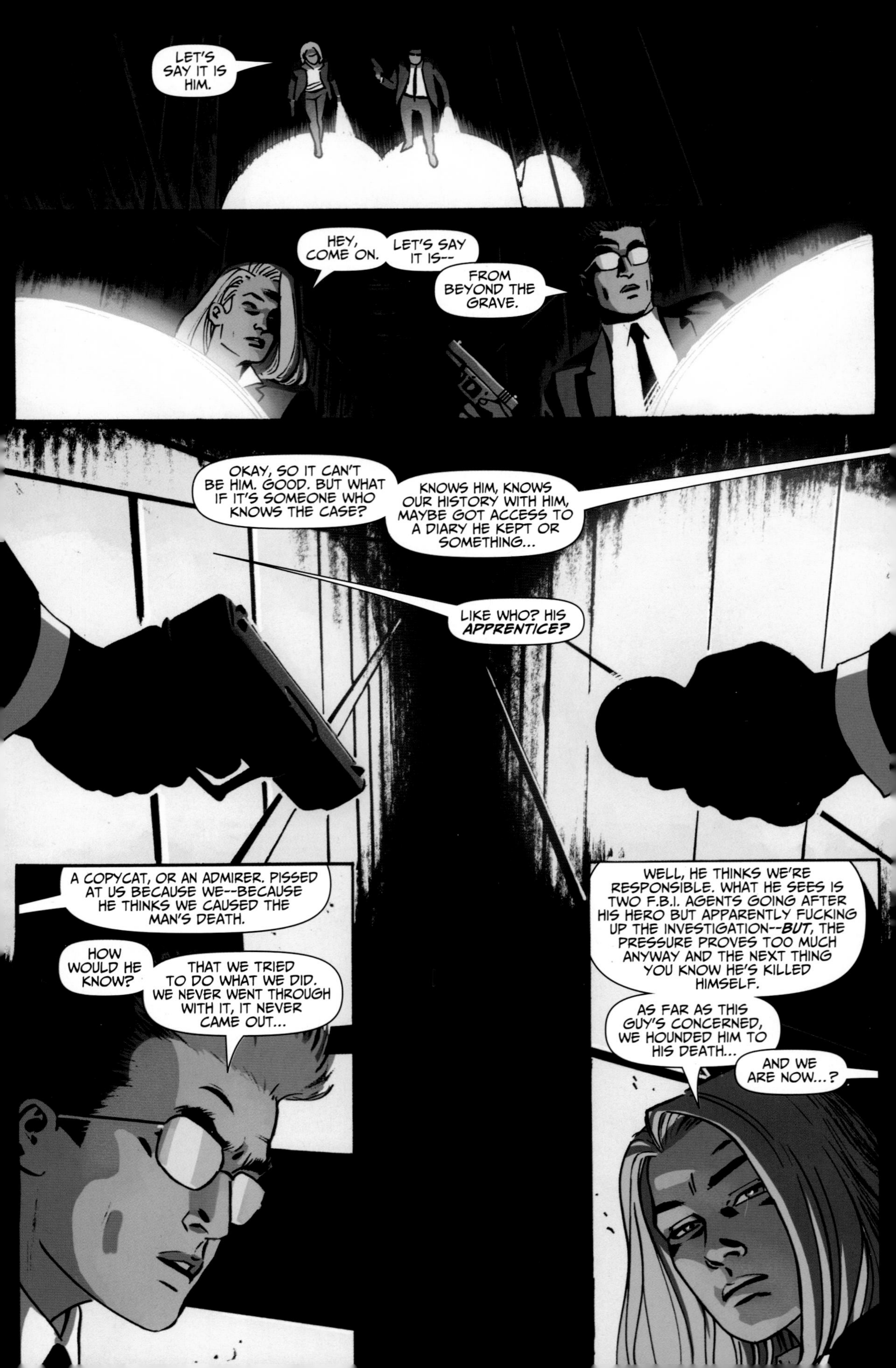
LET'S SAY IT IS HIM.
HEY, COME ON.
LET'S SAY IT IS--
FROM BEYOND THE GRAVE.
OKAY, SO IT CAN'T BE HIM. GOOD. BUT WHAT IF IT'S SOMEONE WHO KNOWS THE CASE?
KNOWS HIM, KNOWS OUR HISTORY WITH HIM, MAYBE GOT ACCESS TO A DIARY HE KEPT OR SOMETHING...
LIKE WHO? HIS *APPRENTICE?*
A COPYCAT, OR AN ADMIRER. PISSED AT US BECAUSE WE--BECAUSE HE THINKS WE CAUSED THE MAN'S DEATH.
HOW WOULD HE KNOW?
THAT WE TRIED TO DO WHAT WE DID. WE NEVER WENT THROUGH WITH IT, IT NEVER CAME OUT...
WELL, HE THINKS WE'RE RESPONSIBLE. WHAT HE SEES IS TWO F.B.I. AGENTS GOING AFTER HIS HERO BUT APPARENTLY FUCKING UP THE INVESTIGATION--*BUT*, THE PRESSURE PROVES TOO MUCH ANYWAY AND THE NEXT THING YOU KNOW HE'S KILLED HIMSELF.
AS FAR AS THIS GUY'S CONCERNED, WE HOUNDED HIM TO HIS DEATH...
AND WE ARE NOW...?

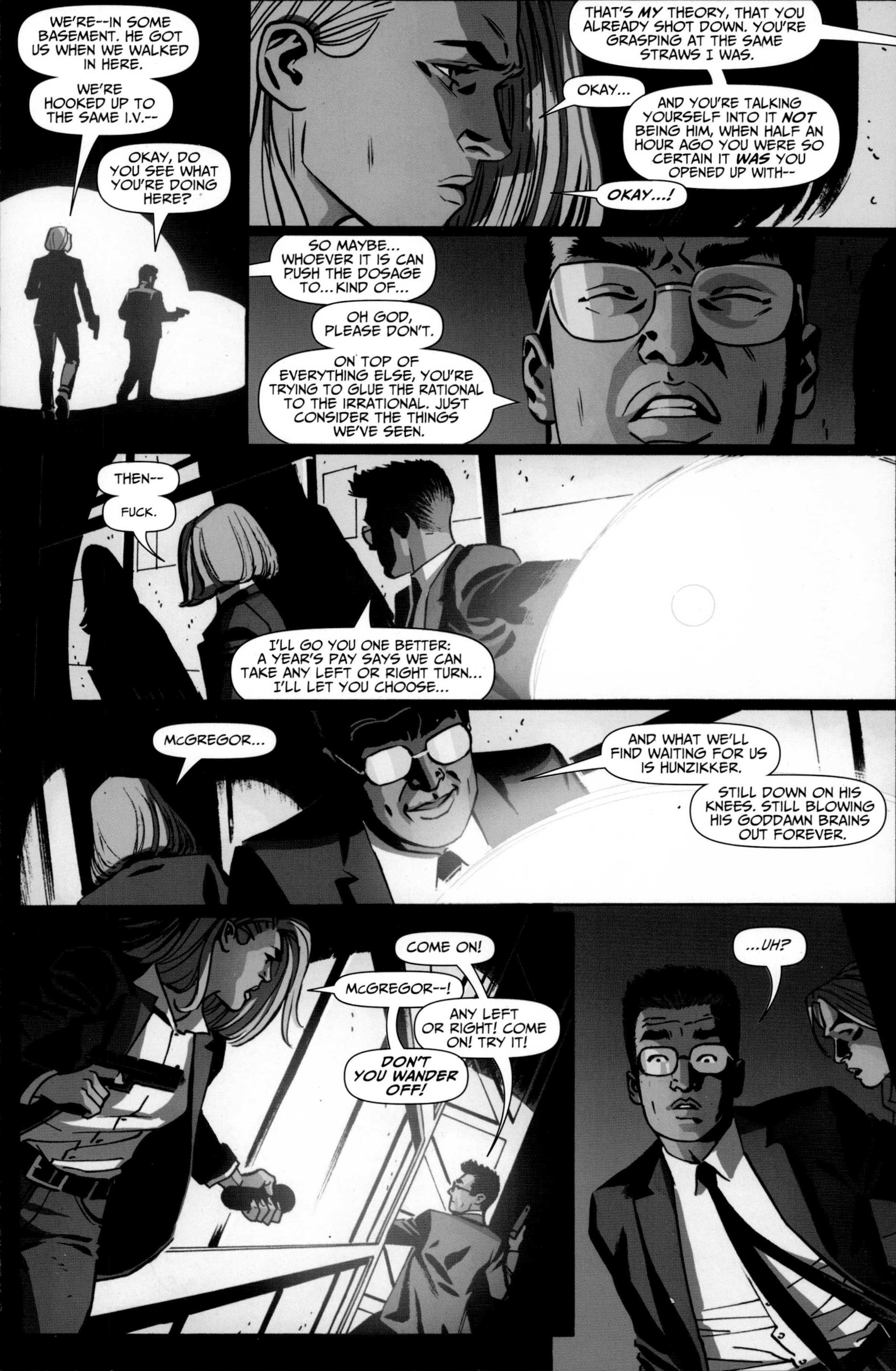
WE'RE--IN SOME BASEMENT. HE GOT US WHEN WE WALKED IN HERE.
WE'RE HOOKED UP TO THE SAME I.V.--
OKAY, DO YOU SEE WHAT YOU'RE DOING HERE?
THAT'S MY THEORY, THAT YOU ALREADY SHOT DOWN. YOU'RE GRASPING AT THE SAME STRAWS I WAS.
OKAY...
AND YOU'RE TALKING YOURSELF INTO IT NOT BEING HIM, WHEN HALF AN HOUR AGO YOU WERE SO CERTAIN IT WAS YOU OPENED UP WITH--
OKAY...!
SO MAYBE... WHOEVER IT IS CAN PUSH THE DOSAGE TO... KIND OF...
OH GOD, PLEASE DON'T.
ON TOP OF EVERYTHING ELSE, YOU'RE TRYING TO GLUE THE RATIONAL TO THE IRRATIONAL. JUST CONSIDER THE THINGS WE'VE SEEN.
THEN--
FUCK.
I'LL GO YOU ONE BETTER: A YEAR'S PAY SAYS WE CAN TAKE ANY LEFT OR RIGHT TURN... I'LL LET YOU CHOOSE...
McGREGOR...
AND WHAT WE'LL FIND WAITING FOR US IS HUNZIKKER.
STILL DOWN ON HIS KNEES. STILL BLOWING HIS GODDAMN BRAINS OUT FOREVER.
COME ON!
McGREGOR--!
ANY LEFT OR RIGHT! COME ON! TRY IT!
DON'T YOU WANDER OFF!
...UH?

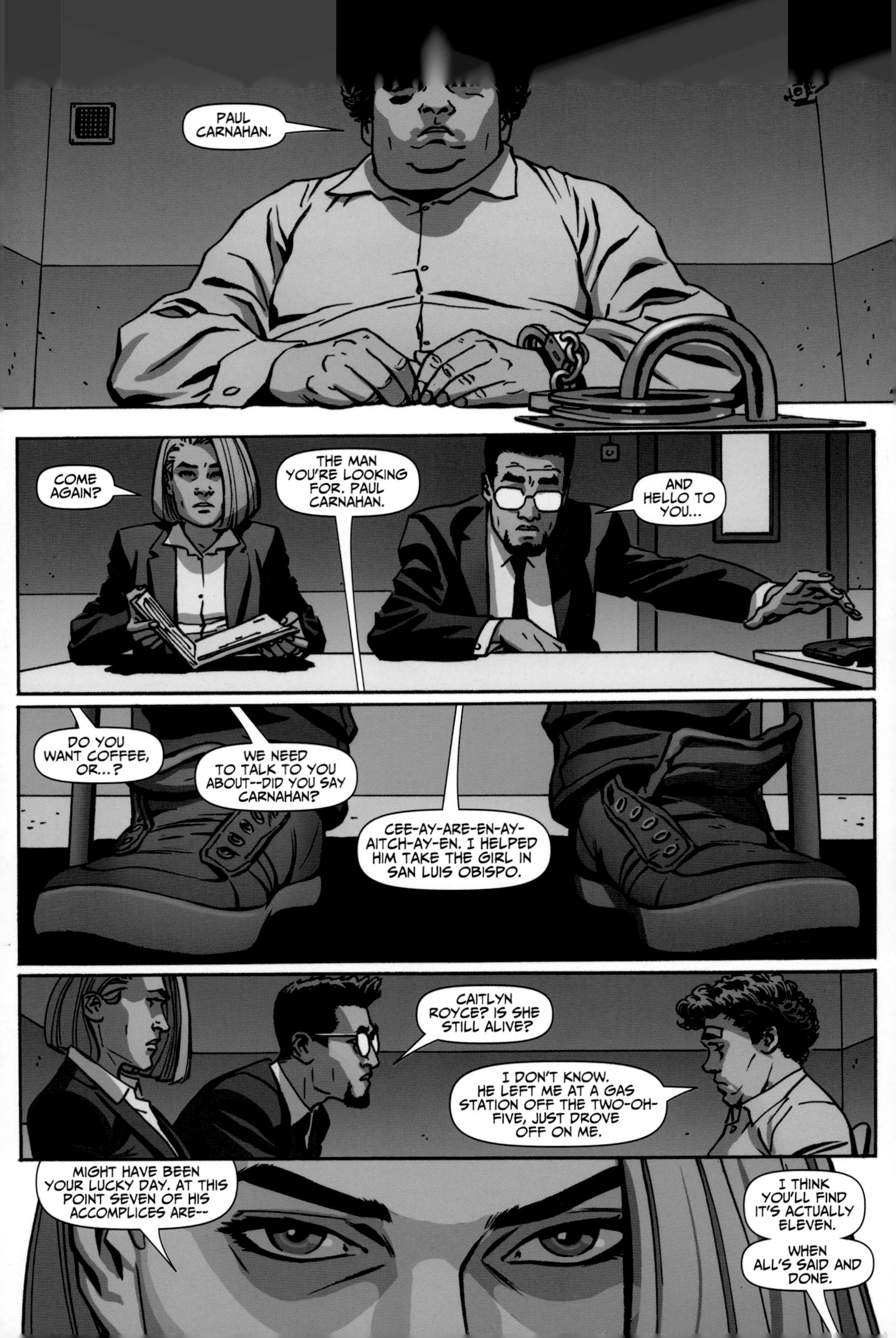
PAUL CARNAHAN.
COME AGAIN?
THE MAN YOU'RE LOOKING FOR. PAUL CARNAHAN.
AND HELLO TO YOU...
DO YOU WANT COFFEE, OR...?
WE NEED TO TALK TO YOU ABOUT--DID YOU SAY CARNAHAN?
CEE-AY-ARE-EN-AY-AITCH-AY-EN. I HELPED HIM TAKE THE GIRL IN SAN LUIS OBISPO.
CAITLYN ROYCE? IS SHE STILL ALIVE?
I DON'T KNOW. HE LEFT ME AT A GAS STATION OFF THE TWO-OH-FIVE, JUST DROVE OFF ON ME.
MIGHT HAVE BEEN YOUR LUCKY DAY. AT THIS POINT SEVEN OF HIS ACCOMPLICES ARE--
I THINK YOU'LL FIND IT'S ACTUALLY ELEVEN.
WHEN ALL'S SAID AND DONE.

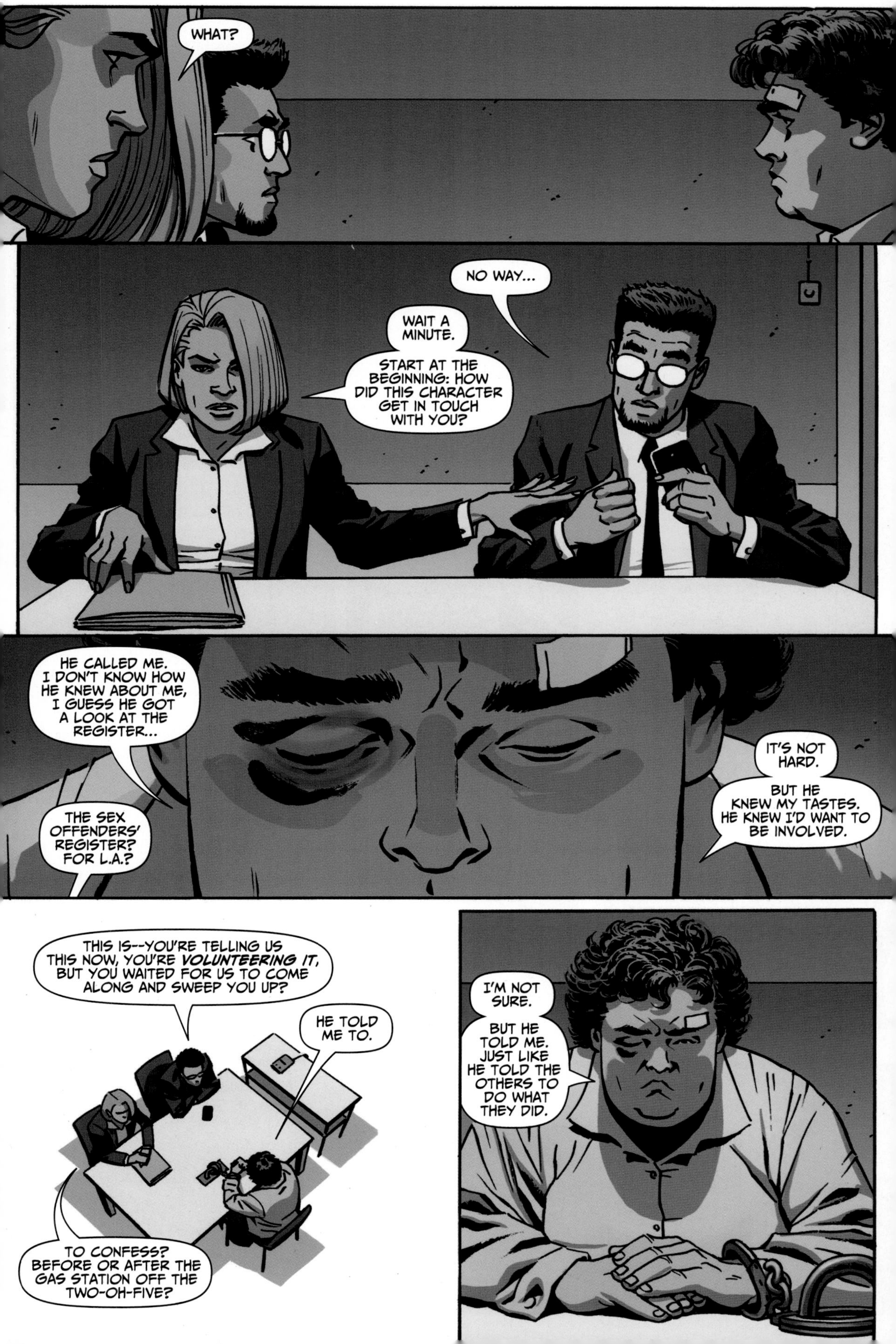
WHAT?
NO WAY...
WAIT A MINUTE.
START AT THE BEGINNING: HOW DID THIS CHARACTER GET IN TOUCH WITH YOU?
HE CALLED ME. I DON'T KNOW HOW HE KNEW ABOUT ME, I GUESS HE GOT A LOOK AT THE REGISTER...
THE SEX OFFENDERS' REGISTER? FOR L.A.?
IT'S NOT HARD.
BUT HE KNEW MY TASTES. HE KNEW I'D WANT TO BE INVOLVED.
THIS IS--YOU'RE TELLING US THIS NOW, YOU'RE *VOLUNTEERING IT*, BUT YOU WAITED FOR US TO COME ALONG AND SWEEP YOU UP?
HE TOLD ME TO.
TO CONFESS? BEFORE OR AFTER THE GAS STATION OFF THE TWO-OH-FIVE?
I'M NOT SURE.
BUT HE TOLD ME. JUST LIKE HE TOLD THE OTHERS TO DO WHAT THEY DID.

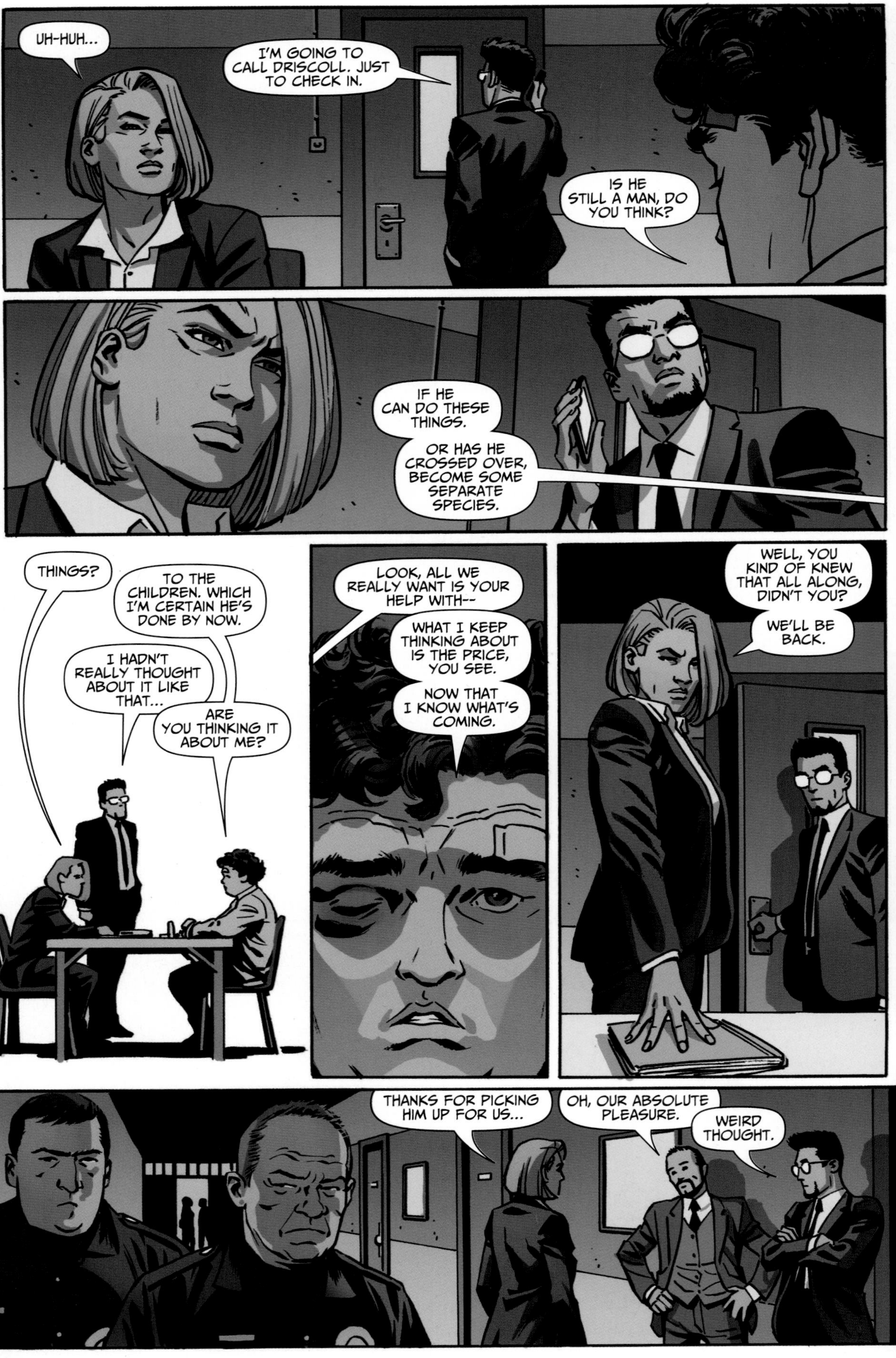
UH-HUH...
I'M GOING TO CALL DRISCOLL. JUST TO CHECK IN.
IS HE STILL A MAN, DO YOU THINK?
IF HE CAN DO THESE THINGS.
OR HAS HE CROSSED OVER, BECOME SOME SEPARATE SPECIES.
THINGS?
TO THE CHILDREN. WHICH I'M CERTAIN HE'S DONE BY NOW.
I HADN'T REALLY THOUGHT ABOUT IT LIKE THAT...
ARE YOU THINKING IT ABOUT ME?
LOOK, ALL WE REALLY WANT IS YOUR HELP WITH--
WHAT I KEEP THINKING ABOUT IS THE PRICE, YOU SEE.
NOW THAT I KNOW WHAT'S COMING.
WELL, YOU KIND OF KNEW THAT ALL ALONG, DIDN'T YOU?
WE'LL BE BACK.
THANKS FOR PICKING HIM UP FOR US...
OH, OUR ABSOLUTE PLEASURE.
WEIRD THOUGHT.

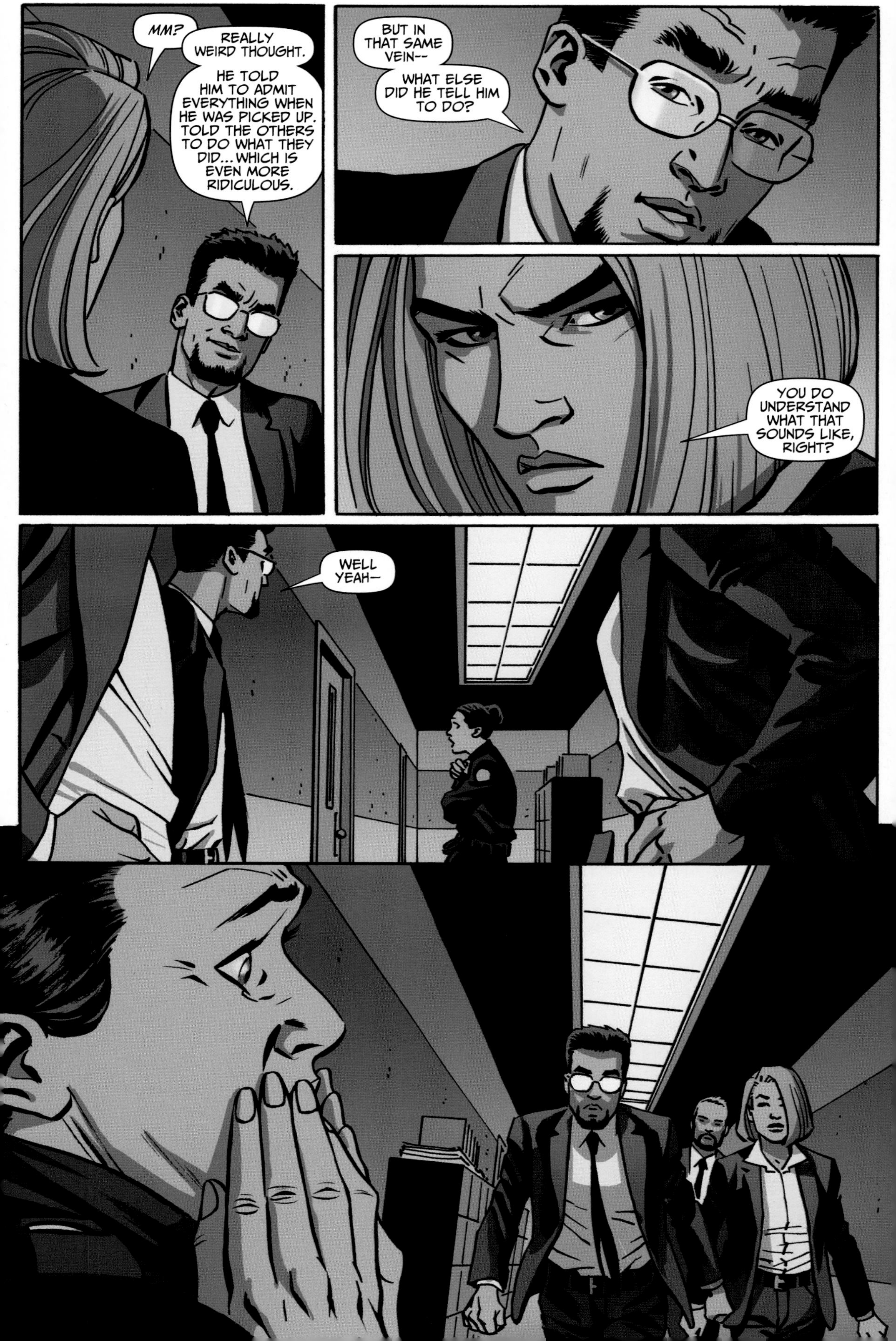
MM?
REALLY WEIRD THOUGHT.
HE TOLD HIM TO ADMIT EVERYTHING WHEN HE WAS PICKED UP. TOLD THE OTHERS TO DO WHAT THEY DID...WHICH IS EVEN MORE RIDICULOUS.
BUT IN THAT SAME VEIN--
WHAT ELSE DID HE TELL HIM TO DO?
YOU DO UNDERSTAND WHAT THAT SOUNDS LIKE, RIGHT?
WELL YEAH—

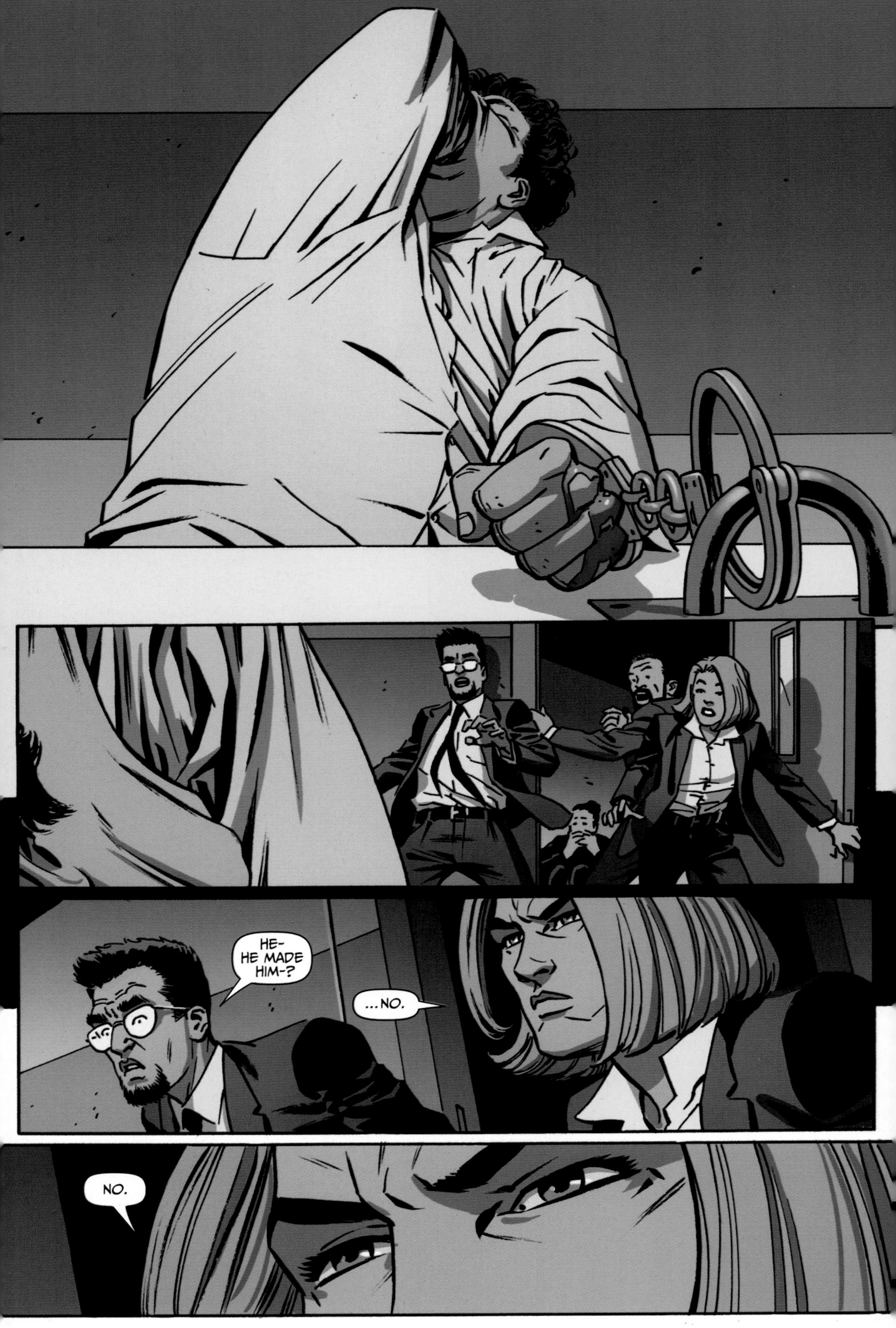
HE-
HE MADE
HIM-?
...NO.
NO.

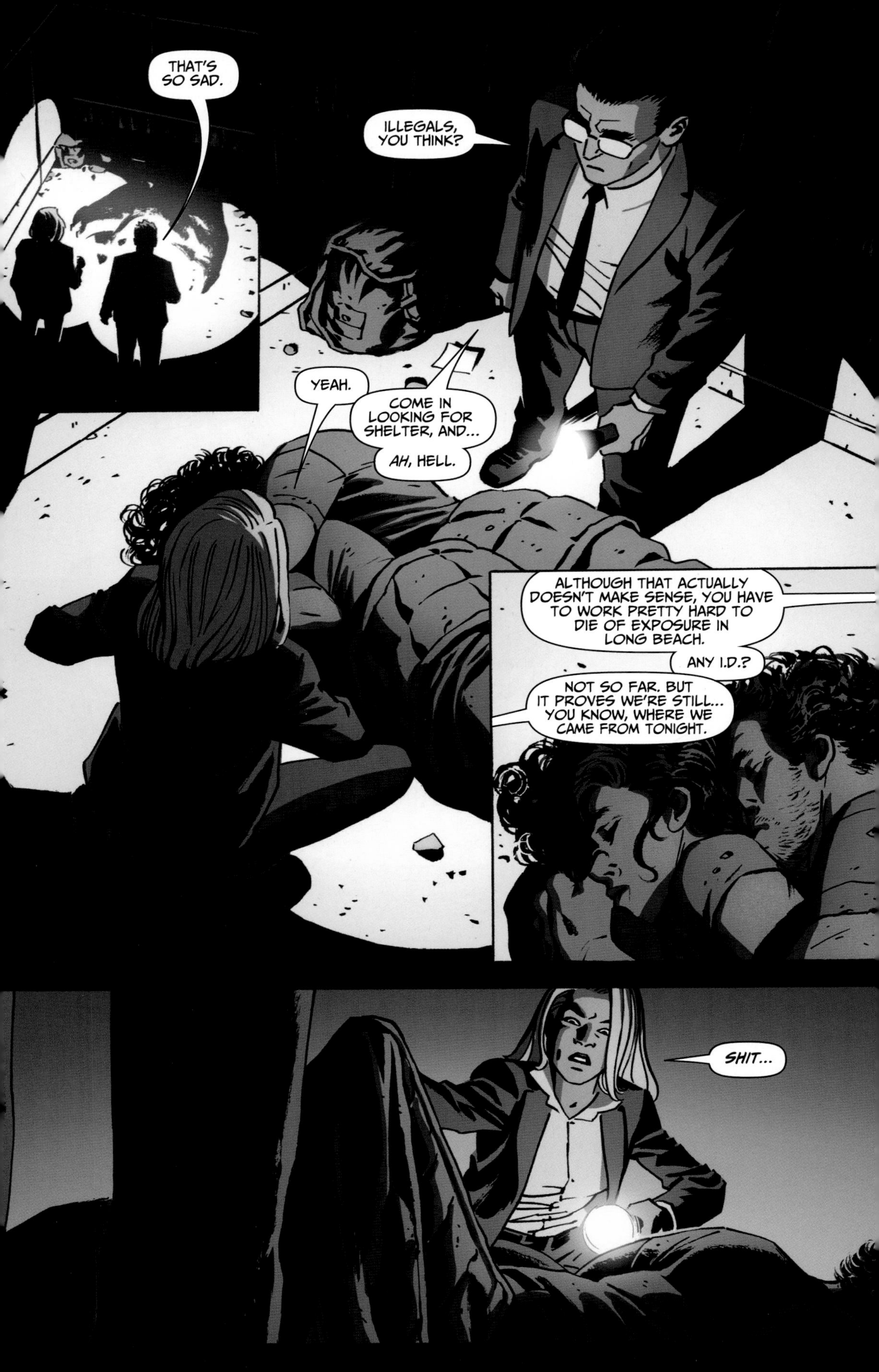
THAT'S SO SAD.
ILLEGALS, YOU THINK?
YEAH.
COME IN LOOKING FOR SHELTER, AND...
AH, HELL.
ALTHOUGH THAT ACTUALLY DOESN'T MAKE SENSE, YOU HAVE TO WORK PRETTY HARD TO DIE OF EXPOSURE IN LONG BEACH.
ANY I.D.?
NOT SO FAR. BUT IT PROVES WE'RE STILL... YOU KNOW, WHERE WE CAME FROM TONIGHT.
SHIT...

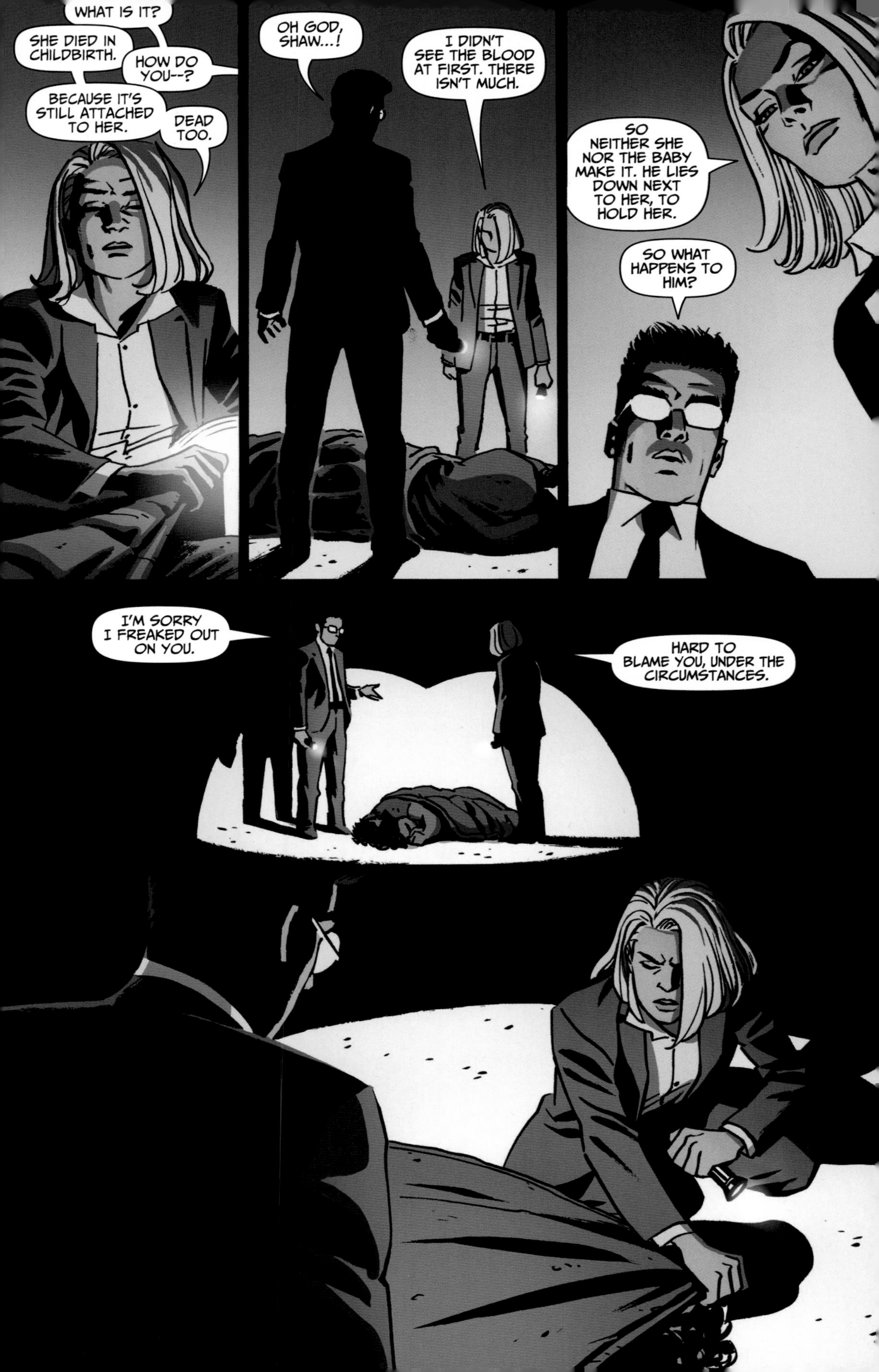
WHAT IS IT?
SHE DIED IN CHILDBIRTH.
HOW DO YOU--?
BECAUSE IT'S STILL ATTACHED TO HER.
DEAD TOO.
OH GOD, SHAW...!
I DIDN'T SEE THE BLOOD AT FIRST. THERE ISN'T MUCH.
SO NEITHER SHE NOR THE BABY MAKE IT. HE LIES DOWN NEXT TO HER, TO HOLD HER.
SO WHAT HAPPENS TO HIM?
I'M SORRY I FREAKED OUT ON YOU.
HARD TO BLAME YOU, UNDER THE CIRCUMSTANCES.

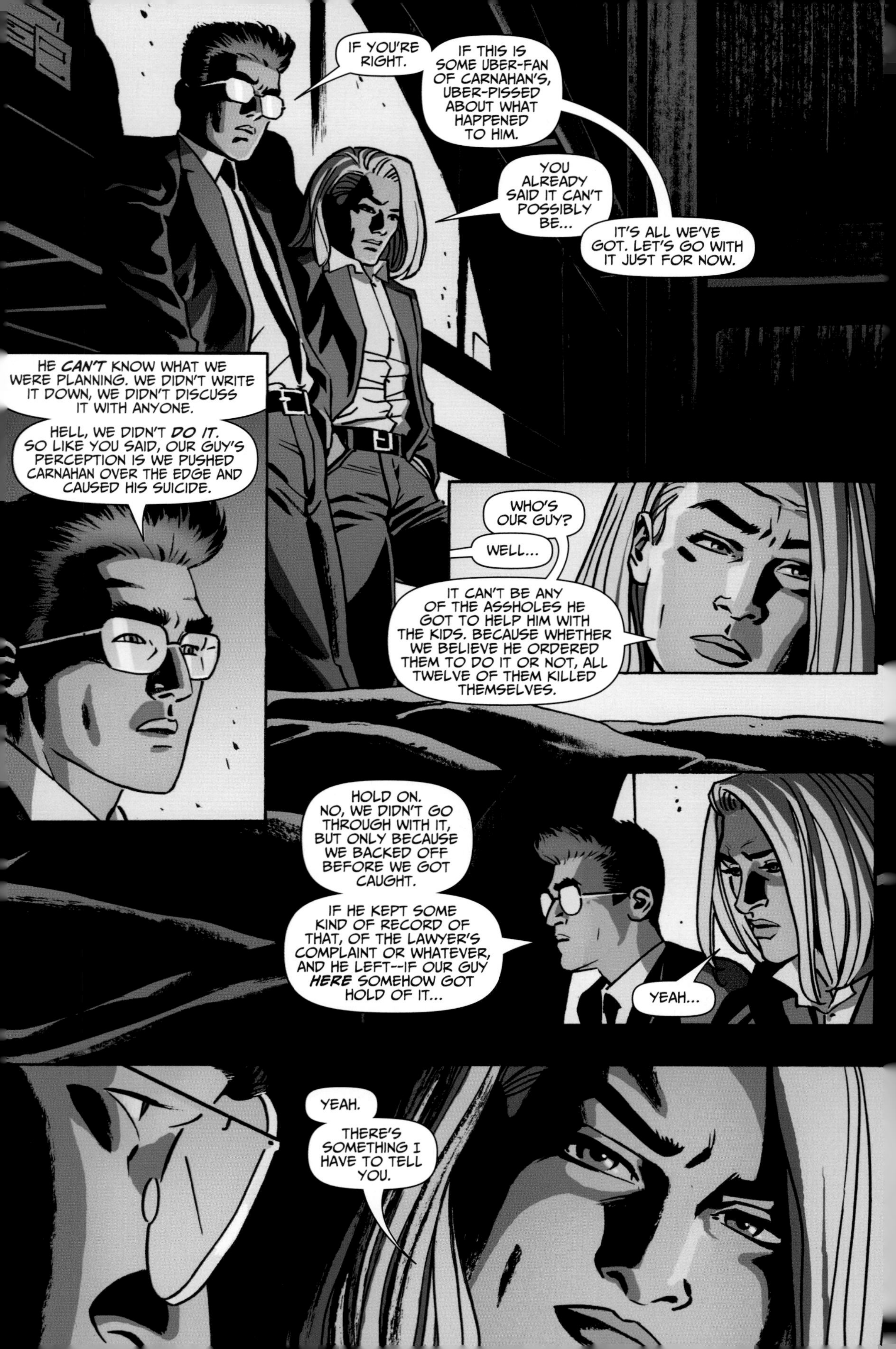
IF YOU'RE RIGHT.
IF THIS IS SOME UBER-FAN OF CARNAHAN'S, UBER-PISSED ABOUT WHAT HAPPENED TO HIM.
YOU ALREADY SAID IT CAN'T POSSIBLY BE...
IT'S ALL WE'VE GOT. LET'S GO WITH IT JUST FOR NOW.
HE *CAN'T* KNOW WHAT WE WERE PLANNING. WE DIDN'T WRITE IT DOWN, WE DIDN'T DISCUSS IT WITH ANYONE.
HELL, WE DIDN'T *DO IT*. SO LIKE YOU SAID, OUR GUY'S PERCEPTION IS WE PUSHED CARNAHAN OVER THE EDGE AND CAUSED HIS SUICIDE.
WHO'S OUR GUY?
WELL...
IT CAN'T BE ANY OF THE ASSHOLES HE GOT TO HELP HIM WITH THE KIDS. BECAUSE WHETHER WE BELIEVE HE ORDERED THEM TO DO IT OR NOT, ALL TWELVE OF THEM KILLED THEMSELVES.
HOLD ON. NO, WE DIDN'T GO THROUGH WITH IT, BUT ONLY BECAUSE WE BACKED OFF BEFORE WE GOT CAUGHT.
IF HE KEPT SOME KIND OF RECORD OF THAT, OF THE LAWYER'S COMPLAINT OR WHATEVER, AND HE LEFT--IF OUR GUY *HERE* SOMEHOW GOT HOLD OF IT...
YEAH...
YEAH.
THERE'S SOMETHING I HAVE TO TELL YOU.

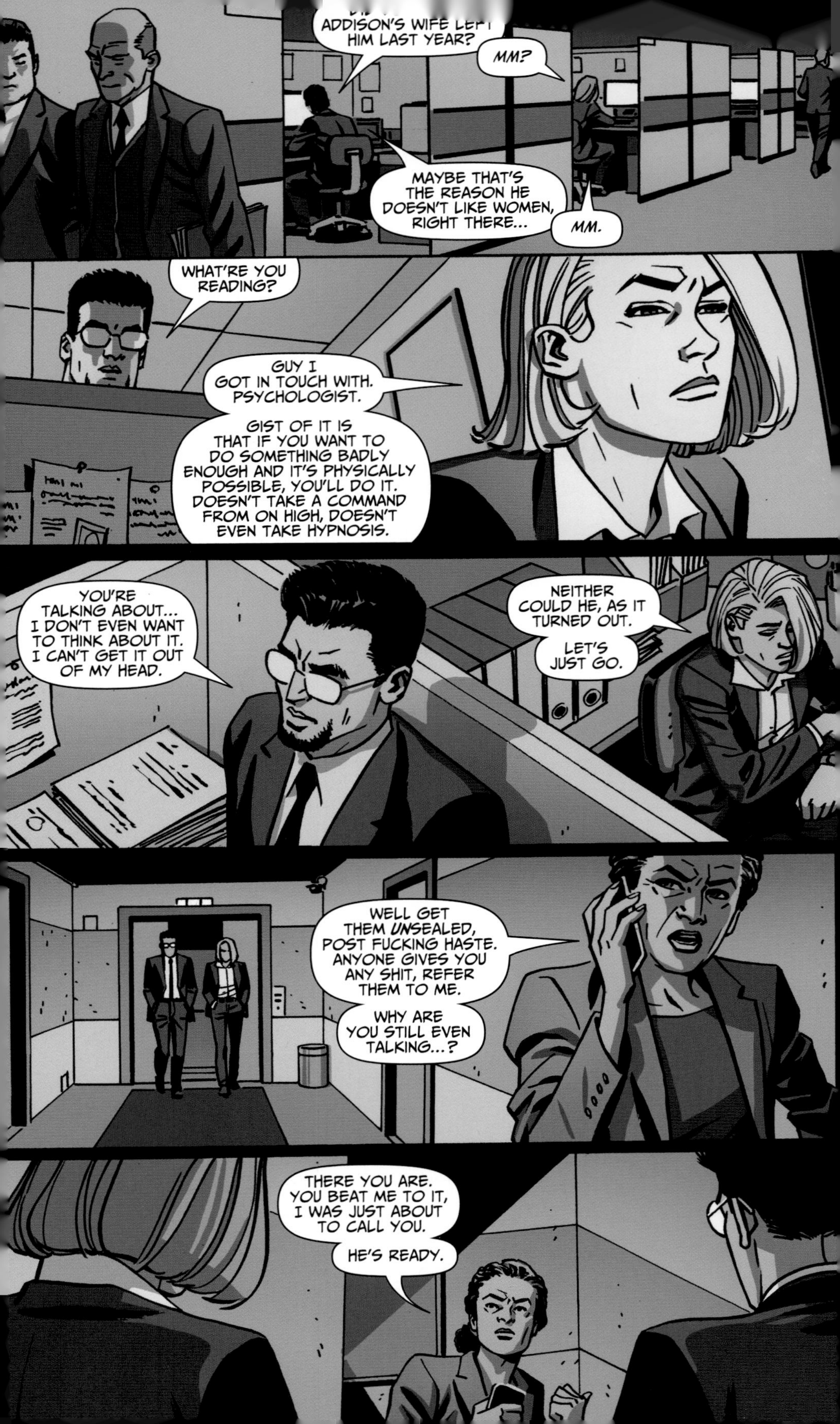
ADDISON'S WIFE LEFT HIM LAST YEAR?
MM?
MAYBE THAT'S THE REASON HE DOESN'T LIKE WOMEN, RIGHT THERE...
MM.
WHAT'RE YOU READING?
GUY I GOT IN TOUCH WITH. PSYCHOLOGIST.
GIST OF IT IS THAT IF YOU WANT TO DO SOMETHING BADLY ENOUGH AND IT'S PHYSICALLY POSSIBLE, YOU'LL DO IT. DOESN'T TAKE A COMMAND FROM ON HIGH, DOESN'T EVEN TAKE HYPNOSIS.
YOU'RE TALKING ABOUT... I DON'T EVEN WANT TO THINK ABOUT IT. I CAN'T GET IT OUT OF MY HEAD.
NEITHER COULD HE, AS IT TURNED OUT.
LET'S JUST GO.
WELL GET THEM *UNSEALED*, POST FUCKING HASTE. ANYONE GIVES YOU ANY SHIT, REFER THEM TO ME.
WHY ARE YOU STILL EVEN TALKING...?
THERE YOU ARE. YOU BEAT ME TO IT, I WAS JUST ABOUT TO CALL YOU.
HE'S READY.

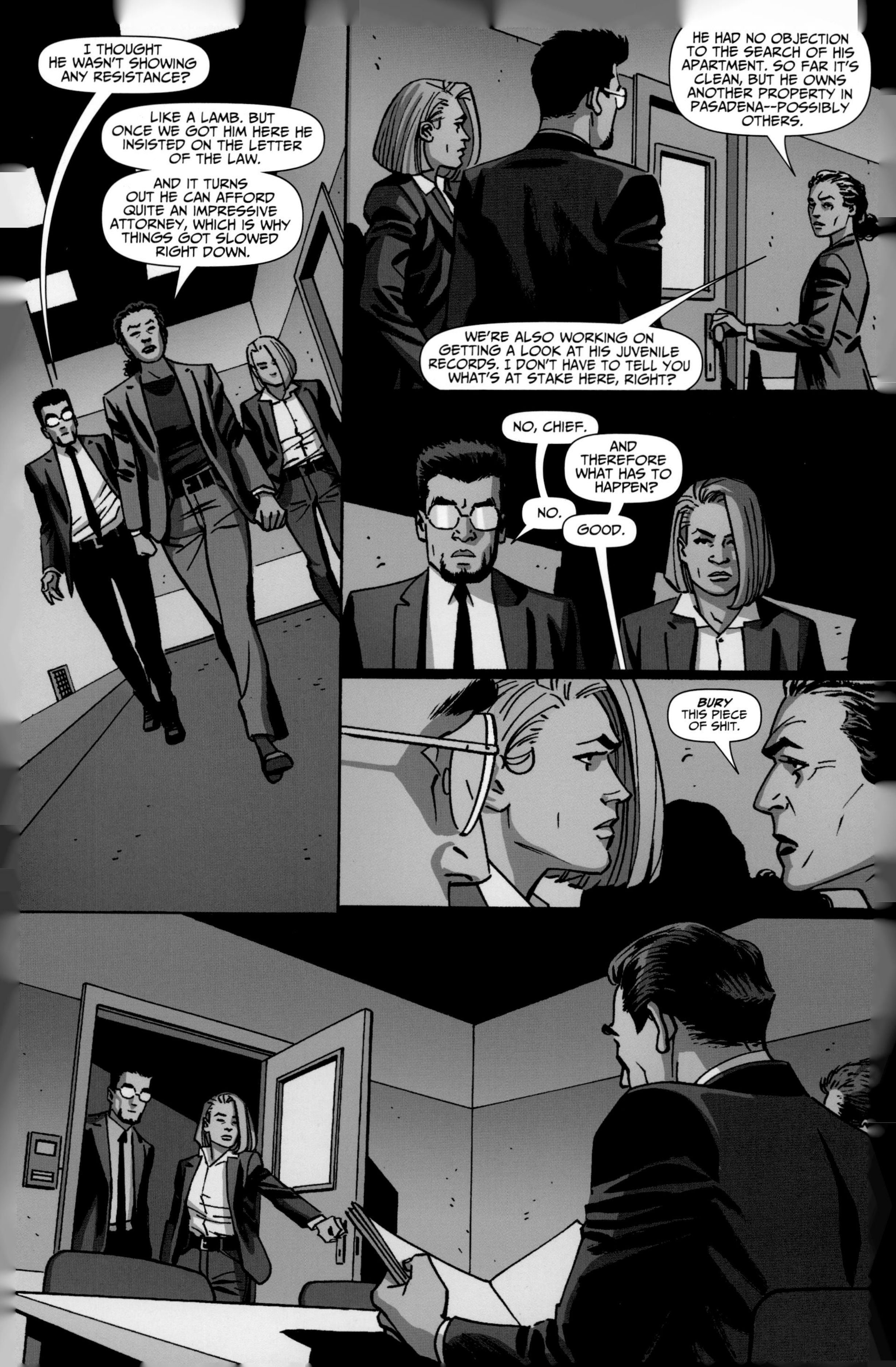
I THOUGHT HE WASN'T SHOWING ANY RESISTANCE?
LIKE A LAMB. BUT ONCE WE GOT HIM HERE HE INSISTED ON THE LETTER OF THE LAW.
AND IT TURNS OUT HE CAN AFFORD QUITE AN IMPRESSIVE ATTORNEY, WHICH IS WHY THINGS GOT SLOWED RIGHT DOWN.
HE HAD NO OBJECTION TO THE SEARCH OF HIS APARTMENT. SO FAR IT'S CLEAN, BUT HE OWNS ANOTHER PROPERTY IN PASADENA--POSSIBLY OTHERS.
WE'RE ALSO WORKING ON GETTING A LOOK AT HIS JUVENILE RECORDS. I DON'T HAVE TO TELL YOU WHAT'S AT STAKE HERE, RIGHT?
NO, CHIEF.
AND THEREFORE WHAT HAS TO HAPPEN?
NO.
GOOD.
BURY THIS PIECE OF SHIT.

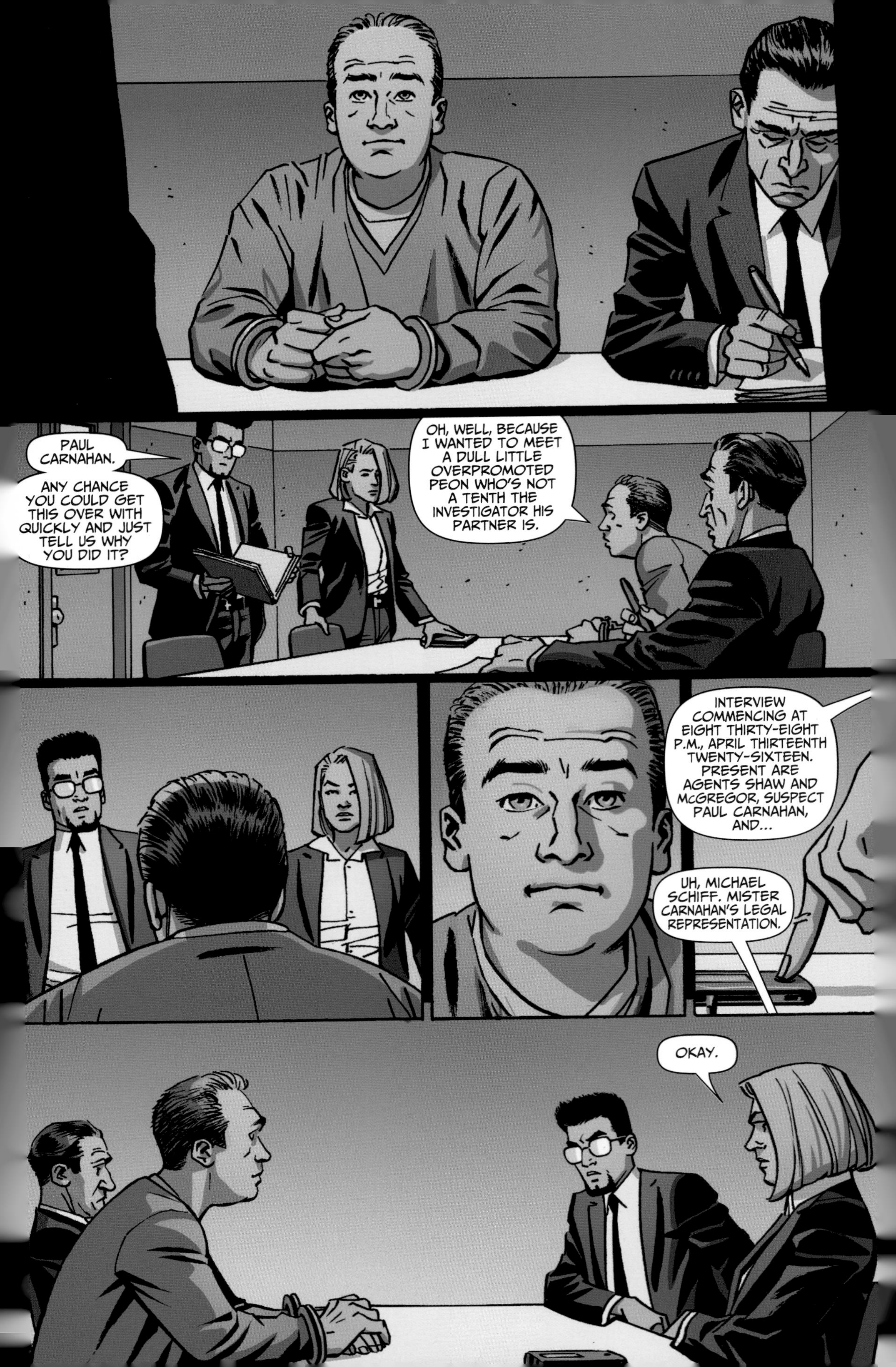
PAUL CARNAHAN.
ANY CHANCE YOU COULD GET THIS OVER WITH QUICKLY AND JUST TELL US WHY YOU DID IT?
OH, WELL, BECAUSE I WANTED TO MEET A DULL LITTLE OVERPROMOTED PEON WHO'S NOT A TENTH THE INVESTIGATOR HIS PARTNER IS.
INTERVIEW COMMENCING AT EIGHT THIRTY-EIGHT P.M., APRIL THIRTEENTH TWENTY-SIXTEEN. PRESENT ARE AGENTS SHAW AND McGREGOR, SUSPECT PAUL CARNAHAN, AND...
UH, MICHAEL SCHIFF. MISTER CARNAHAN'S LEGAL REPRESENTATION.
OKAY.

4

FOUR

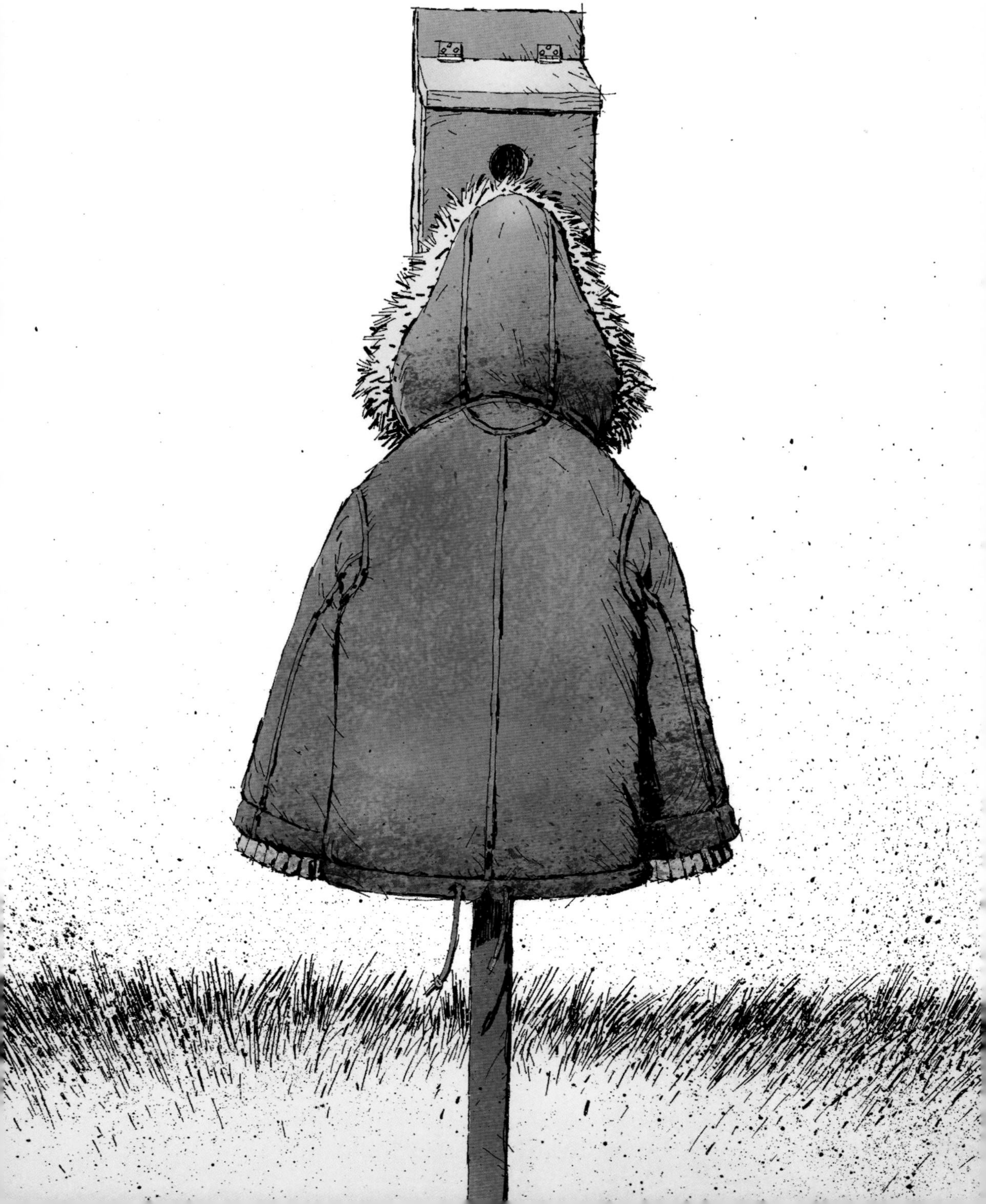

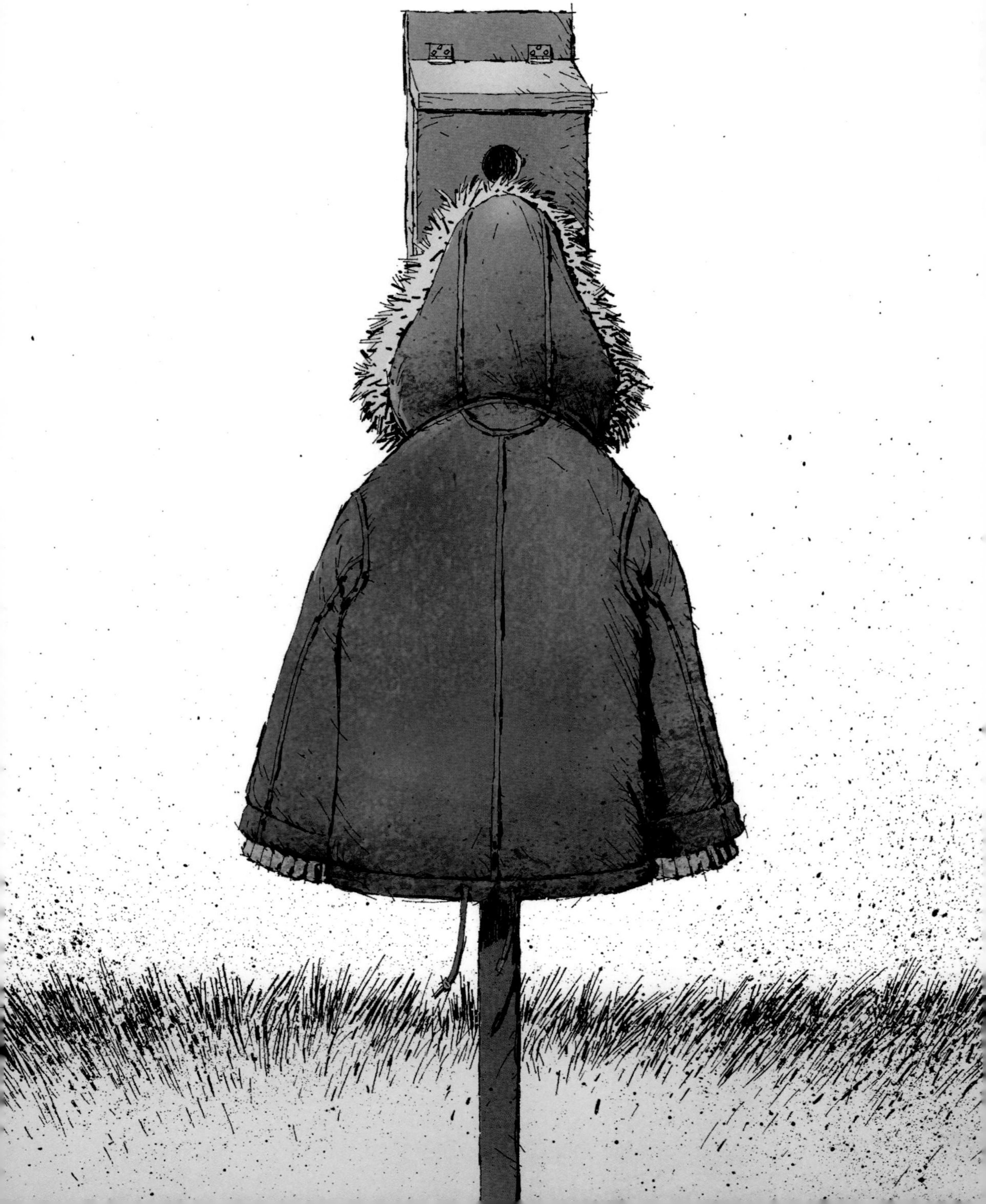

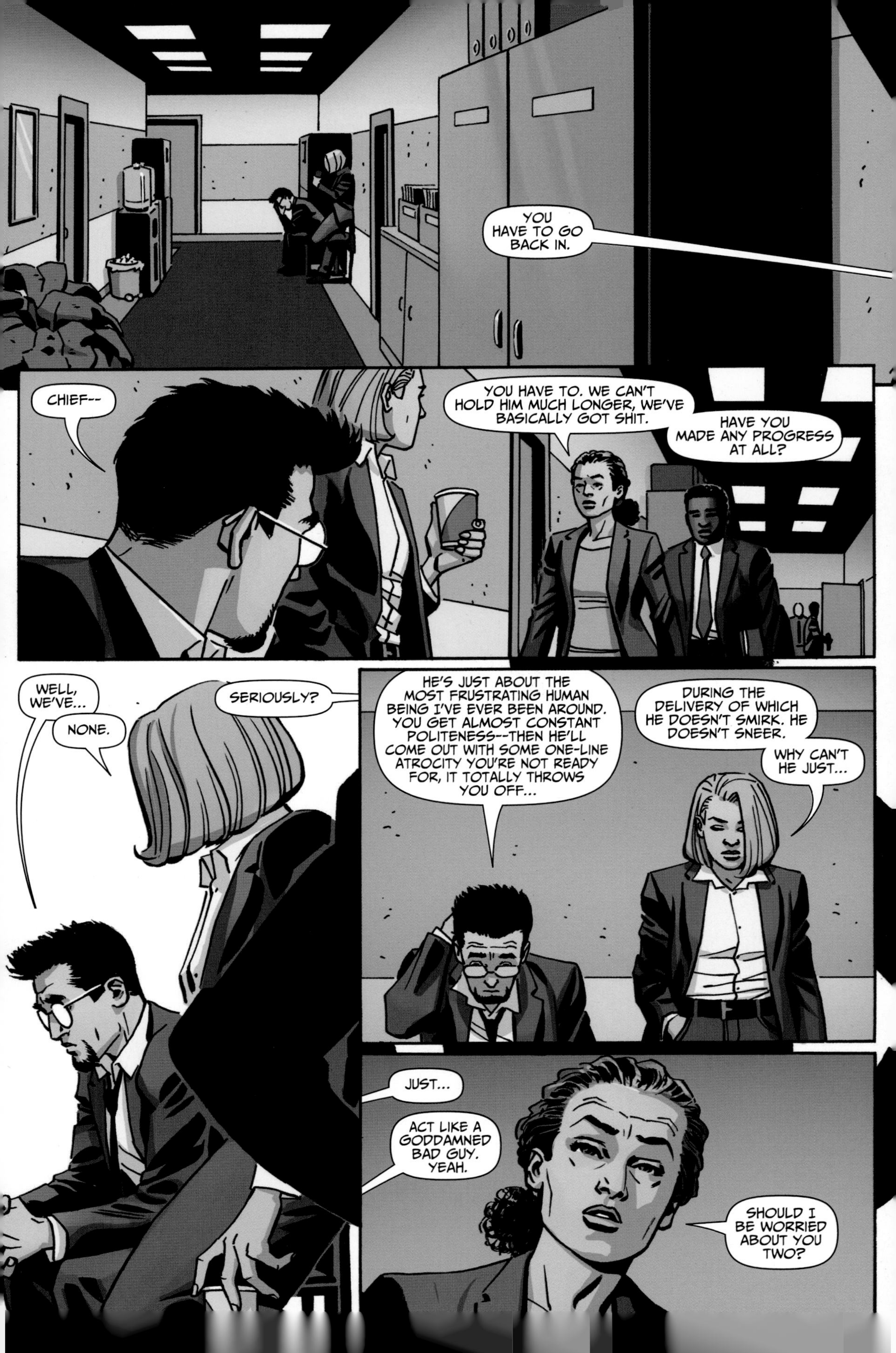
YOU HAVE TO GO BACK IN.
CHIEF--
YOU HAVE TO. WE CAN'T HOLD HIM MUCH LONGER, WE'VE BASICALLY GOT SHIT.
HAVE YOU MADE ANY PROGRESS AT ALL?
WELL, WE'VE...
NONE.
SERIOUSLY?
HE'S JUST ABOUT THE MOST FRUSTRATING HUMAN BEING I'VE EVER BEEN AROUND. YOU GET ALMOST CONSTANT POLITENESS--THEN HE'LL COME OUT WITH SOME ONE-LINE ATROCITY YOU'RE NOT READY FOR, IT TOTALLY THROWS YOU OFF...
DURING THE DELIVERY OF WHICH HE DOESN'T SMIRK. HE DOESN'T SNEER.
WHY CAN'T HE JUST...
JUST...
ACT LIKE A GODDAMNED BAD GUY. YEAH.
SHOULD I BE WORRIED ABOUT YOU TWO?

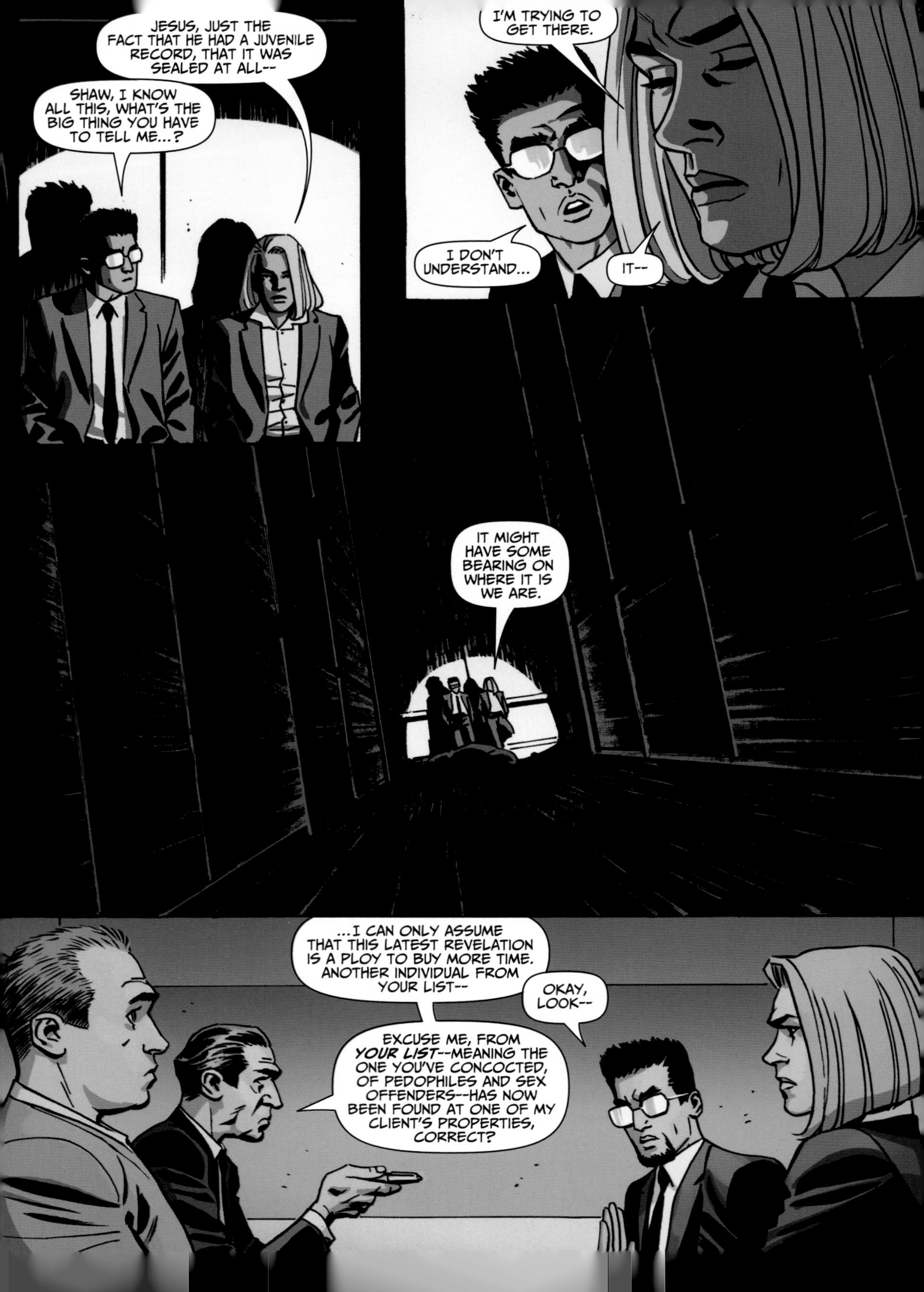
JESUS, JUST THE FACT THAT HE HAD A JUVENILE RECORD, THAT IT WAS SEALED AT ALL--
SHAW, I KNOW ALL THIS, WHAT'S THE BIG THING YOU HAVE TO TELL ME...?
I'M TRYING TO GET THERE.
I DON'T UNDERSTAND...
IT--
IT MIGHT HAVE SOME BEARING ON WHERE IT IS WE ARE.
...I CAN ONLY ASSUME THAT THIS LATEST REVELATION IS A PLOY TO BUY MORE TIME. ANOTHER INDIVIDUAL FROM YOUR LIST--
OKAY, LOOK--
EXCUSE ME, FROM *YOUR LIST*--MEANING THE ONE YOU'VE CONCOCTED, OF PEDOPHILES AND SEX OFFENDERS--HAS NOW BEEN FOUND AT ONE OF MY CLIENT'S PROPERTIES, CORRECT?

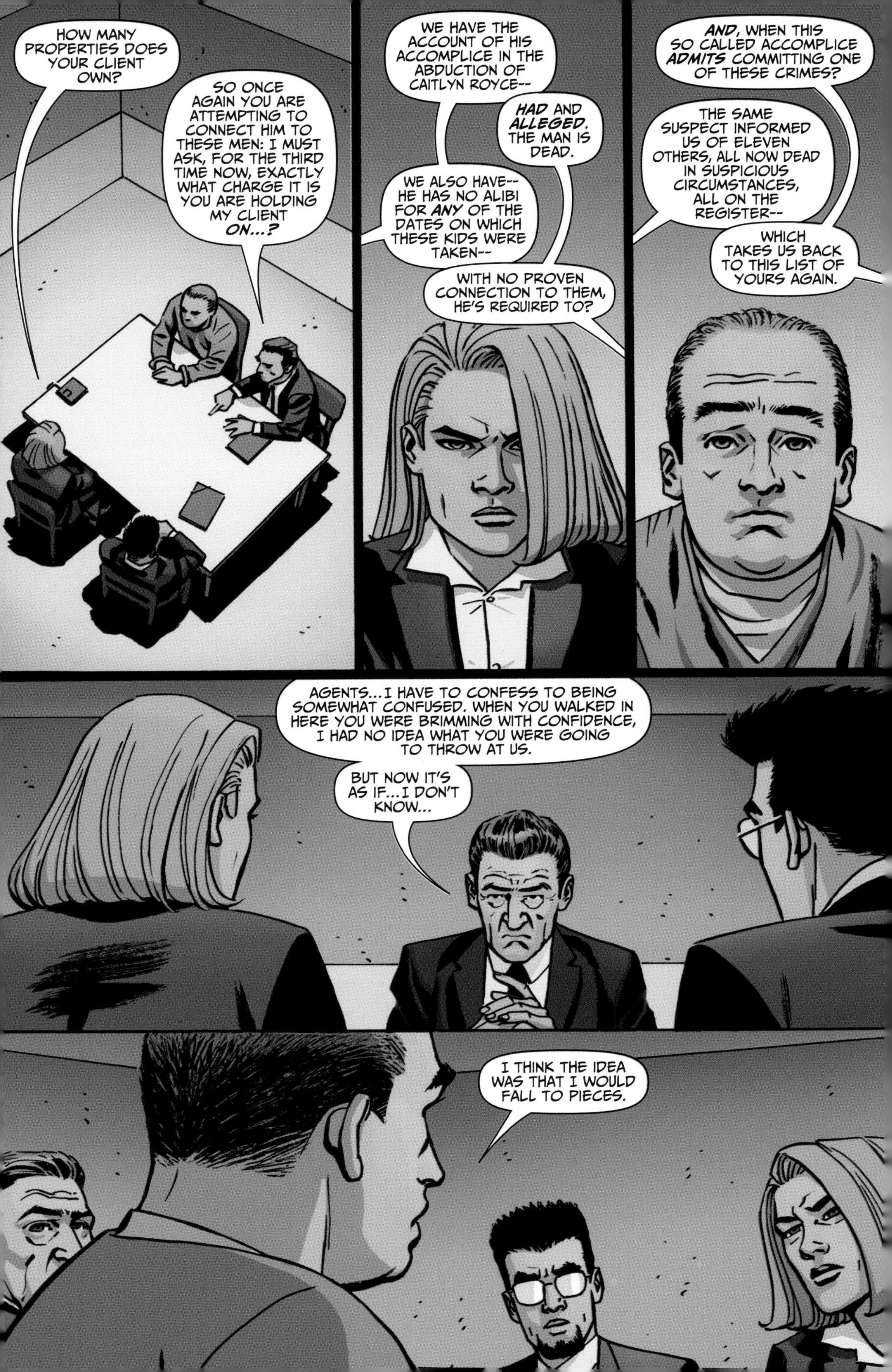
HOW MANY PROPERTIES DOES YOUR CLIENT OWN?
SO ONCE AGAIN YOU ARE ATTEMPTING TO CONNECT HIM TO THESE MEN: I MUST ASK, FOR THE THIRD TIME NOW, EXACTLY WHAT CHARGE IT IS YOU ARE HOLDING MY CLIENT ON...?
WE HAVE THE ACCOUNT OF HIS ACCOMPLICE IN THE ABDUCTION OF CAITLYN ROYCE--
HAD AND ALLEGED. THE MAN IS DEAD.
WE ALSO HAVE-- HE HAS NO ALIBI FOR ANY OF THE DATES ON WHICH THESE KIDS WERE TAKEN--
WITH NO PROVEN CONNECTION TO THEM, HE'S REQUIRED TO?
AND, WHEN THIS SO CALLED ACCOMPLICE ADMITS COMMITTING ONE OF THESE CRIMES?
THE SAME SUSPECT INFORMED US OF ELEVEN OTHERS, ALL NOW DEAD IN SUSPICIOUS CIRCUMSTANCES, ALL ON THE REGISTER--
WHICH TAKES US BACK TO THIS LIST OF YOURS AGAIN.
AGENTS...I HAVE TO CONFESS TO BEING SOMEWHAT CONFUSED. WHEN YOU WALKED IN HERE YOU WERE BRIMMING WITH CONFIDENCE, I HAD NO IDEA WHAT YOU WERE GOING TO THROW AT US.
BUT NOW IT'S AS IF...I DON'T KNOW...
I THINK THE IDEA WAS THAT I WOULD FALL TO PIECES.

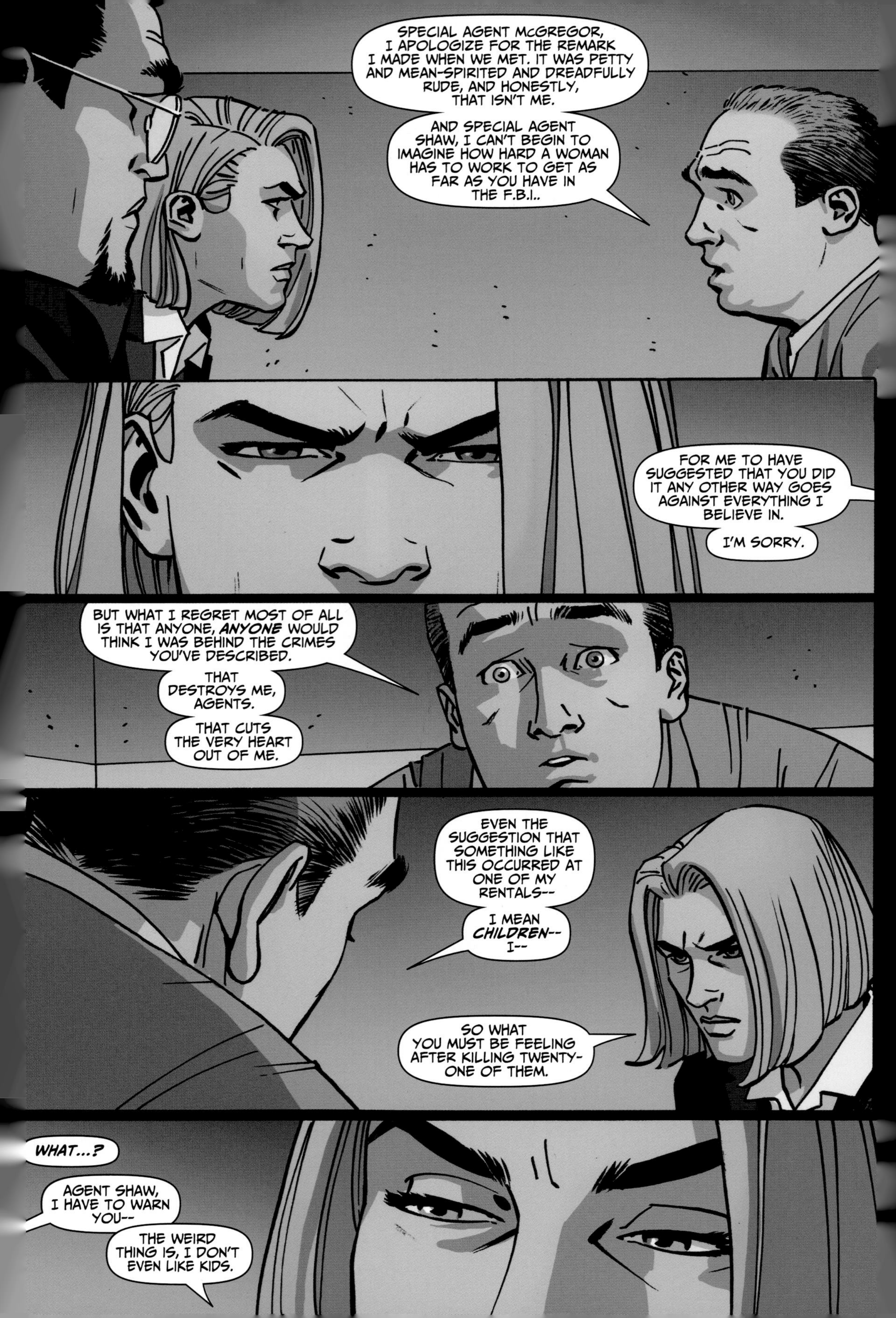
SPECIAL AGENT McGREGOR, I APOLOGIZE FOR THE REMARK I MADE WHEN WE MET. IT WAS PETTY AND MEAN-SPIRITED AND DREADFULLY RUDE, AND HONESTLY, THAT ISN'T ME.
AND SPECIAL AGENT SHAW, I CAN'T BEGIN TO IMAGINE HOW HARD A WOMAN HAS TO WORK TO GET AS FAR AS YOU HAVE IN THE F.B.I..
FOR ME TO HAVE SUGGESTED THAT YOU DID IT ANY OTHER WAY GOES AGAINST EVERYTHING I BELIEVE IN.
I'M SORRY.
BUT WHAT I REGRET MOST OF ALL IS THAT ANYONE, *ANYONE* WOULD THINK I WAS BEHIND THE CRIMES YOU'VE DESCRIBED.
THAT DESTROYS ME, AGENTS.
THAT CUTS THE VERY HEART OUT OF ME.
EVEN THE SUGGESTION THAT SOMETHING LIKE THIS OCCURRED AT ONE OF MY RENTALS--
I MEAN *CHILDREN*-- I--
SO WHAT YOU MUST BE FEELING AFTER KILLING TWENTY-ONE OF THEM.
WHAT...?
AGENT SHAW, I HAVE TO WARN YOU--
THE WEIRD THING IS, I DON'T EVEN LIKE KIDS.

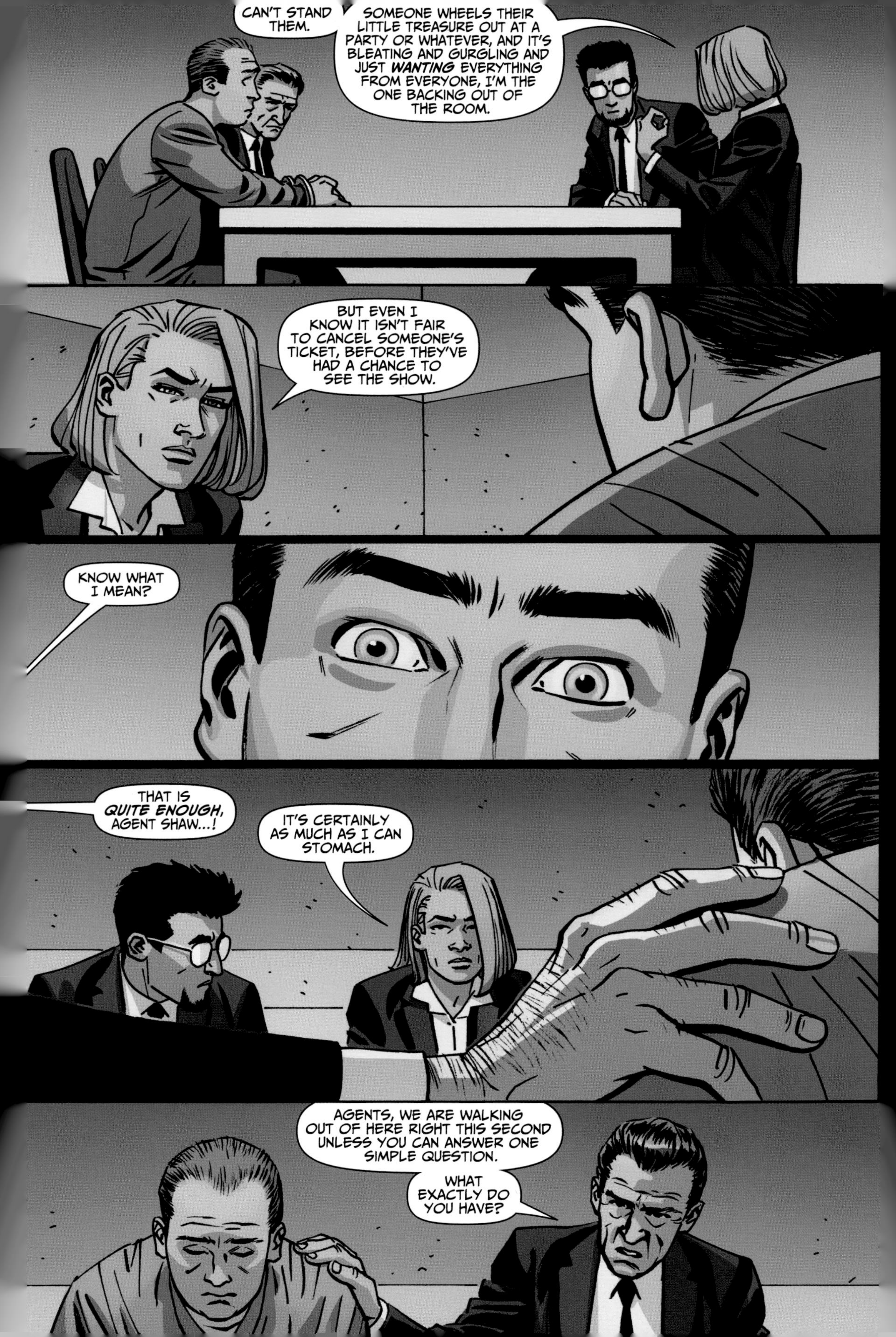
CAN'T STAND THEM.
SOMEONE WHEELS THEIR LITTLE TREASURE OUT AT A PARTY OR WHATEVER, AND IT'S BLEATING AND GURGLING AND JUST WANTING EVERYTHING FROM EVERYONE, I'M THE ONE BACKING OUT OF THE ROOM.
BUT EVEN I KNOW IT ISN'T FAIR TO CANCEL SOMEONE'S TICKET, BEFORE THEY'VE HAD A CHANCE TO SEE THE SHOW.
KNOW WHAT I MEAN?
THAT IS QUITE ENOUGH, AGENT SHAW...!
IT'S CERTAINLY AS MUCH AS I CAN STOMACH.
AGENTS, WE ARE WALKING OUT OF HERE RIGHT THIS SECOND UNLESS YOU CAN ANSWER ONE SIMPLE QUESTION.
WHAT EXACTLY DO YOU HAVE?

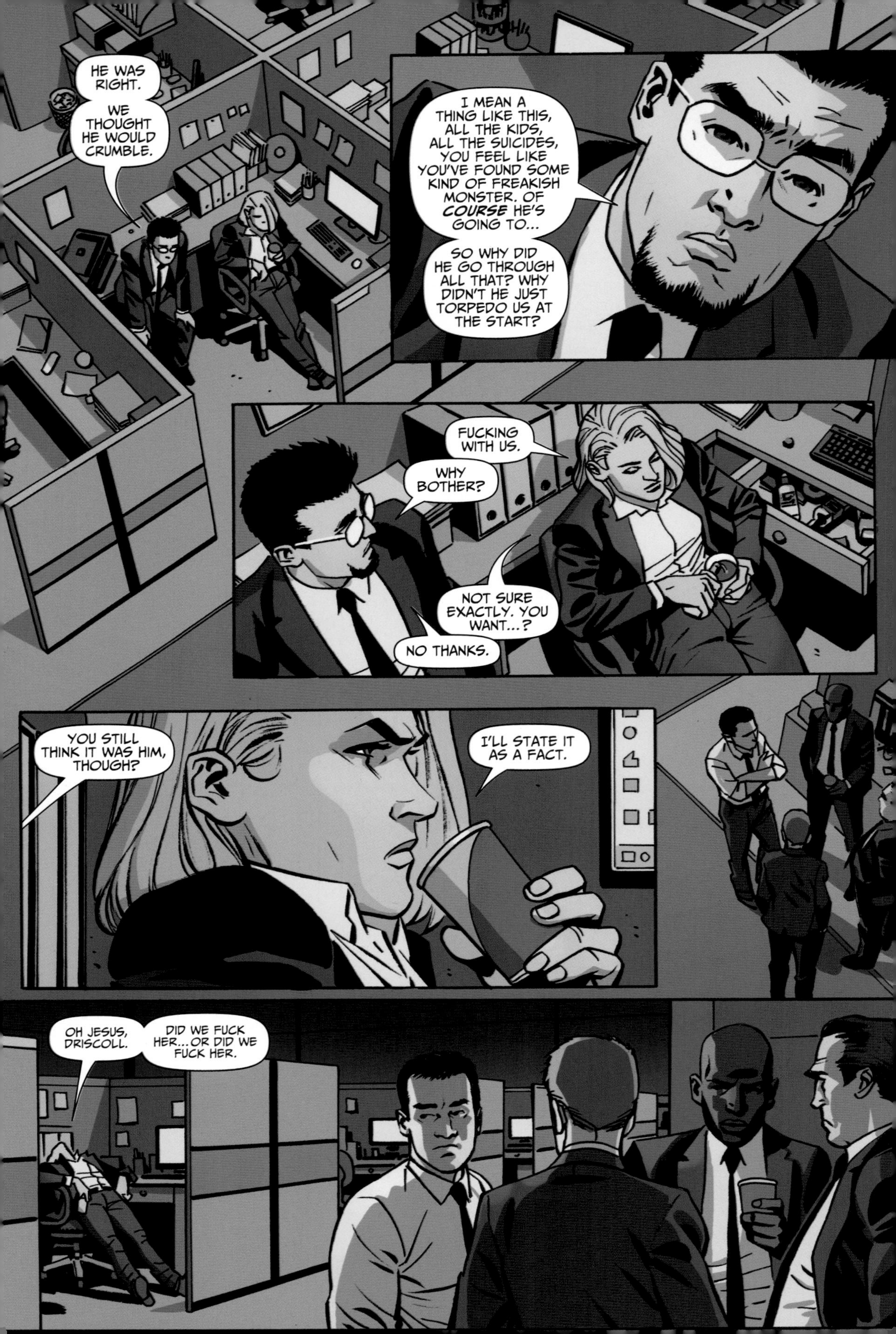
HE WAS RIGHT.
WE THOUGHT HE WOULD CRUMBLE.
I MEAN A THING LIKE THIS, ALL THE KIDS, ALL THE SUICIDES, YOU FEEL LIKE YOU'VE FOUND SOME KIND OF FREAKISH MONSTER. OF *COURSE* HE'S GOING TO...
SO WHY DID HE GO THROUGH ALL THAT? WHY DIDN'T HE JUST TORPEDO US AT THE START?
FUCKING WITH US.
WHY BOTHER?
NOT SURE EXACTLY. YOU WANT...?
NO THANKS.
YOU STILL THINK IT WAS HIM, THOUGH?
I'LL STATE IT AS A FACT.
OH JESUS, DRISCOLL.
DID WE FUCK HER...OR DID WE FUCK HER.

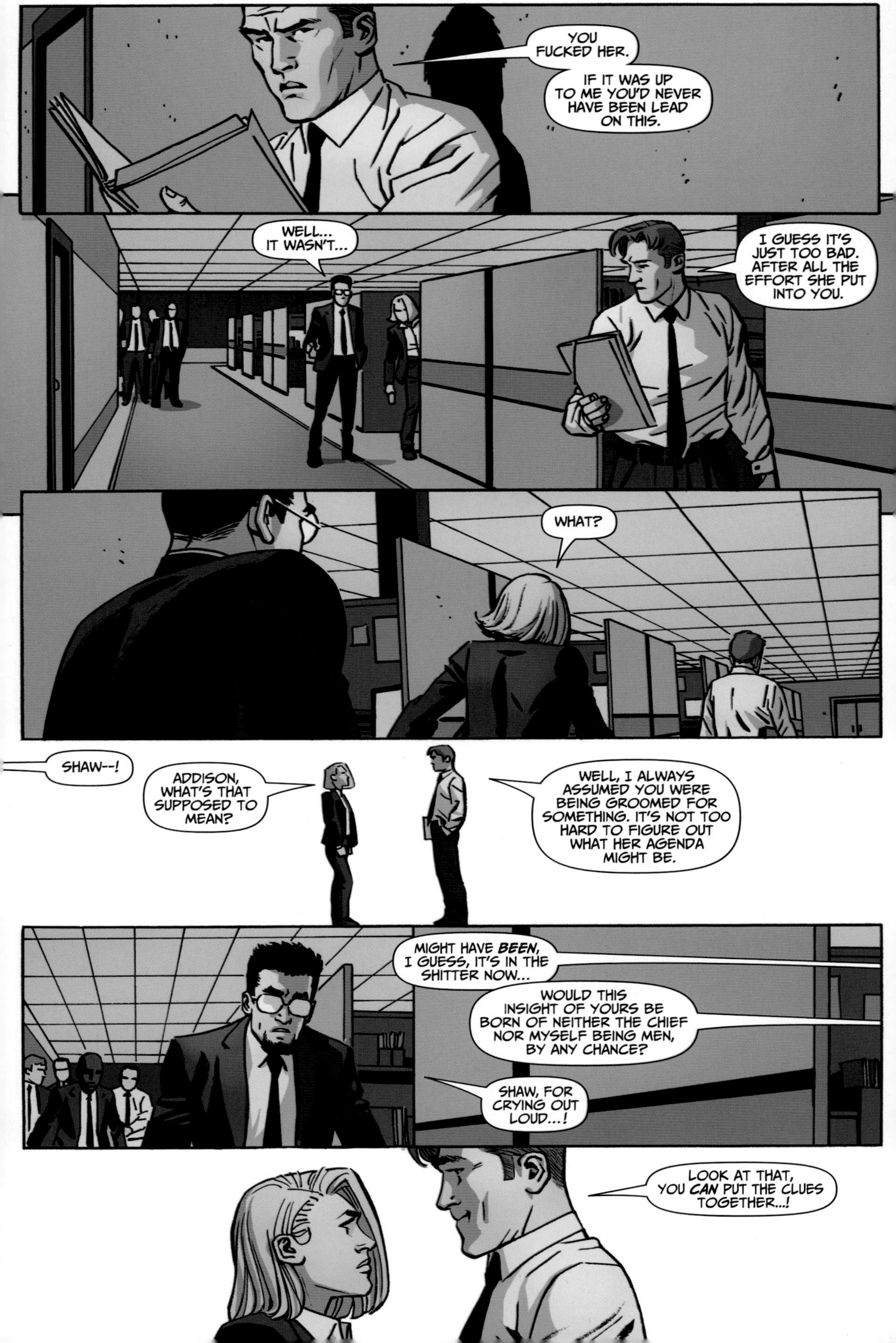
YOU FUCKED HER.
IF IT WAS UP TO ME YOU'D NEVER HAVE BEEN LEAD ON THIS.
WELL... IT WASN'T...
I GUESS IT'S JUST TOO BAD. AFTER ALL THE EFFORT SHE PUT INTO YOU.
WHAT?
SHAW--!
ADDISON, WHAT'S THAT SUPPOSED TO MEAN?
WELL, I ALWAYS ASSUMED YOU WERE BEING GROOMED FOR SOMETHING. IT'S NOT TOO HARD TO FIGURE OUT WHAT HER AGENDA MIGHT BE.
MIGHT HAVE *BEEN*, I GUESS, IT'S IN THE SHITTER NOW...
WOULD THIS INSIGHT OF YOURS BE BORN OF NEITHER THE CHIEF NOR MYSELF BEING MEN, BY ANY CHANCE?
SHAW, FOR CRYING OUT LOUD...!
LOOK AT THAT, YOU *CAN* PUT THE CLUES TOGETHER...!

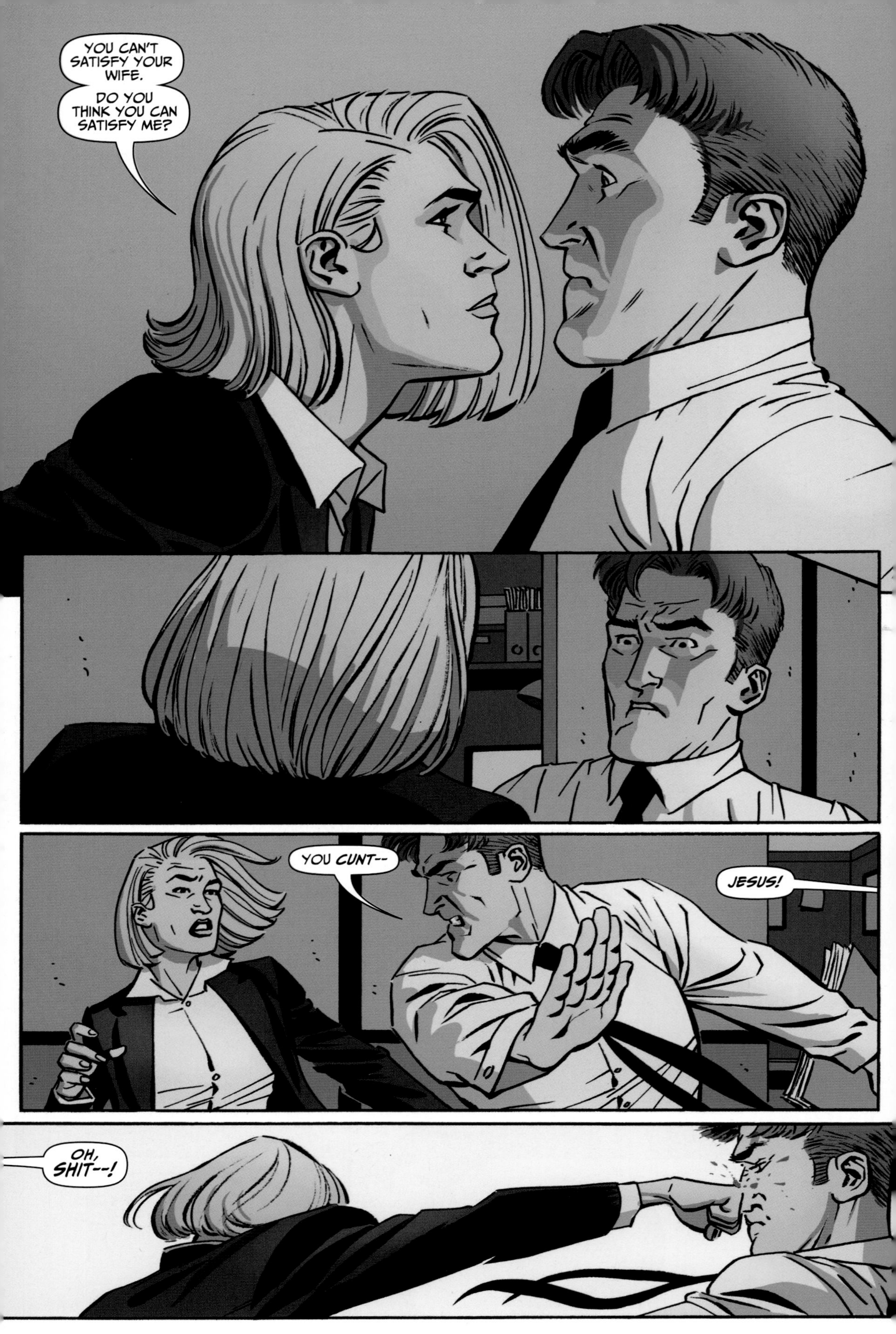
YOU CAN'T SATISFY YOUR WIFE.
DO YOU THINK YOU CAN SATISFY ME?
YOU CUNT--
JESUS!
OH, SHIT--!

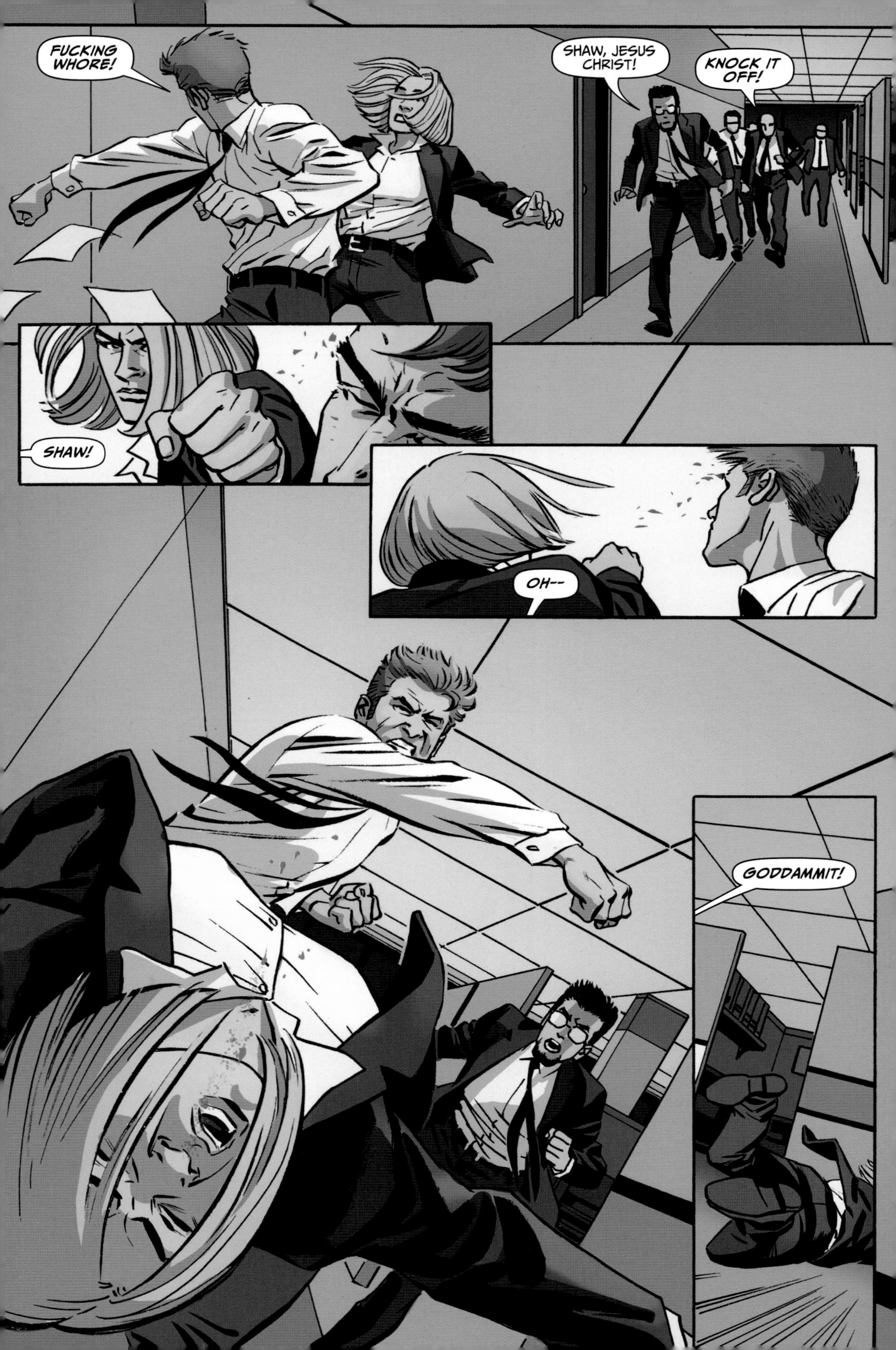
FUCKING WHORE!
SHAW, JESUS CHRIST!
KNOCK IT OFF!
SHAW!
OH--
GODDAMMIT!

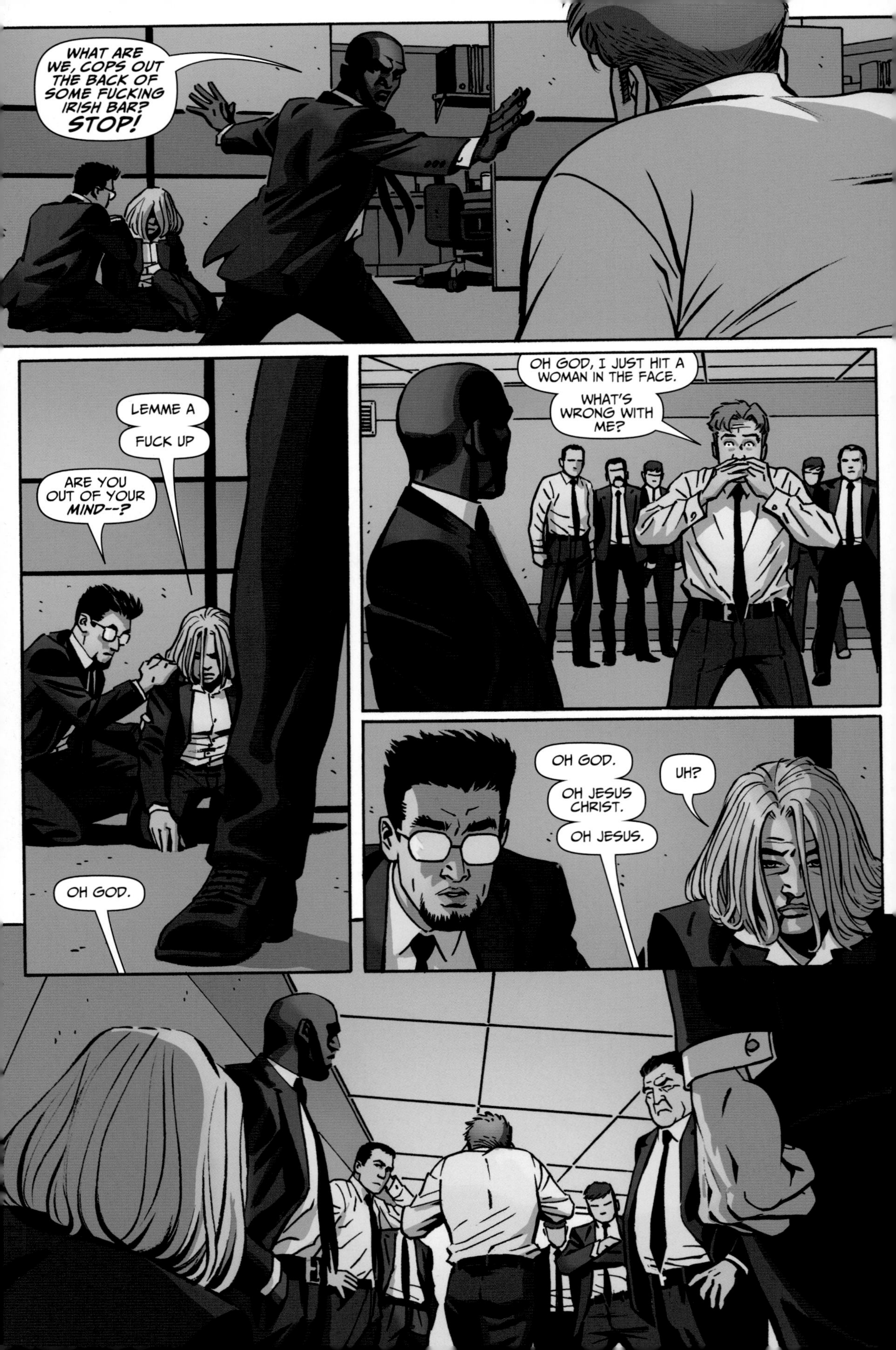
WHAT ARE WE, COPS OUT THE BACK OF SOME FUCKING IRISH BAR? STOP!
LEMME A
FUCK UP
ARE YOU OUT OF YOUR MIND--?
OH GOD.
OH GOD, I JUST HIT A WOMAN IN THE FACE.
WHAT'S WRONG WITH ME?
OH GOD.
OH JESUS CHRIST.
OH JESUS.
UH?

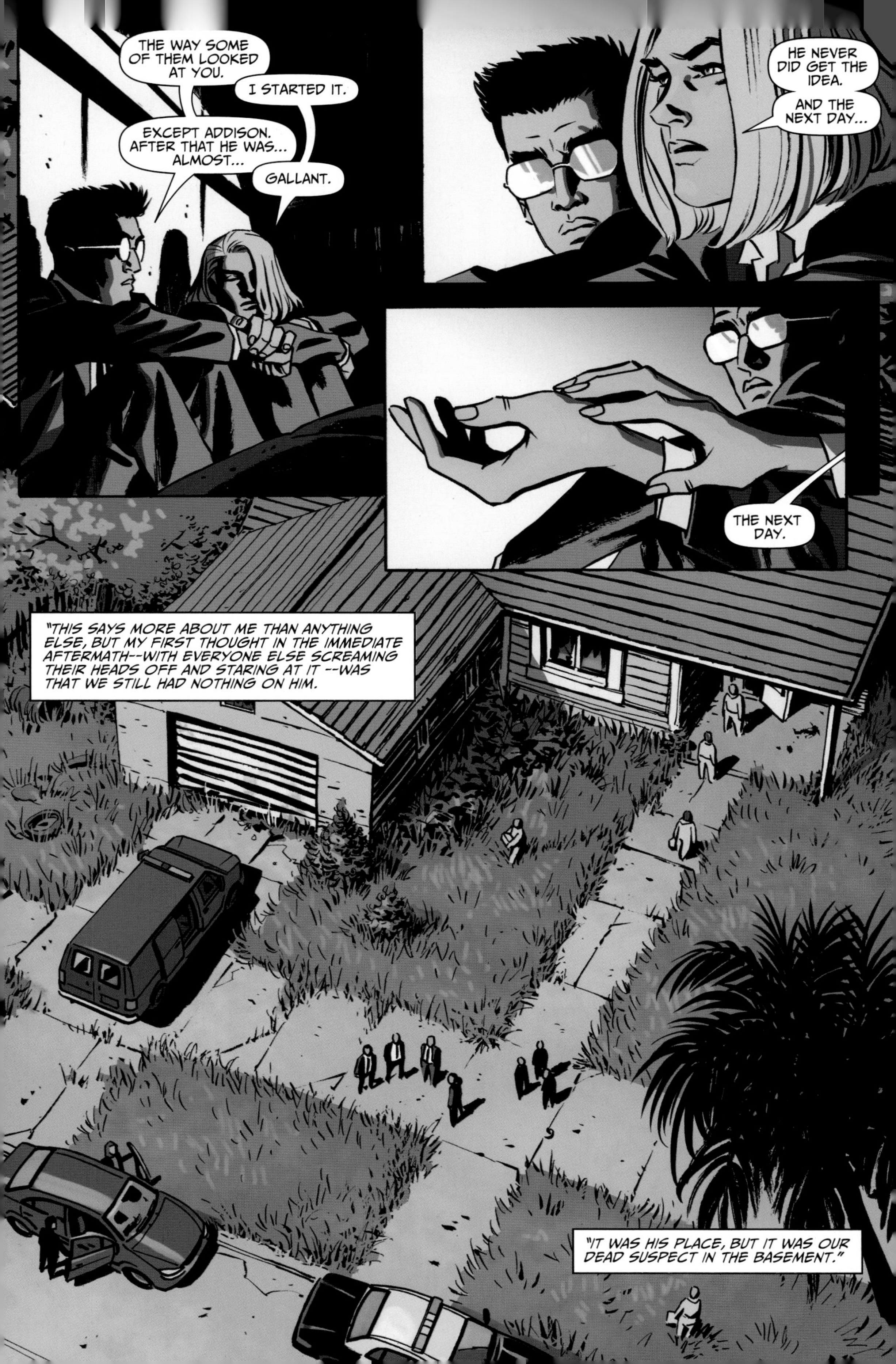
THE WAY SOME OF THEM LOOKED AT YOU.
I STARTED IT.
EXCEPT ADDISON. AFTER THAT HE WAS... ALMOST...
GALLANT.
HE NEVER DID GET THE IDEA.
AND THE NEXT DAY...
THE NEXT DAY.
"THIS SAYS MORE ABOUT ME THAN ANYTHING ELSE, BUT MY FIRST THOUGHT IN THE IMMEDIATE AFTERMATH--WITH EVERYONE ELSE SCREAMING THEIR HEADS OFF AND STARING AT IT --WAS THAT WE STILL HAD NOTHING ON HIM.
"IT WAS HIS PLACE, BUT IT WAS OUR DEAD SUSPECT IN THE BASEMENT."

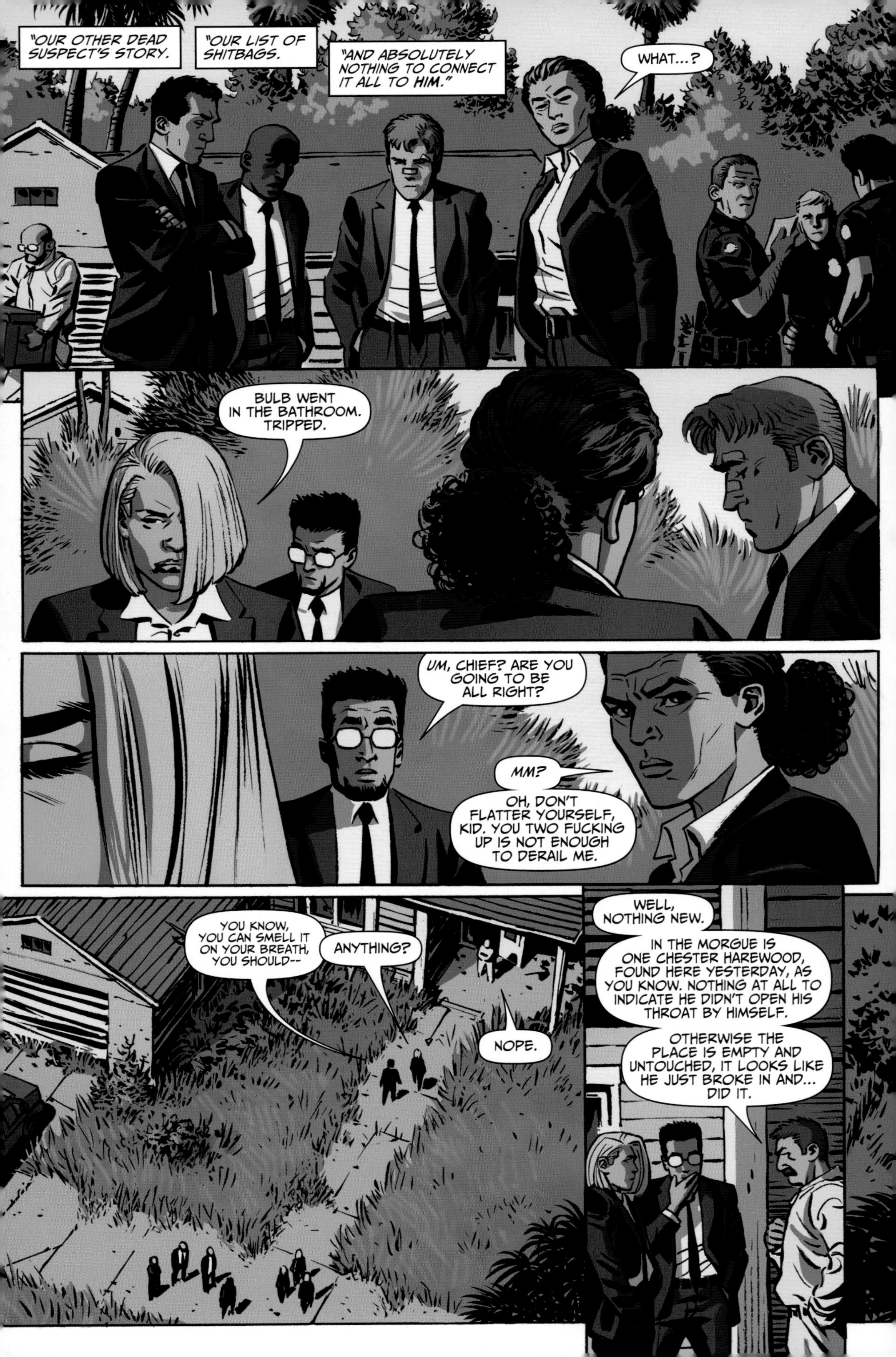
"OUR OTHER DEAD SUSPECT'S STORY.
"OUR LIST OF SHITBAGS.
"AND ABSOLUTELY NOTHING TO CONNECT IT ALL TO HIM."
WHAT...?
BULB WENT IN THE BATHROOM. TRIPPED.
UM, CHIEF? ARE YOU GOING TO BE ALL RIGHT?
MM?
OH, DON'T FLATTER YOURSELF, KID. YOU TWO FUCKING UP IS NOT ENOUGH TO DERAIL ME.
YOU KNOW, YOU CAN SMELL IT ON YOUR BREATH, YOU SHOULD--
ANYTHING?
NOPE.
WELL, NOTHING NEW.
IN THE MORGUE IS ONE CHESTER HAREWOOD, FOUND HERE YESTERDAY, AS YOU KNOW. NOTHING AT ALL TO INDICATE HE DIDN'T OPEN HIS THROAT BY HIMSELF.
OTHERWISE THE PLACE IS EMPTY AND UNTOUCHED, IT LOOKS LIKE HE JUST BROKE IN AND... DID IT.

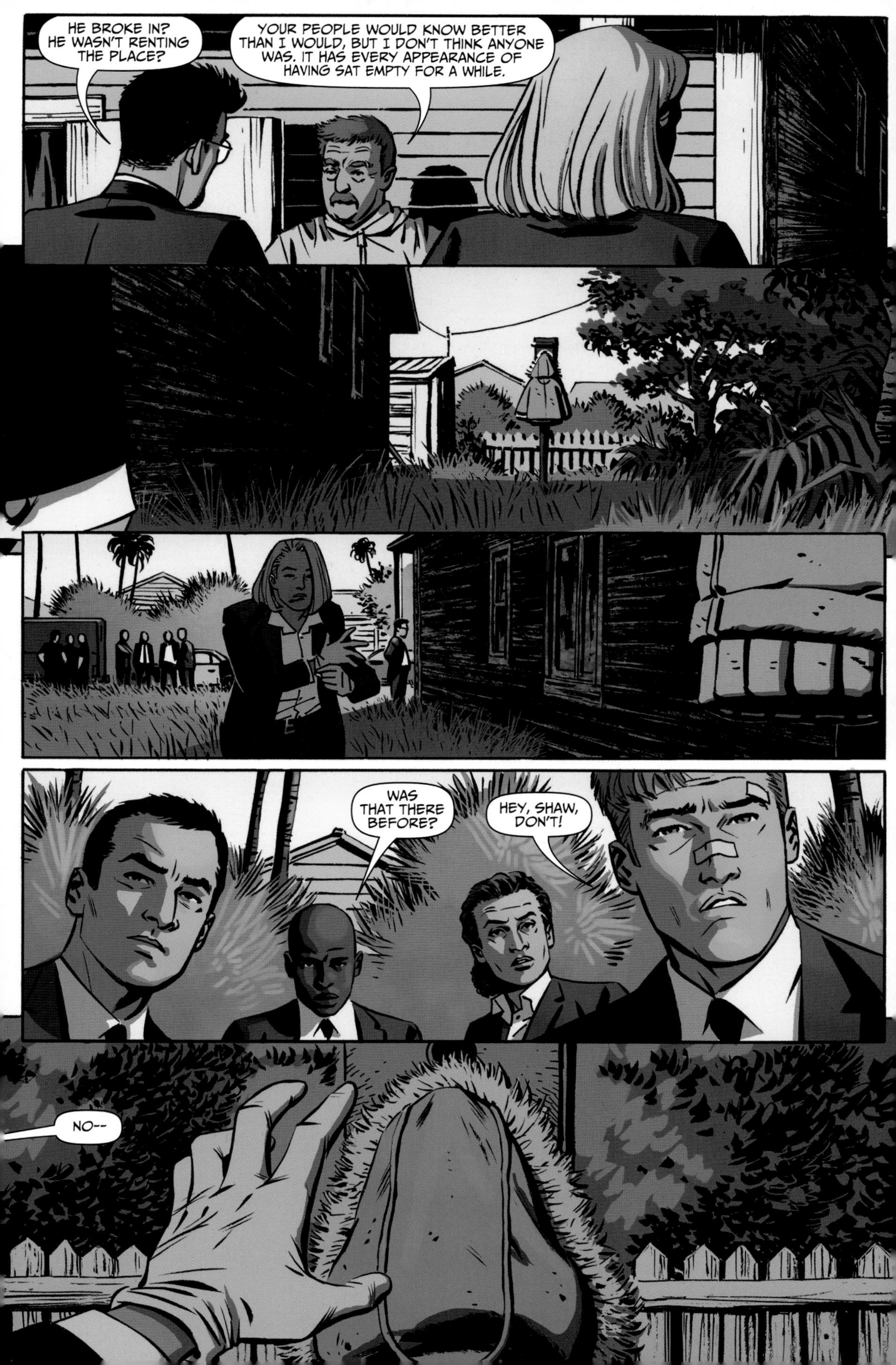
HE BROKE IN? HE WASN'T RENTING THE PLACE?
YOUR PEOPLE WOULD KNOW BETTER THAN I WOULD, BUT I DON'T THINK ANYONE WAS. IT HAS EVERY APPEARANCE OF HAVING SAT EMPTY FOR A WHILE.
WAS THAT THERE BEFORE?
HEY, SHAW, DON'T!
NO--

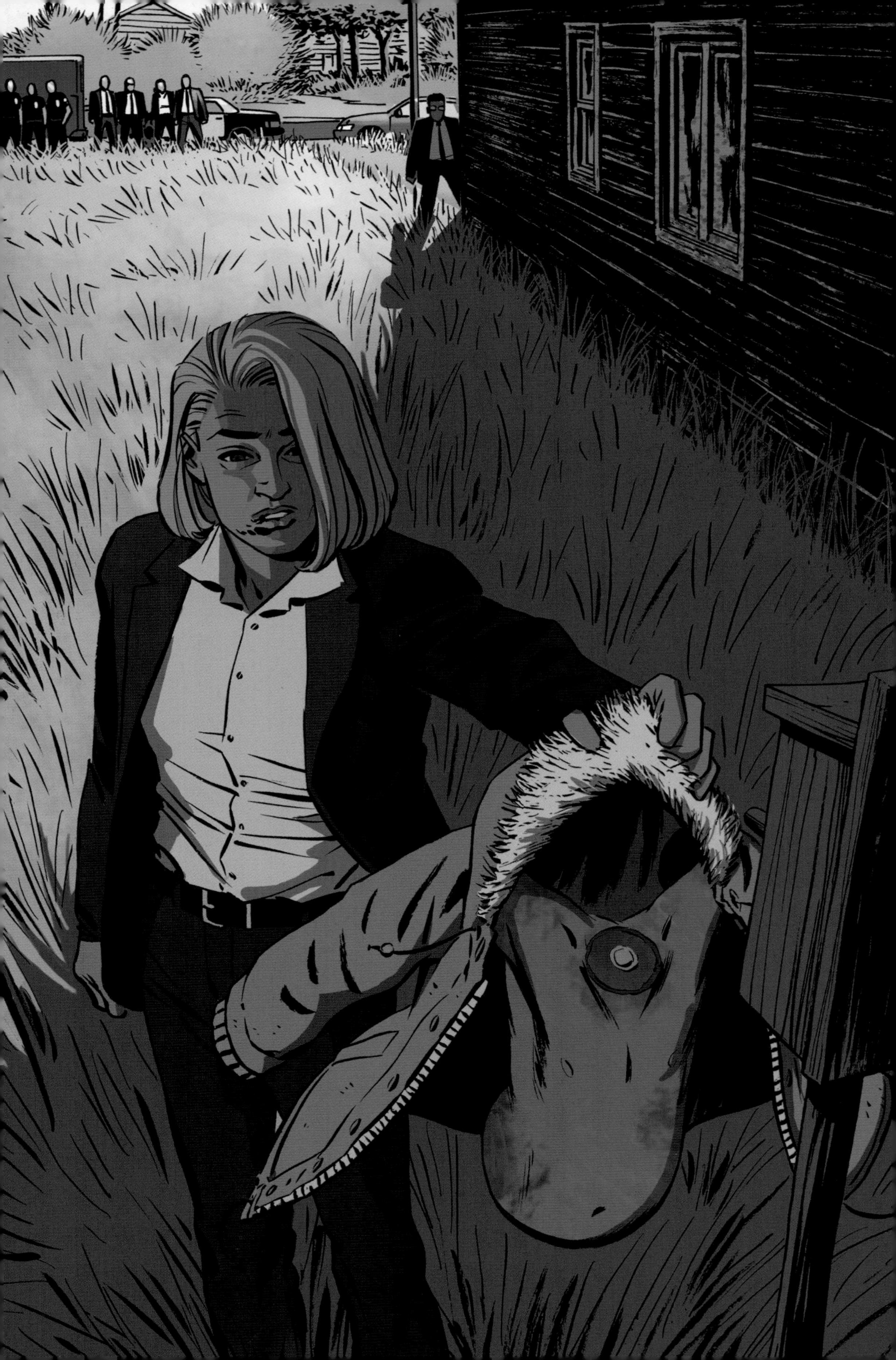

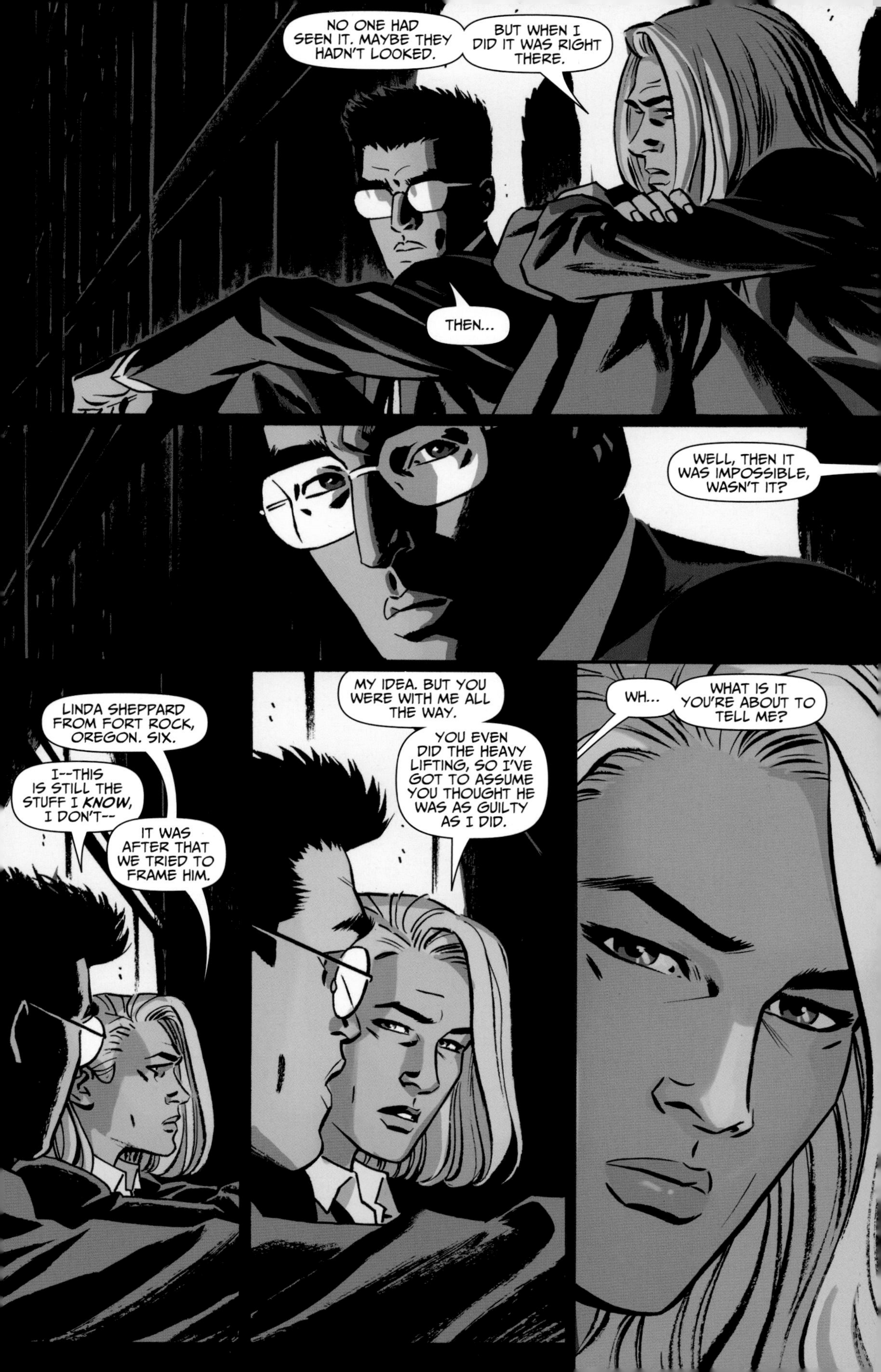
NO ONE HAD SEEN IT. MAYBE THEY HADN'T LOOKED.
BUT WHEN I DID IT WAS RIGHT THERE.
THEN...
WELL, THEN IT WAS IMPOSSIBLE, WASN'T IT?
LINDA SHEPPARD FROM FORT ROCK, OREGON. SIX.
I--THIS IS STILL THE STUFF I *KNOW*, I DON'T--
IT WAS AFTER THAT WE TRIED TO FRAME HIM.
MY IDEA. BUT YOU WERE WITH ME ALL THE WAY.
YOU EVEN DID THE HEAVY LIFTING, SO I'VE GOT TO ASSUME YOU THOUGHT HE WAS AS GUILTY AS I DID.
WH...
WHAT IS IT YOU'RE ABOUT TO TELL ME?

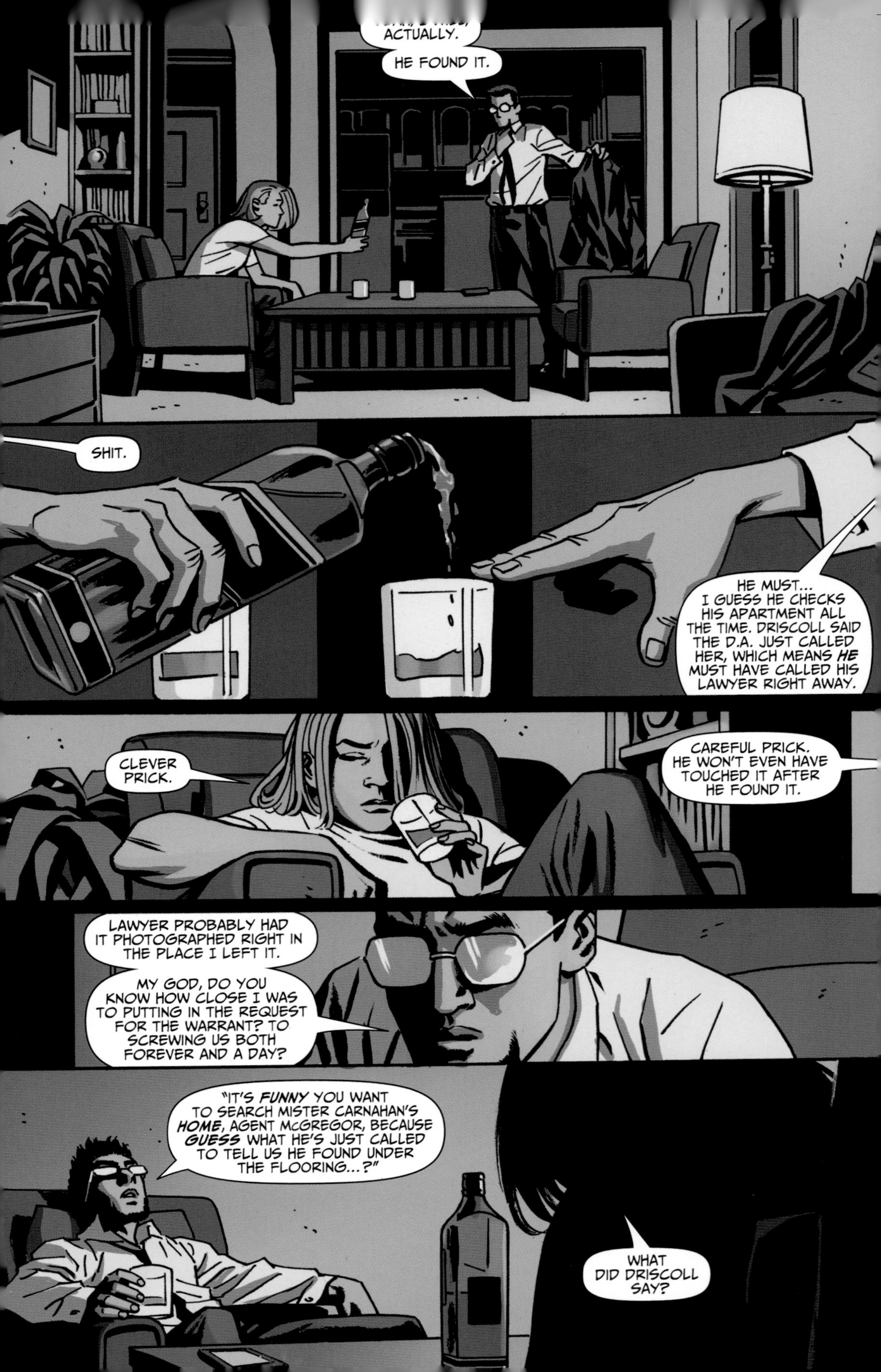
ACTUALLY.
HE FOUND IT.
SHIT.
HE MUST... I GUESS HE CHECKS HIS APARTMENT ALL THE TIME. DRISCOLL SAID THE D.A. JUST CALLED HER, WHICH MEANS *HE* MUST HAVE CALLED HIS LAWYER RIGHT AWAY.
CLEVER PRICK.
CAREFUL PRICK. HE WON'T EVEN HAVE TOUCHED IT AFTER HE FOUND IT.
LAWYER PROBABLY HAD IT PHOTOGRAPHED RIGHT IN THE PLACE I LEFT IT.
MY GOD, DO YOU KNOW HOW CLOSE I WAS TO PUTTING IN THE REQUEST FOR THE WARRANT? TO SCREWING US BOTH FOREVER AND A DAY?
"IT'S *FUNNY* YOU WANT TO SEARCH MISTER CARNAHAN'S *HOME*, AGENT McGREGOR, BECAUSE *GUESS* WHAT HE'S JUST CALLED TO TELL US HE FOUND UNDER THE FLOORING...?"
WHAT DID DRISCOLL SAY?

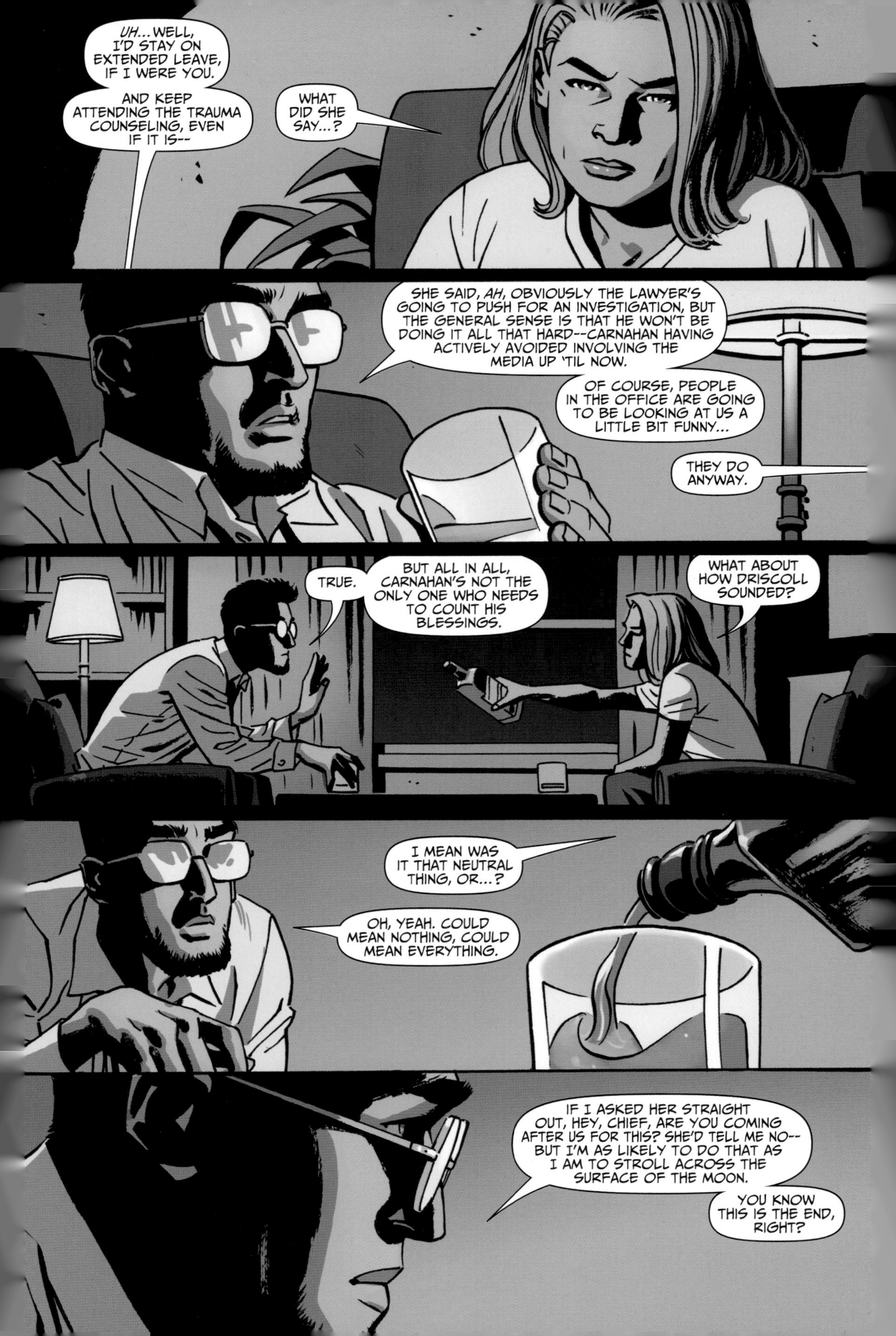

UH...WELL, I'D STAY ON EXTENDED LEAVE, IF I WERE YOU.
AND KEEP ATTENDING THE TRAUMA COUNSELING, EVEN IF IT IS--
WHAT DID SHE SAY...?
SHE SAID, AH, OBVIOUSLY THE LAWYER'S GOING TO PUSH FOR AN INVESTIGATION, BUT THE GENERAL SENSE IS THAT HE WON'T BE DOING IT ALL THAT HARD--CARNAHAN HAVING ACTIVELY AVOIDED INVOLVING THE MEDIA UP 'TIL NOW.
OF COURSE, PEOPLE IN THE OFFICE ARE GOING TO BE LOOKING AT US A LITTLE BIT FUNNY...
THEY DO ANYWAY.
TRUE.
BUT ALL IN ALL, CARNAHAN'S NOT THE ONLY ONE WHO NEEDS TO COUNT HIS BLESSINGS.
WHAT ABOUT HOW DRISCOLL SOUNDED?
I MEAN WAS IT THAT NEUTRAL THING, OR...?
OH, YEAH. COULD MEAN NOTHING, COULD MEAN EVERYTHING.
IF I ASKED HER STRAIGHT OUT, HEY, CHIEF, ARE YOU COMING AFTER US FOR THIS? SHE'D TELL ME NO--BUT I'M AS LIKELY TO DO THAT AS I AM TO STROLL ACROSS THE SURFACE OF THE MOON.
YOU KNOW THIS IS THE END, RIGHT?

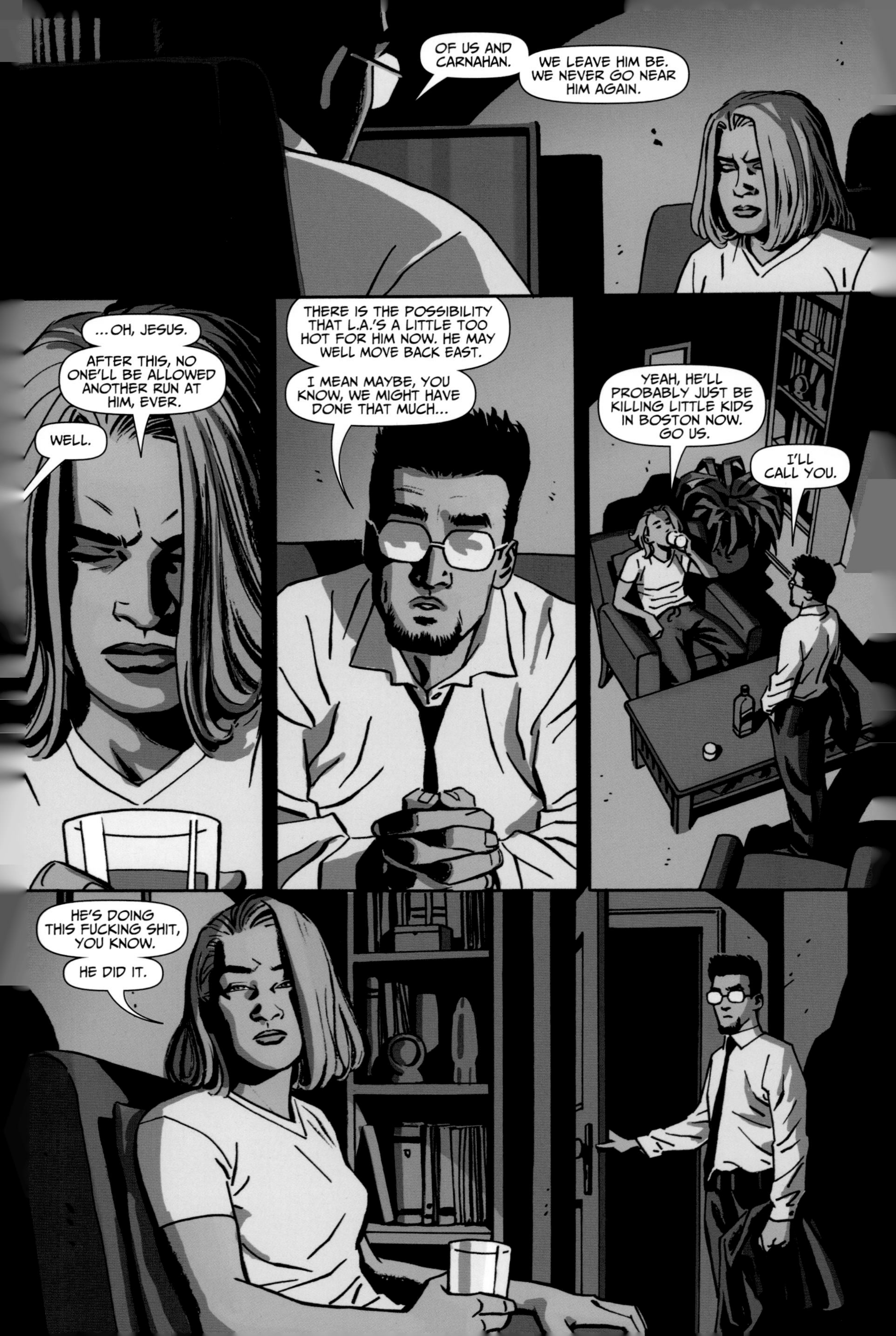
OF US AND CARNAHAN.
WE LEAVE HIM BE. WE NEVER GO NEAR HIM AGAIN.
...OH, JESUS.
AFTER THIS, NO ONE'LL BE ALLOWED ANOTHER RUN AT HIM, EVER.
WELL.
THERE IS THE POSSIBILITY THAT L.A.'S A LITTLE TOO HOT FOR HIM NOW. HE MAY WELL MOVE BACK EAST.
I MEAN MAYBE, YOU KNOW, WE MIGHT HAVE DONE THAT MUCH...
YEAH, HE'LL PROBABLY JUST BE KILLING LITTLE KIDS IN BOSTON NOW. GO US.
I'LL CALL YOU.
HE'S DOING THIS FUCKING SHIT, YOU KNOW.
HE DID IT.

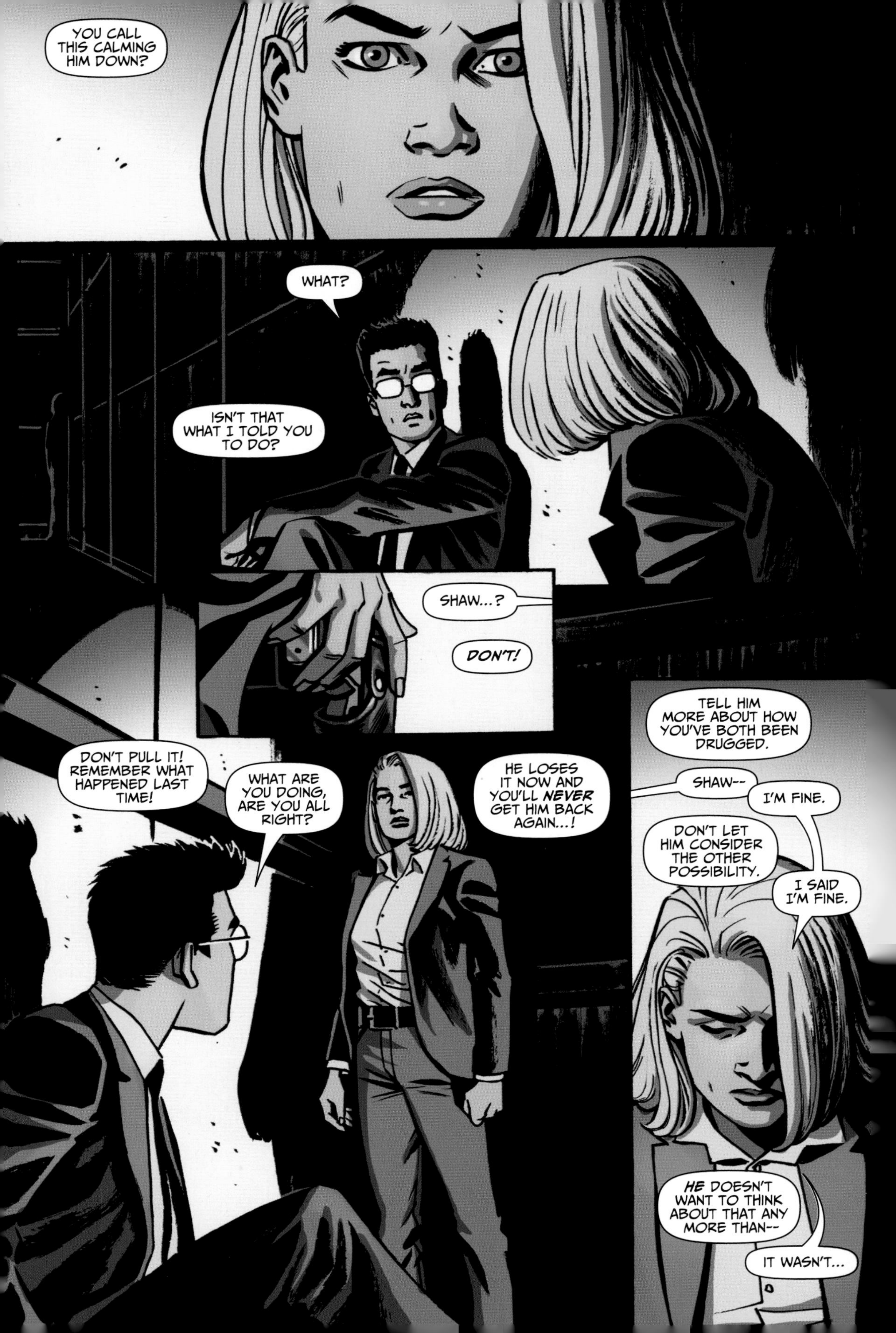

YOU CALL THIS CALMING HIM DOWN?
WHAT?
ISN'T THAT WHAT I TOLD YOU TO DO?
SHAW...?
DON'T!
DON'T PULL IT! REMEMBER WHAT HAPPENED LAST TIME!
WHAT ARE YOU DOING, ARE YOU ALL RIGHT?
HE LOSES IT NOW AND YOU'LL NEVER GET HIM BACK AGAIN...!
TELL HIM MORE ABOUT HOW YOU'VE BOTH BEEN DRUGGED.
SHAW--
I'M FINE.
DON'T LET HIM CONSIDER THE OTHER POSSIBILITY.
I SAID I'M FINE.
HE DOESN'T WANT TO THINK ABOUT THAT ANY MORE THAN--
IT WASN'T...

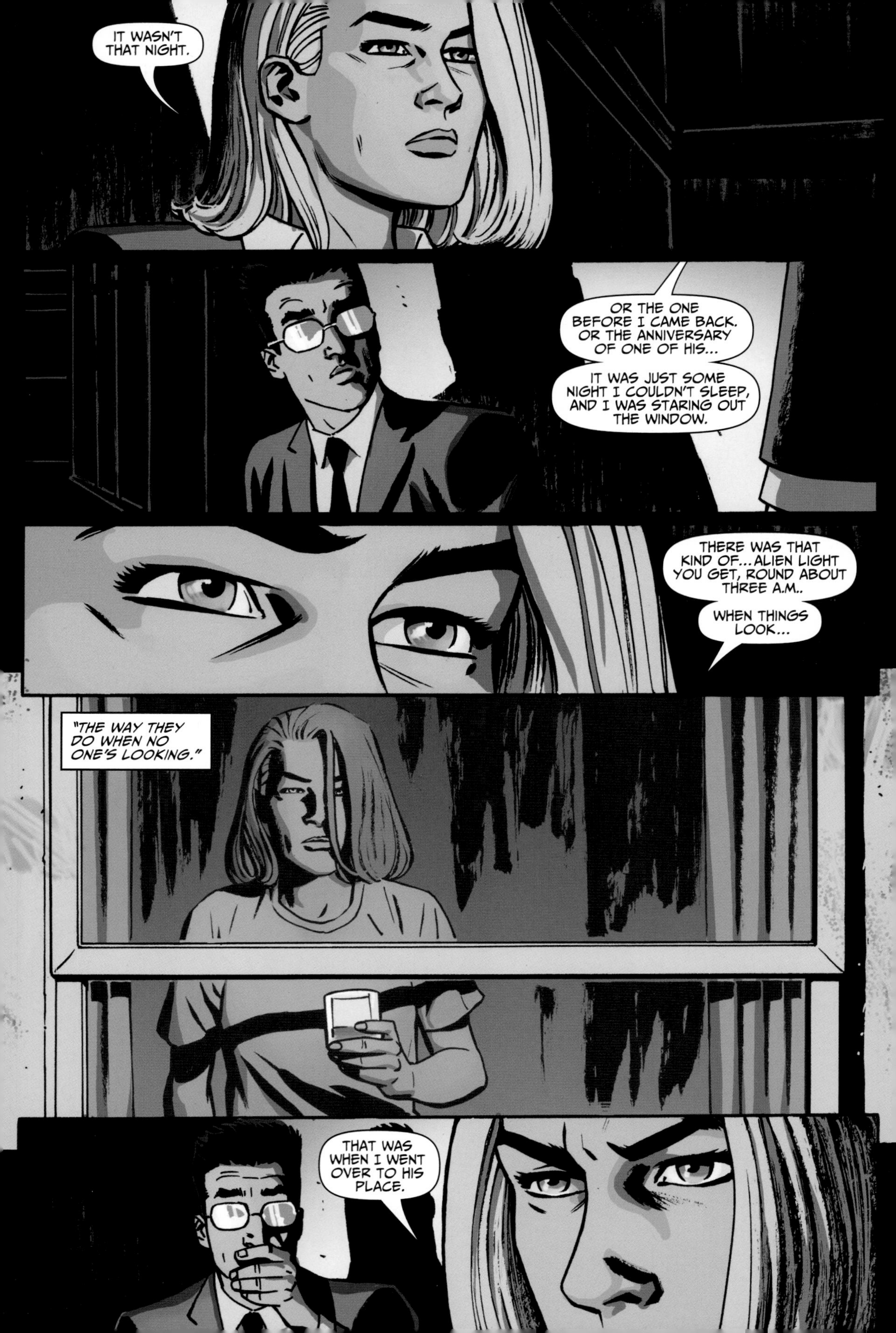
IT WASN'T THAT NIGHT.
OR THE ONE BEFORE I CAME BACK. OR THE ANNIVERSARY OF ONE OF HIS...
IT WAS JUST SOME NIGHT I COULDN'T SLEEP, AND I WAS STARING OUT THE WINDOW.
THERE WAS THAT KIND OF...ALIEN LIGHT YOU GET, ROUND ABOUT THREE A.M..
WHEN THINGS LOOK...
"THE WAY THEY DO WHEN NO ONE'S LOOKING."
THAT WAS WHEN I WENT OVER TO HIS PLACE.

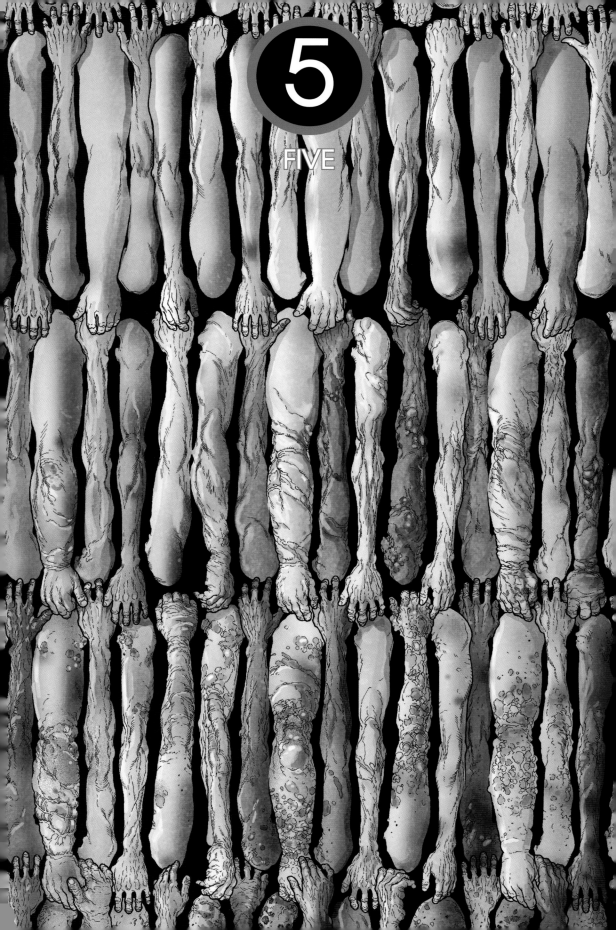

5

FIVE

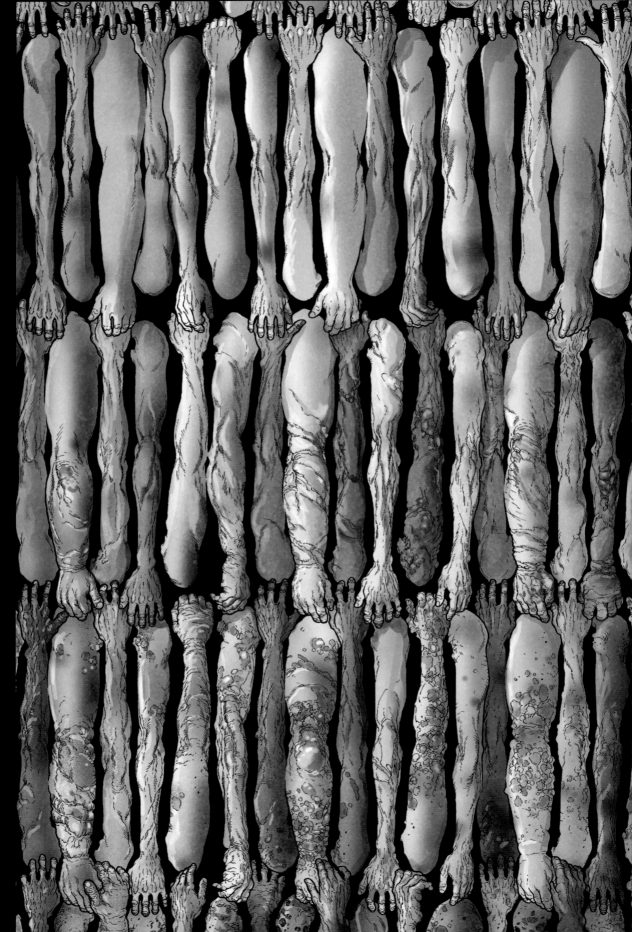

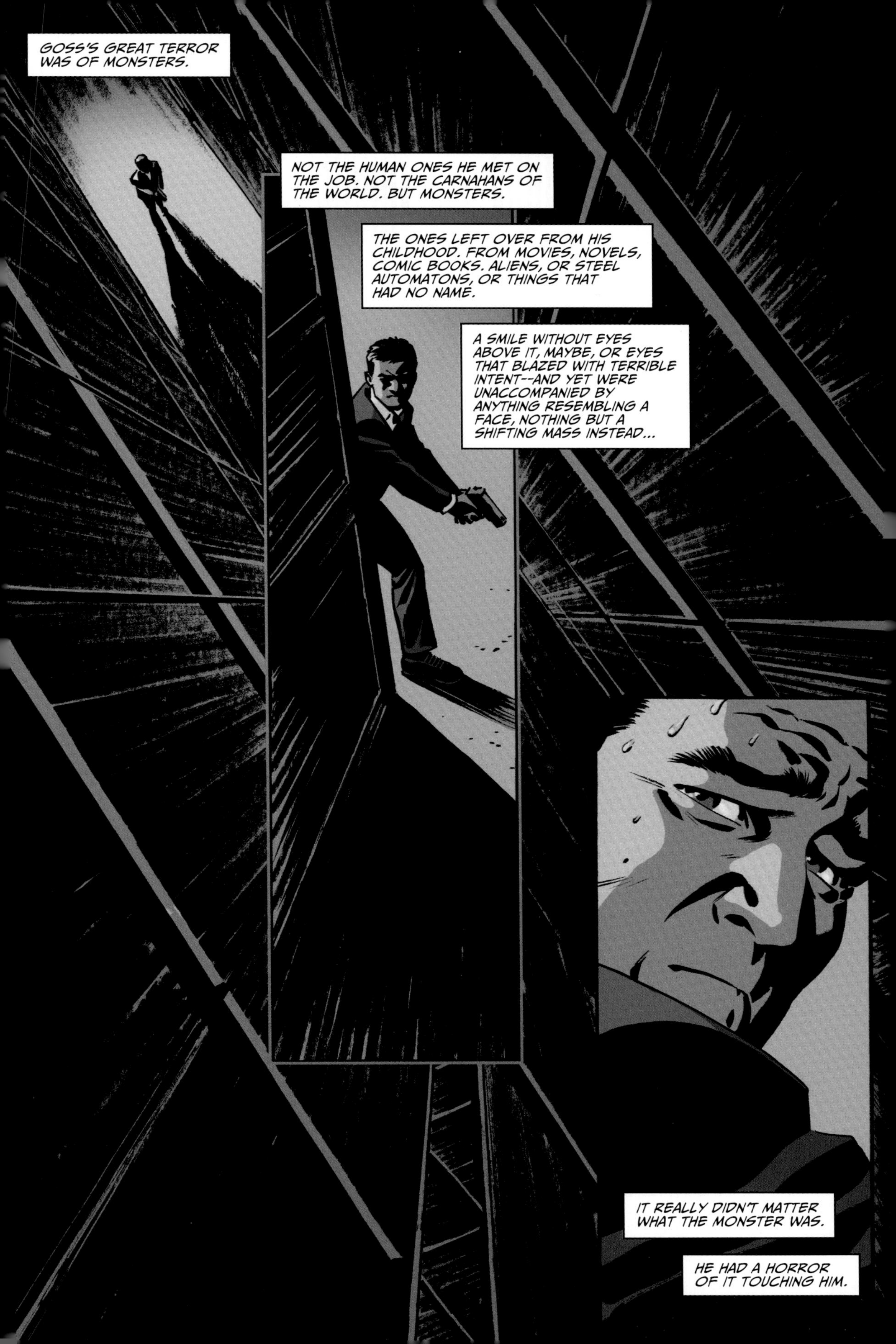
GOSS'S GREAT TERROR WAS OF MONSTERS.
NOT THE HUMAN ONES HE MET ON THE JOB. NOT THE CARNAHANS OF THE WORLD. BUT MONSTERS.
THE ONES LEFT OVER FROM HIS CHILDHOOD. FROM MOVIES, NOVELS, COMIC BOOKS. ALIENS, OR STEEL AUTOMATONS, OR THINGS THAT HAD NO NAME.
A SMILE WITHOUT EYES ABOVE IT, MAYBE, OR EYES THAT BLAZED WITH TERRIBLE INTENT--AND YET WERE UNACCOMPANIED BY ANYTHING RESEMBLING A FACE, NOTHING BUT A SHIFTING MASS INSTEAD...
IT REALLY DIDN'T MATTER WHAT THE MONSTER WAS.
HE HAD A HORROR OF IT TOUCHING HIM.

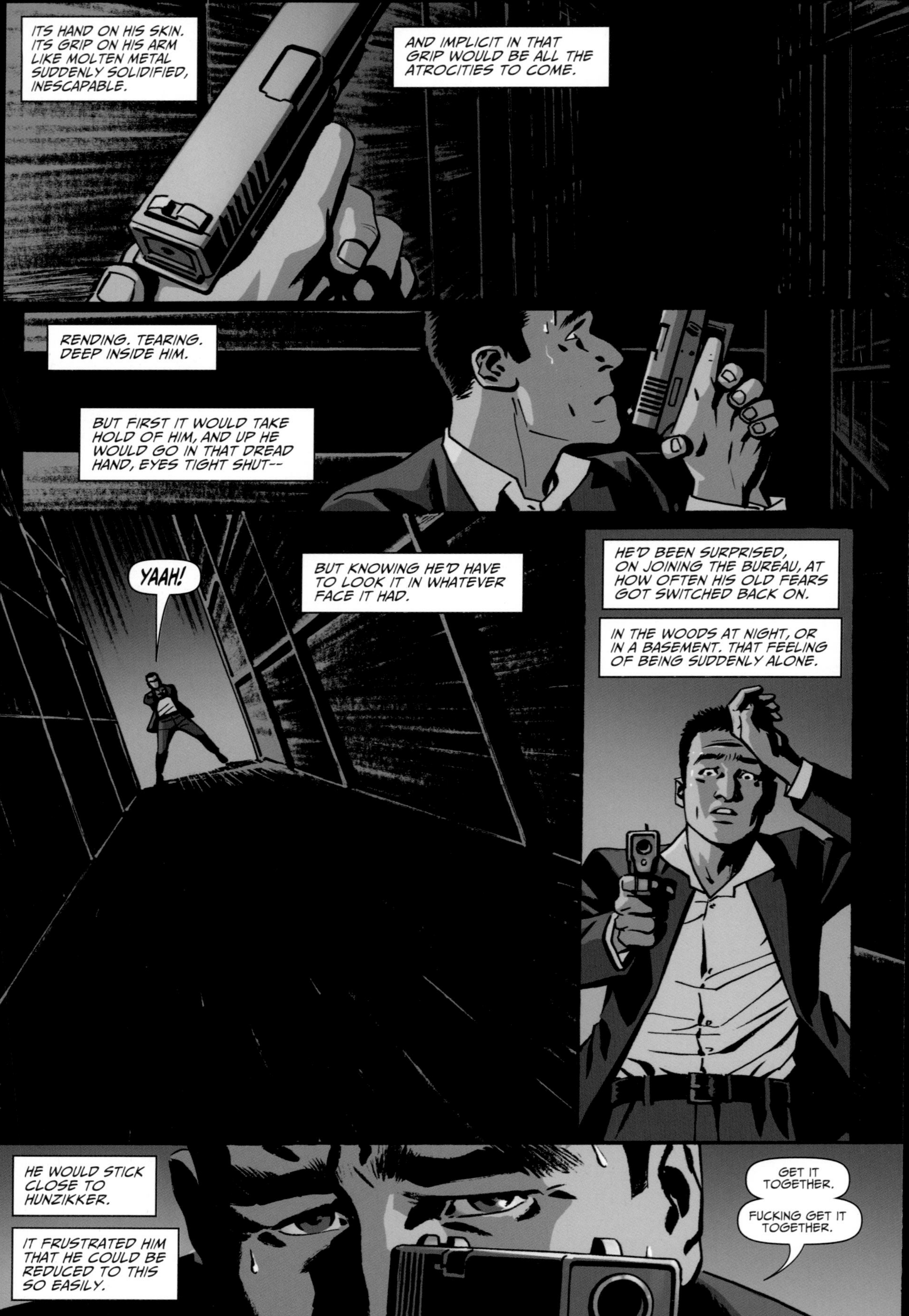

ITS HAND ON HIS SKIN. ITS GRIP ON HIS ARM LIKE MOLTEN METAL SUDDENLY SOLIDIFIED, INESCAPABLE.
AND IMPLICIT IN THAT GRIP WOULD BE ALL THE ATROCITIES TO COME.
RENDING. TEARING. DEEP INSIDE HIM.
BUT FIRST IT WOULD TAKE HOLD OF HIM, AND UP HE WOULD GO IN THAT DREAD HAND, EYES TIGHT SHUT--
YAAH!
BUT KNOWING HE'D HAVE TO LOOK IT IN WHATEVER FACE IT HAD.
HE'D BEEN SURPRISED, ON JOINING THE BUREAU, AT HOW OFTEN HIS OLD FEARS GOT SWITCHED BACK ON.
IN THE WOODS AT NIGHT, OR IN A BASEMENT. THAT FEELING OF BEING SUDDENLY ALONE.
HE WOULD STICK CLOSE TO HUNZIKKER.
IT FRUSTRATED HIM THAT HE COULD BE REDUCED TO THIS SO EASILY.
GET IT TOGETHER.
FUCKING GET IT TOGETHER.

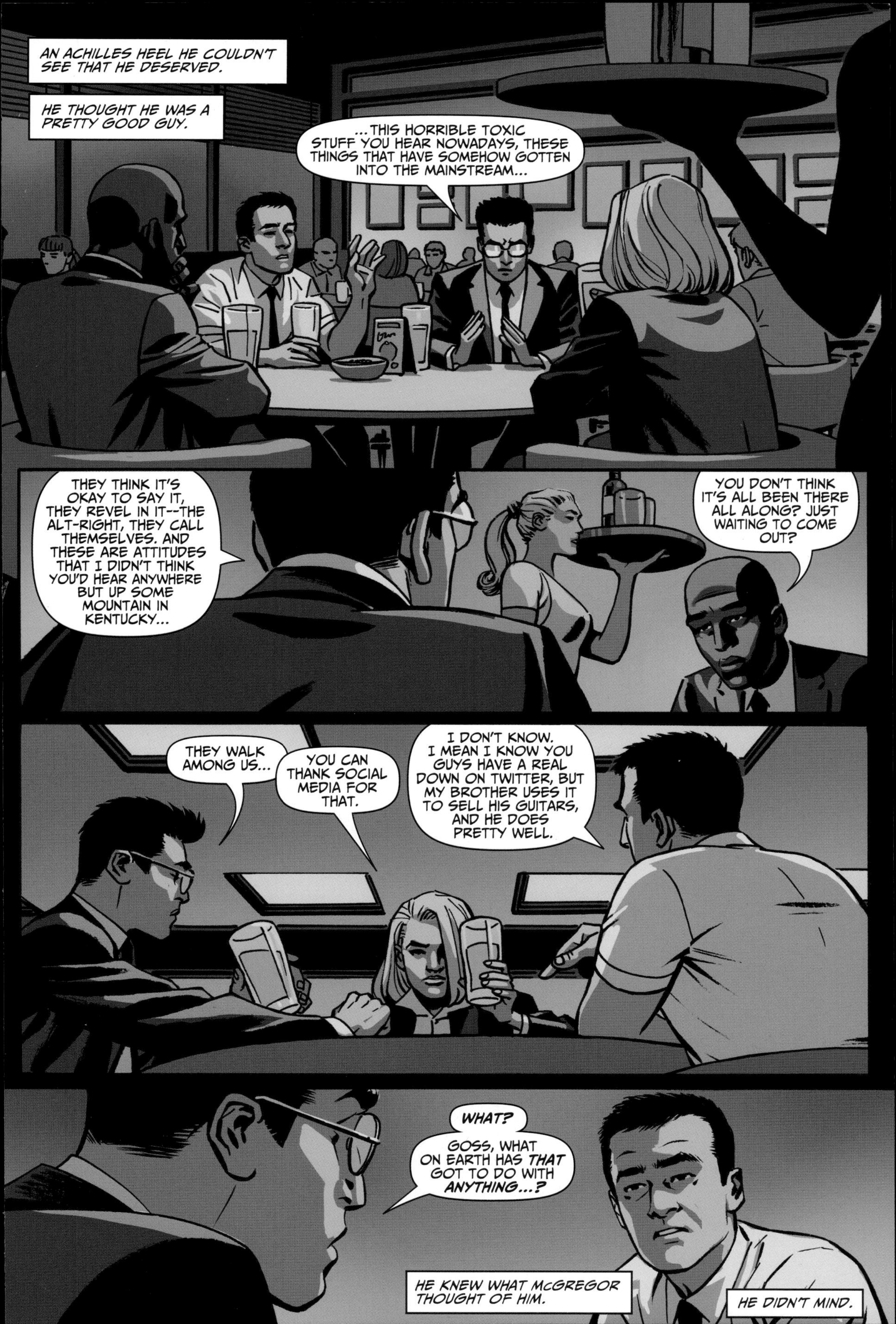

AN ACHILLES HEEL HE COULDN'T SEE THAT HE DESERVED.
HE THOUGHT HE WAS A PRETTY GOOD GUY.
...THIS HORRIBLE TOXIC STUFF YOU HEAR NOWADAYS, THESE THINGS THAT HAVE SOMEHOW GOTTEN INTO THE MAINSTREAM...
THEY THINK IT'S OKAY TO SAY IT, THEY REVEL IN IT--THE ALT-RIGHT, THEY CALL THEMSELVES. AND THESE ARE ATTITUDES THAT I DIDN'T THINK YOU'D HEAR ANYWHERE BUT UP SOME MOUNTAIN IN KENTUCKY...
YOU DON'T THINK IT'S ALL BEEN THERE ALL ALONG? JUST WAITING TO COME OUT?
THEY WALK AMONG US...
YOU CAN THANK SOCIAL MEDIA FOR THAT.
I DON'T KNOW. I MEAN I KNOW YOU GUYS HAVE A REAL DOWN ON TWITTER, BUT MY BROTHER USES IT TO SELL HIS GUITARS, AND HE DOES PRETTY WELL.
WHAT?
GOSS, WHAT ON EARTH HAS *THAT* GOT TO DO WITH *ANYTHING...?*
HE KNEW WHAT McGREGOR THOUGHT OF HIM.
HE DIDN'T MIND.

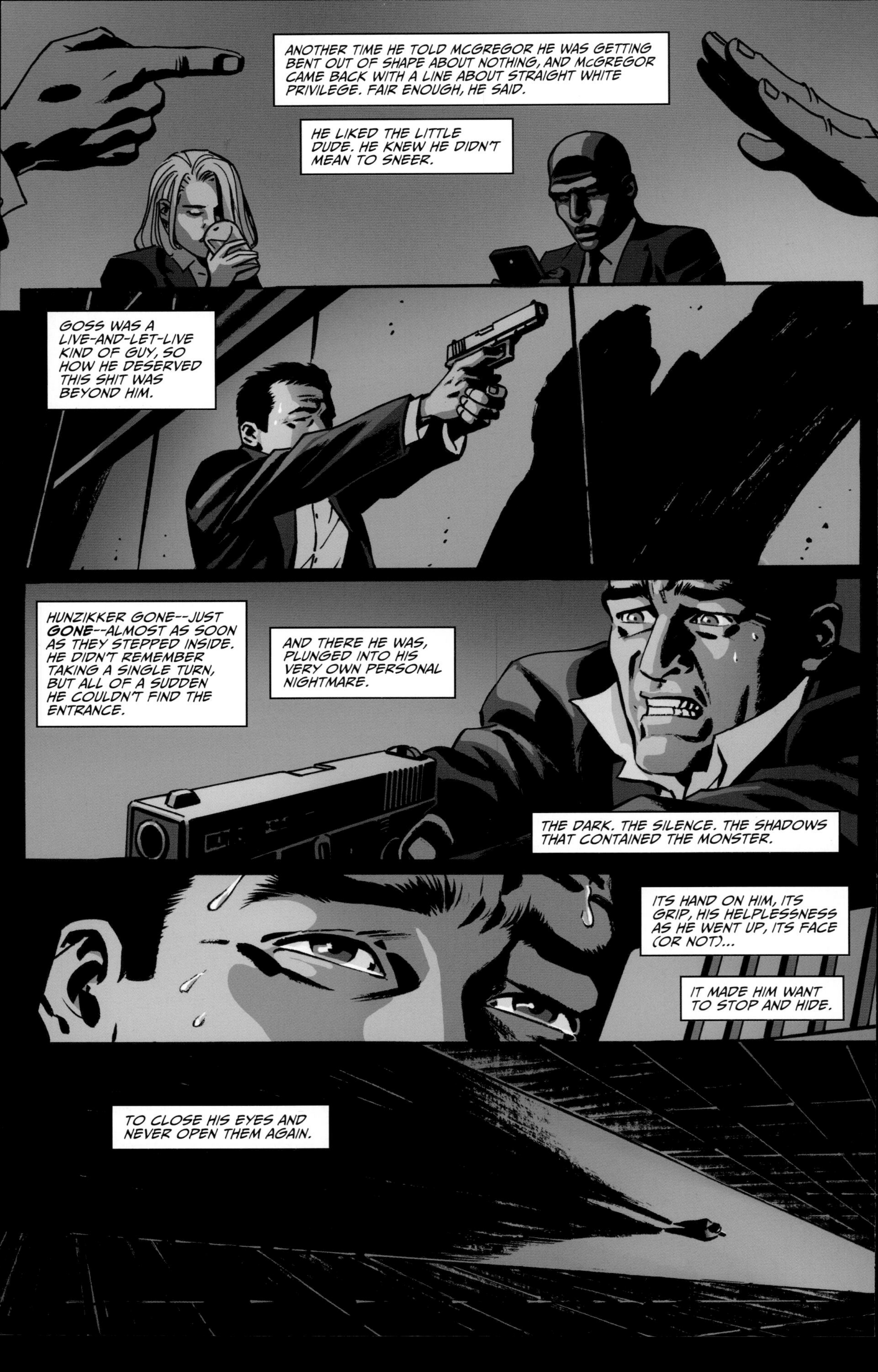

ANOTHER TIME HE TOLD MCGREGOR HE WAS GETTING BENT OUT OF SHAPE ABOUT NOTHING, AND MCGREGOR CAME BACK WITH A LINE ABOUT STRAIGHT WHITE PRIVILEGE. FAIR ENOUGH, HE SAID.
HE LIKED THE LITTLE DUDE. HE KNEW HE DIDN'T MEAN TO SNEER.
GOSS WAS A LIVE-AND-LET-LIVE KIND OF GUY, SO HOW HE DESERVED THIS SHIT WAS BEYOND HIM.
HUNZIKKER GONE--JUST **GONE**--ALMOST AS SOON AS THEY STEPPED INSIDE. HE DIDN'T REMEMBER TAKING A SINGLE TURN, BUT ALL OF A SUDDEN HE COULDN'T FIND THE ENTRANCE.
AND THERE HE WAS, PLUNGED INTO HIS VERY OWN PERSONAL NIGHTMARE.
THE DARK. THE SILENCE. THE SHADOWS THAT CONTAINED THE MONSTER.
ITS HAND ON HIM, ITS GRIP, HIS HELPLESSNESS AS HE WENT UP, ITS FACE (OR NOT)...
IT MADE HIM WANT TO STOP AND HIDE.
TO CLOSE HIS EYES AND NEVER OPEN THEM AGAIN.

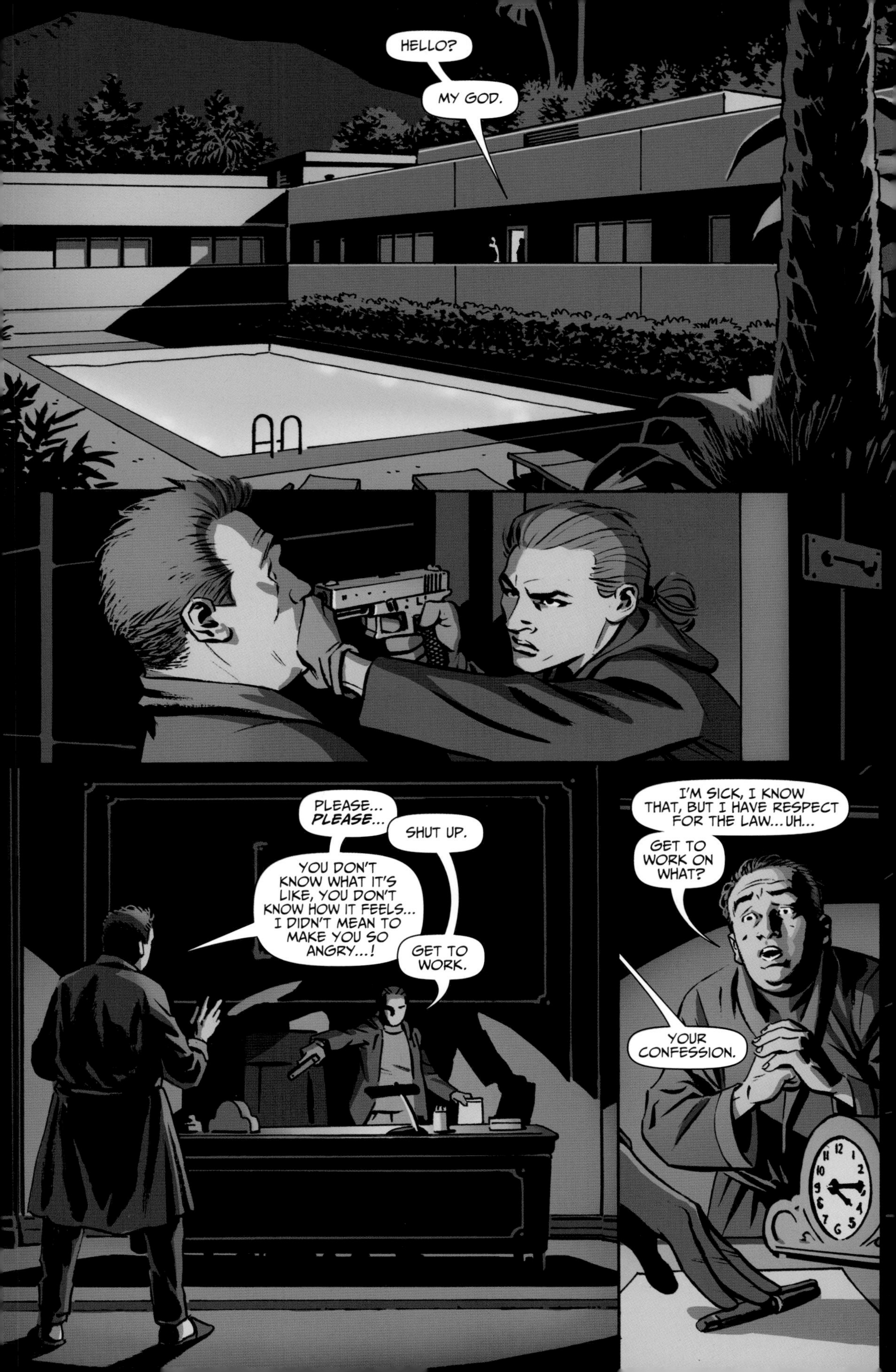
HELLO?
MY GOD.
PLEASE... *PLEASE*...
SHUT UP.
YOU DON'T KNOW WHAT IT'S LIKE, YOU DON'T KNOW HOW IT FEELS... I DIDN'T MEAN TO MAKE YOU SO ANGRY...!
GET TO WORK.
I'M SICK, I KNOW THAT, BUT I HAVE RESPECT FOR THE LAW... UH...
GET TO WORK ON WHAT?
YOUR CONFESSION.

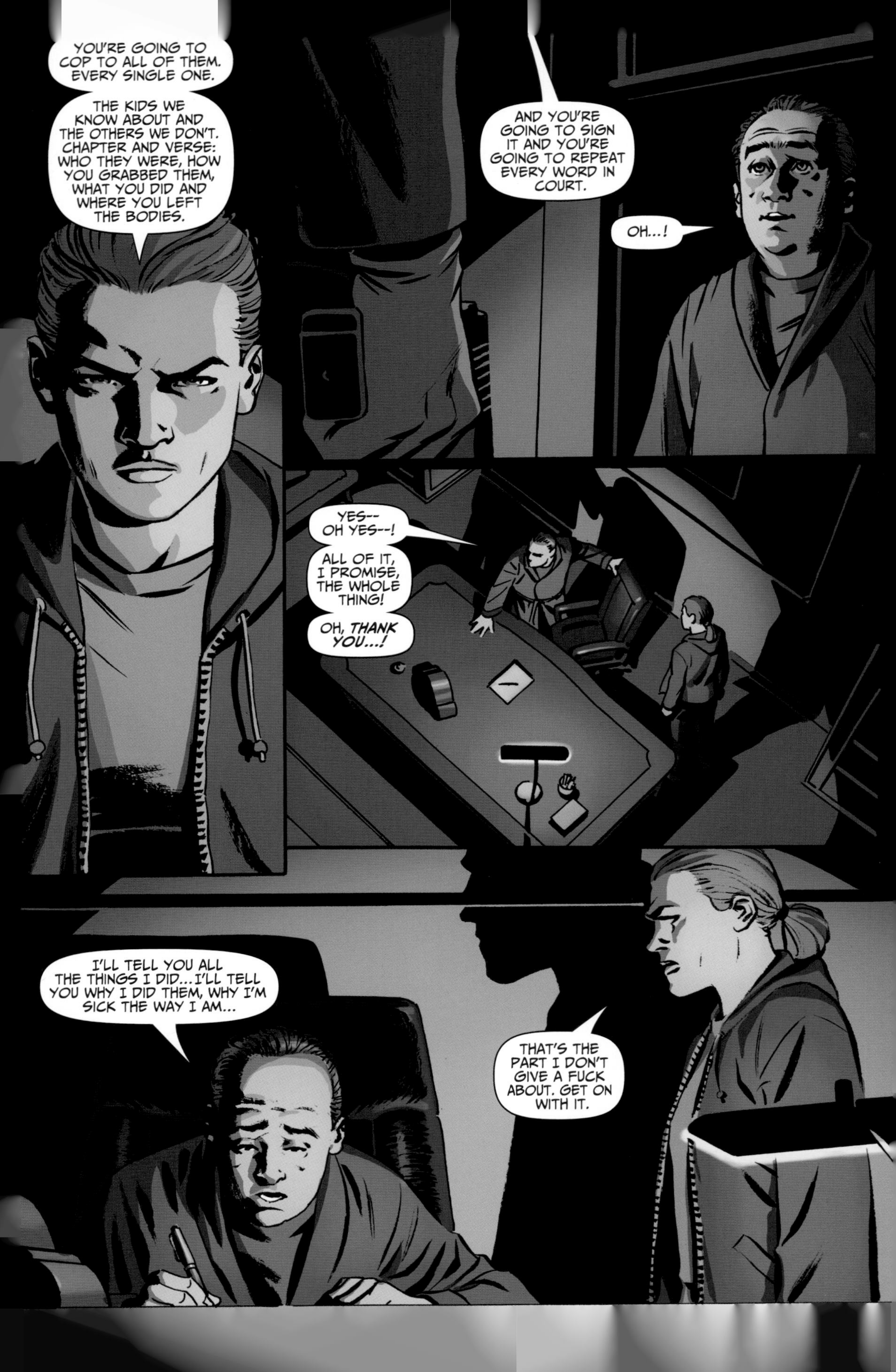
YOU'RE GOING TO COP TO ALL OF THEM. EVERY SINGLE ONE.
THE KIDS WE KNOW ABOUT AND THE OTHERS WE DON'T. CHAPTER AND VERSE: WHO THEY WERE, HOW YOU GRABBED THEM, WHAT YOU DID AND WHERE YOU LEFT THE BODIES.
AND YOU'RE GOING TO SIGN IT AND YOU'RE GOING TO REPEAT EVERY WORD IN COURT.
OH...!
YES-- OH YES--!
ALL OF IT, I PROMISE, THE WHOLE THING!
OH, *THANK YOU...!*
I'LL TELL YOU ALL THE THINGS I DID... I'LL TELL YOU WHY I DID THEM, WHY I'M SICK THE WAY I AM...
THAT'S THE PART I DON'T GIVE A FUCK ABOUT. GET ON WITH IT.

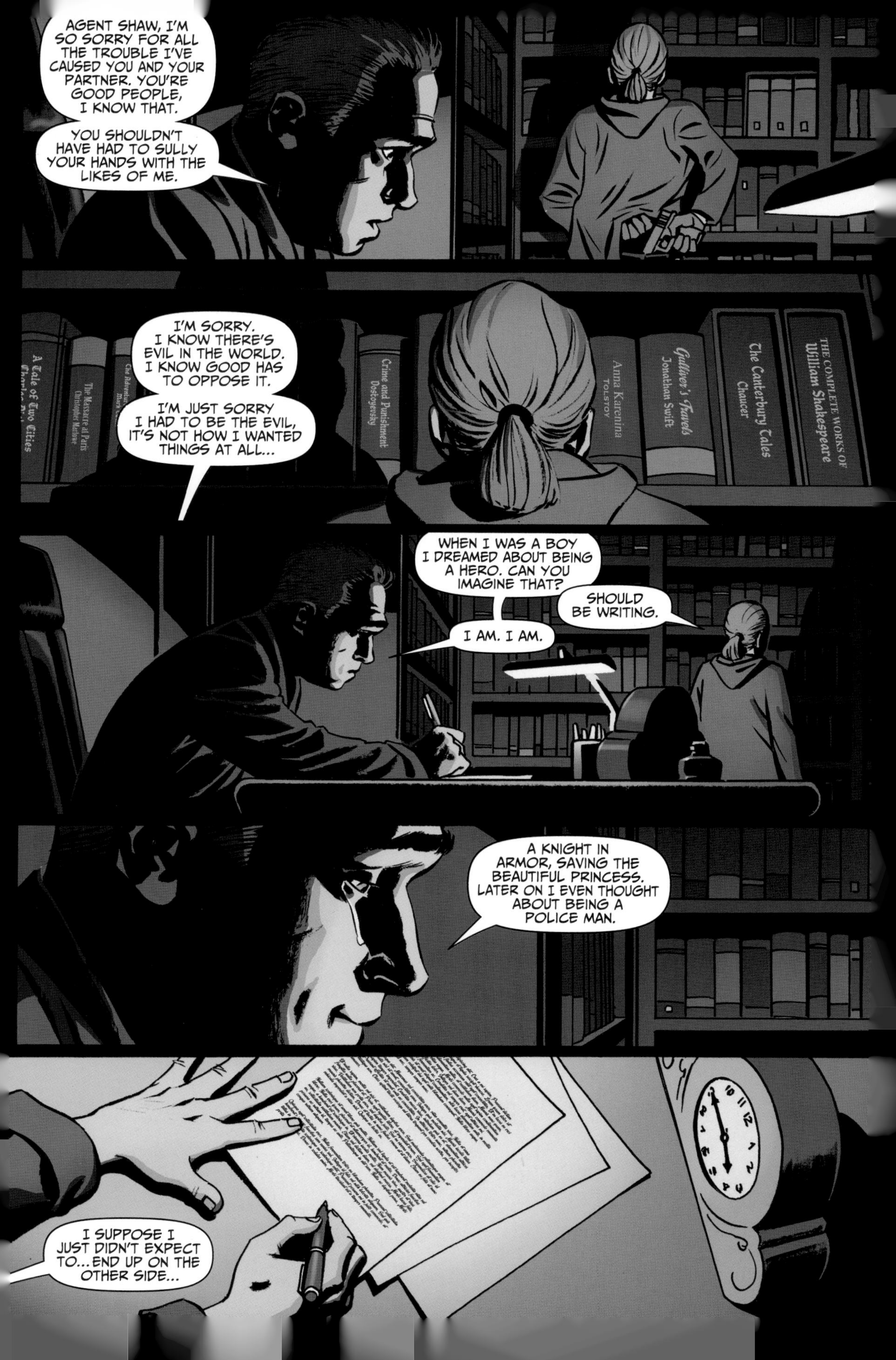
AGENT SHAW, I'M SO SORRY FOR ALL THE TROUBLE I'VE CAUSED YOU AND YOUR PARTNER. YOU'RE GOOD PEOPLE, I KNOW THAT.
YOU SHOULDN'T HAVE HAD TO SULLY YOUR HANDS WITH THE LIKES OF ME.
I'M SORRY. I KNOW THERE'S EVIL IN THE WORLD. I KNOW GOOD HAS TO OPPOSE IT.
I'M JUST SORRY I HAD TO BE THE EVIL, IT'S NOT HOW I WANTED THINGS AT ALL...
A Tale of Two Cities
Crime and Punishment Dostoyevsky
Anna Karenina Tolstoy
Gulliver's Travels Jonathan Swift
The Canterbury Tales Chaucer
THE COMPLETE WORKS OF William Shakespeare
WHEN I WAS A BOY I DREAMED ABOUT BEING A HERO. CAN YOU IMAGINE THAT?
SHOULD BE WRITING.
I AM. I AM.
A KNIGHT IN ARMOR, SAVING THE BEAUTIFUL PRINCESS. LATER ON I EVEN THOUGHT ABOUT BEING A POLICE MAN.
I SUPPOSE I JUST DIDN'T EXPECT TO...END UP ON THE OTHER SIDE...

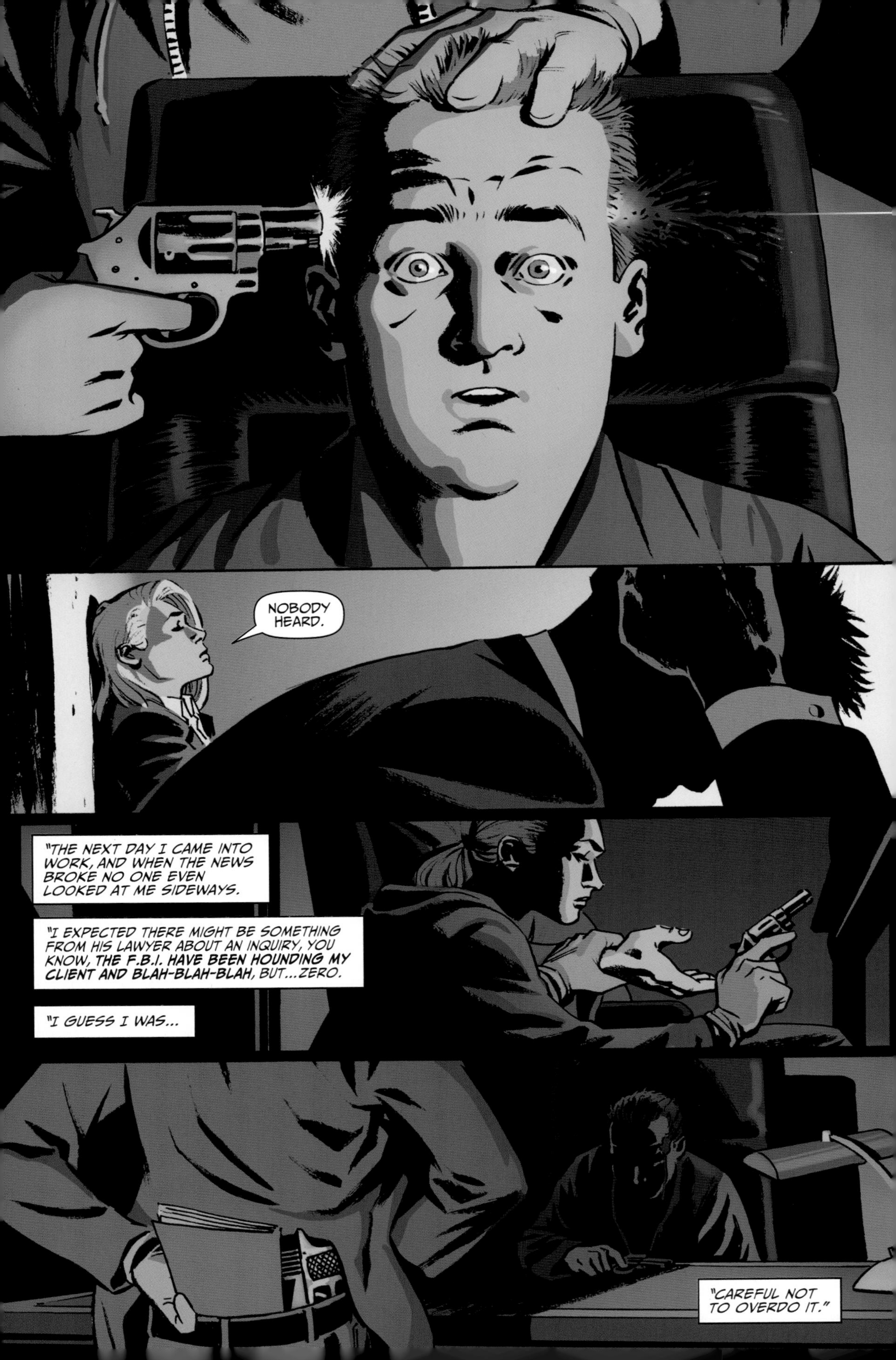
NOBODY HEARD.
"THE NEXT DAY I CAME INTO WORK, AND WHEN THE NEWS BROKE NO ONE EVEN LOOKED AT ME SIDEWAYS.
"I EXPECTED THERE MIGHT BE SOMETHING FROM HIS LAWYER ABOUT AN INQUIRY, YOU KNOW, **THE F.B.I. HAVE BEEN HOUNDING MY CLIENT AND BLAH-BLAH-BLAH**, BUT...ZERO.
"I GUESS I WAS...
"CAREFUL NOT TO OVERDO IT."

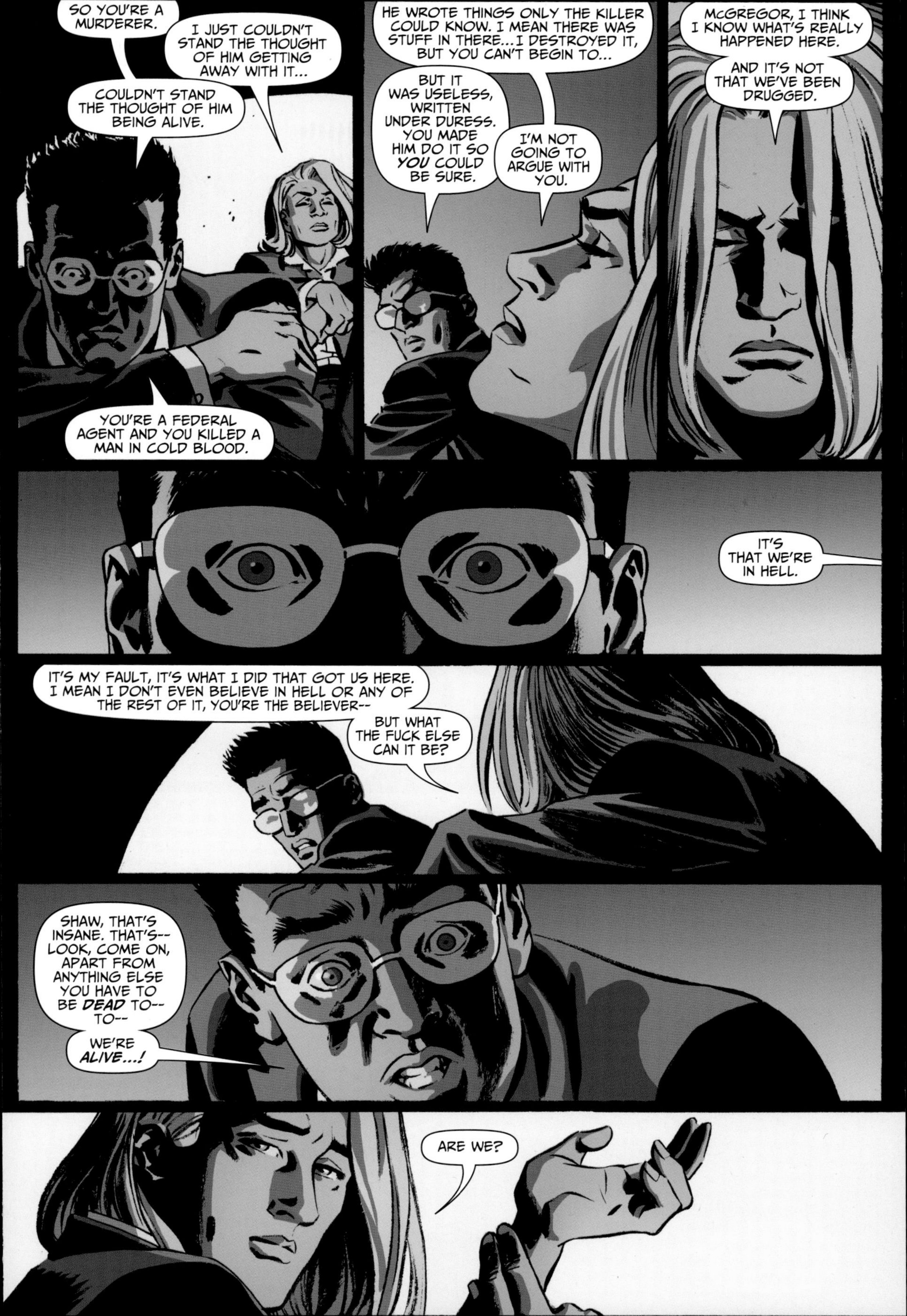
SO YOU'RE A MURDERER.
I JUST COULDN'T STAND THE THOUGHT OF HIM GETTING AWAY WITH IT...
COULDN'T STAND THE THOUGHT OF HIM BEING ALIVE.
YOU'RE A FEDERAL AGENT AND YOU KILLED A MAN IN COLD BLOOD.
HE WROTE THINGS ONLY THE KILLER COULD KNOW. I MEAN THERE WAS STUFF IN THERE... I DESTROYED IT, BUT YOU CAN'T BEGIN TO...
BUT IT WAS USELESS, WRITTEN UNDER DURESS. YOU MADE HIM DO IT SO *YOU* COULD BE SURE.
I'M NOT GOING TO ARGUE WITH YOU.
McGREGOR, I THINK I KNOW WHAT'S REALLY HAPPENED HERE.
AND IT'S NOT THAT WE'VE BEEN DRUGGED.
IT'S THAT WE'RE IN HELL.
IT'S MY FAULT, IT'S WHAT I DID THAT GOT US HERE. I MEAN I DON'T EVEN BELIEVE IN HELL OR ANY OF THE REST OF IT, YOU'RE THE BELIEVER--
BUT WHAT THE FUCK ELSE CAN IT BE?
SHAW, THAT'S INSANE. THAT'S-- LOOK, COME ON, APART FROM ANYTHING ELSE YOU HAVE TO BE *DEAD* TO-- TO--
WE'RE *ALIVE...!*
ARE WE?

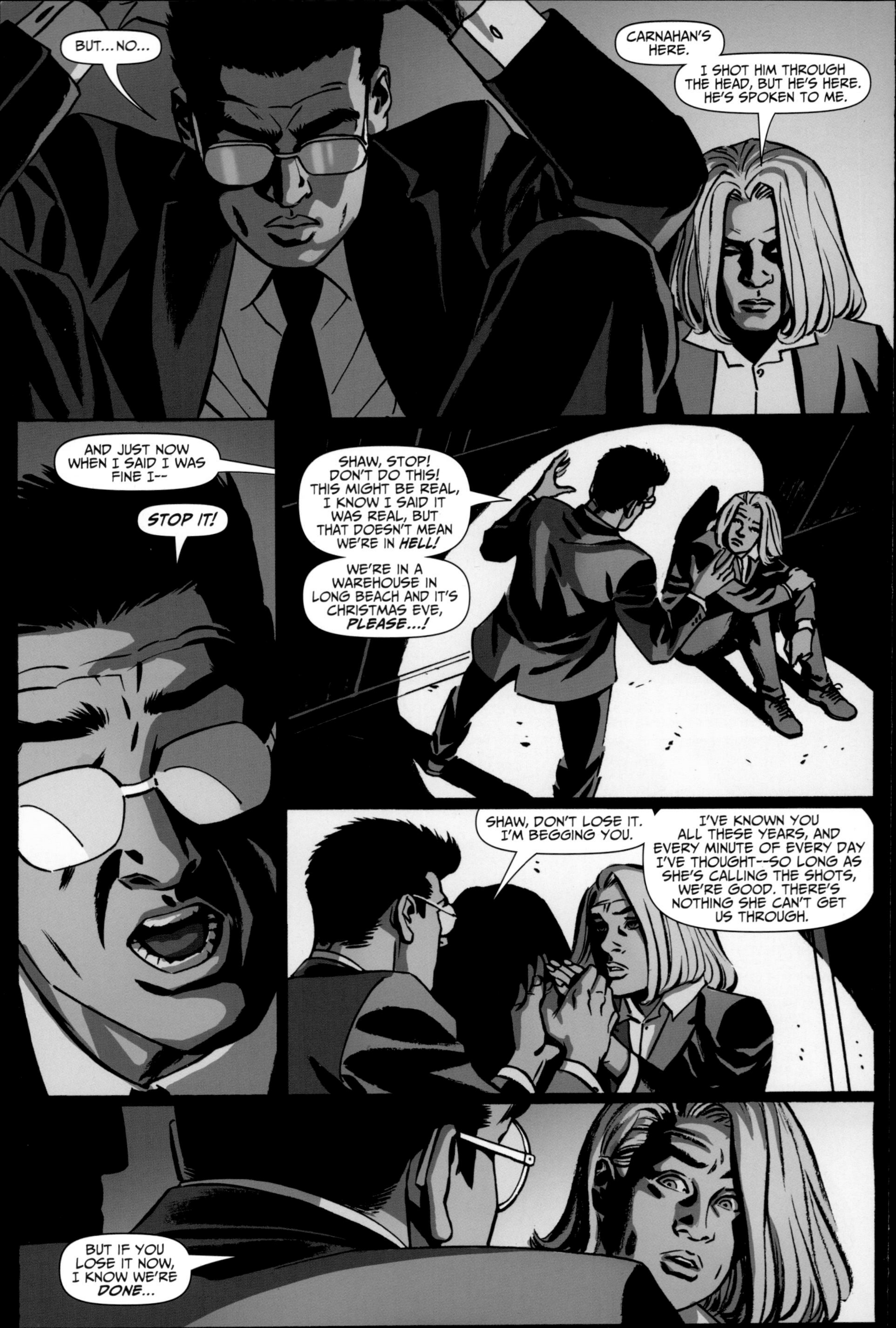
BUT... NO...
CARNAHAN'S HERE.
I SHOT HIM THROUGH THE HEAD, BUT HE'S HERE. HE'S SPOKEN TO ME.
AND JUST NOW WHEN I SAID I WAS FINE I--
STOP IT!
SHAW, STOP! DON'T DO THIS! THIS MIGHT BE REAL, I KNOW I SAID IT WAS REAL, BUT THAT DOESN'T MEAN WE'RE IN HELL!
WE'RE IN A WAREHOUSE IN LONG BEACH AND IT'S CHRISTMAS EVE, PLEASE...!
SHAW, DON'T LOSE IT. I'M BEGGING YOU.
I'VE KNOWN YOU ALL THESE YEARS, AND EVERY MINUTE OF EVERY DAY I'VE THOUGHT--SO LONG AS SHE'S CALLING THE SHOTS, WE'RE GOOD. THERE'S NOTHING SHE CAN'T GET US THROUGH.
BUT IF YOU LOSE IT NOW, I KNOW WE'RE DONE...

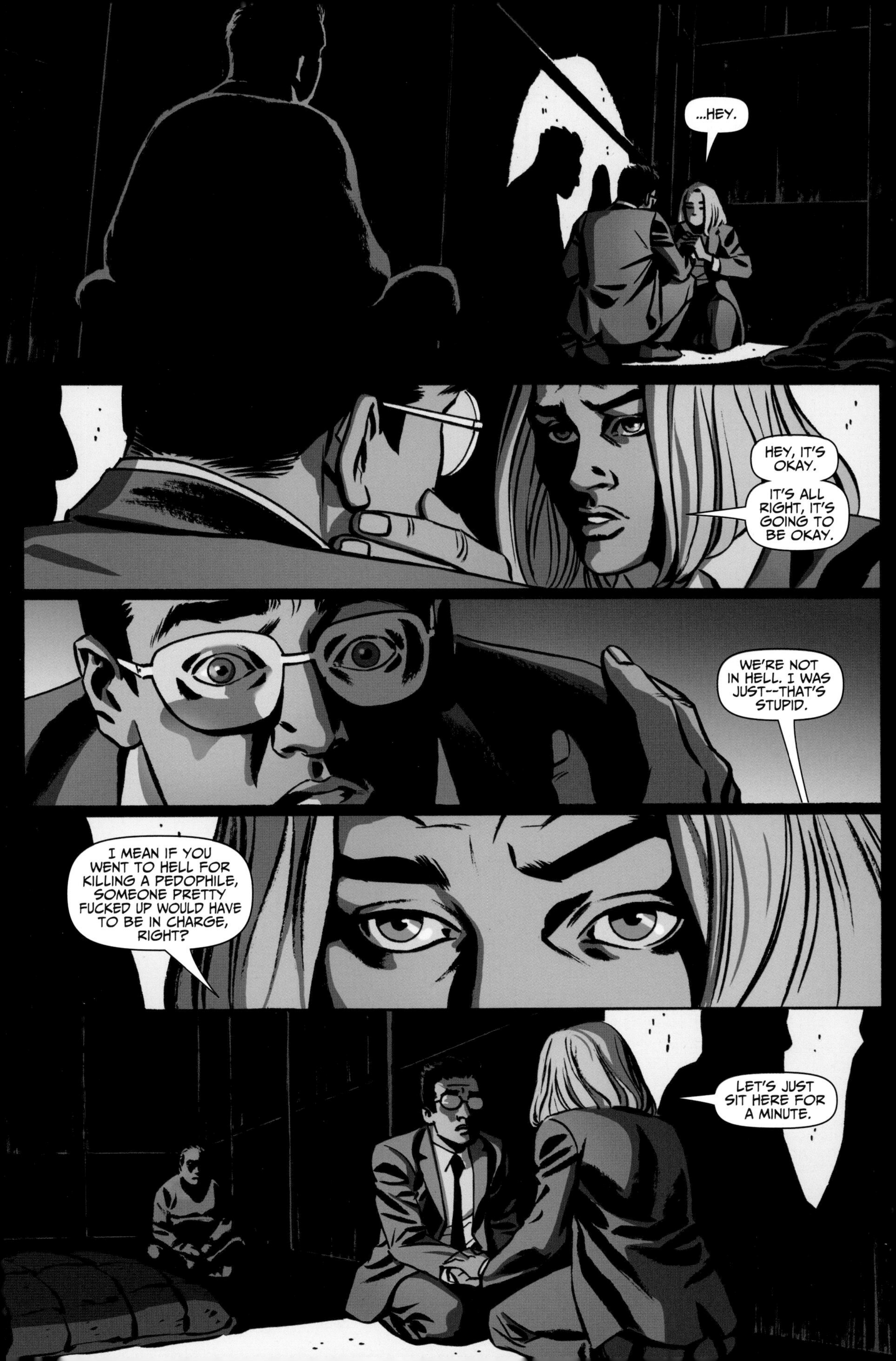
...HEY.
HEY, IT'S OKAY.
IT'S ALL RIGHT, IT'S GOING TO BE OKAY.
WE'RE NOT IN HELL. I WAS JUST--THAT'S STUPID.
I MEAN IF YOU WENT TO HELL FOR KILLING A PEDOPHILE, SOMEONE PRETTY FUCKED UP WOULD HAVE TO BE IN CHARGE, RIGHT?
LET'S JUST SIT HERE FOR A MINUTE.

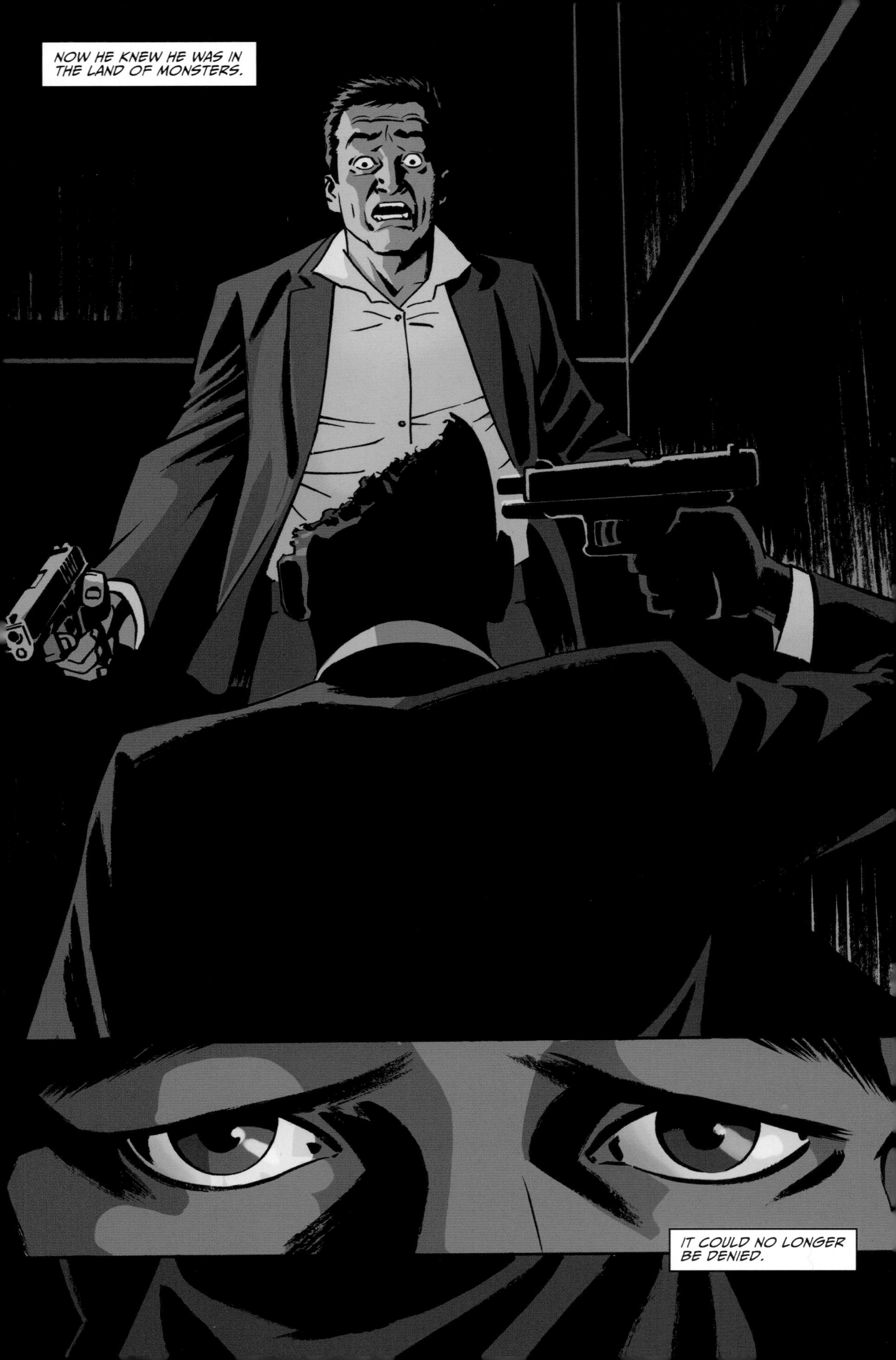
NOW HE KNEW HE WAS IN THE LAND OF MONSTERS.
IT COULD NO LONGER BE DENIED.

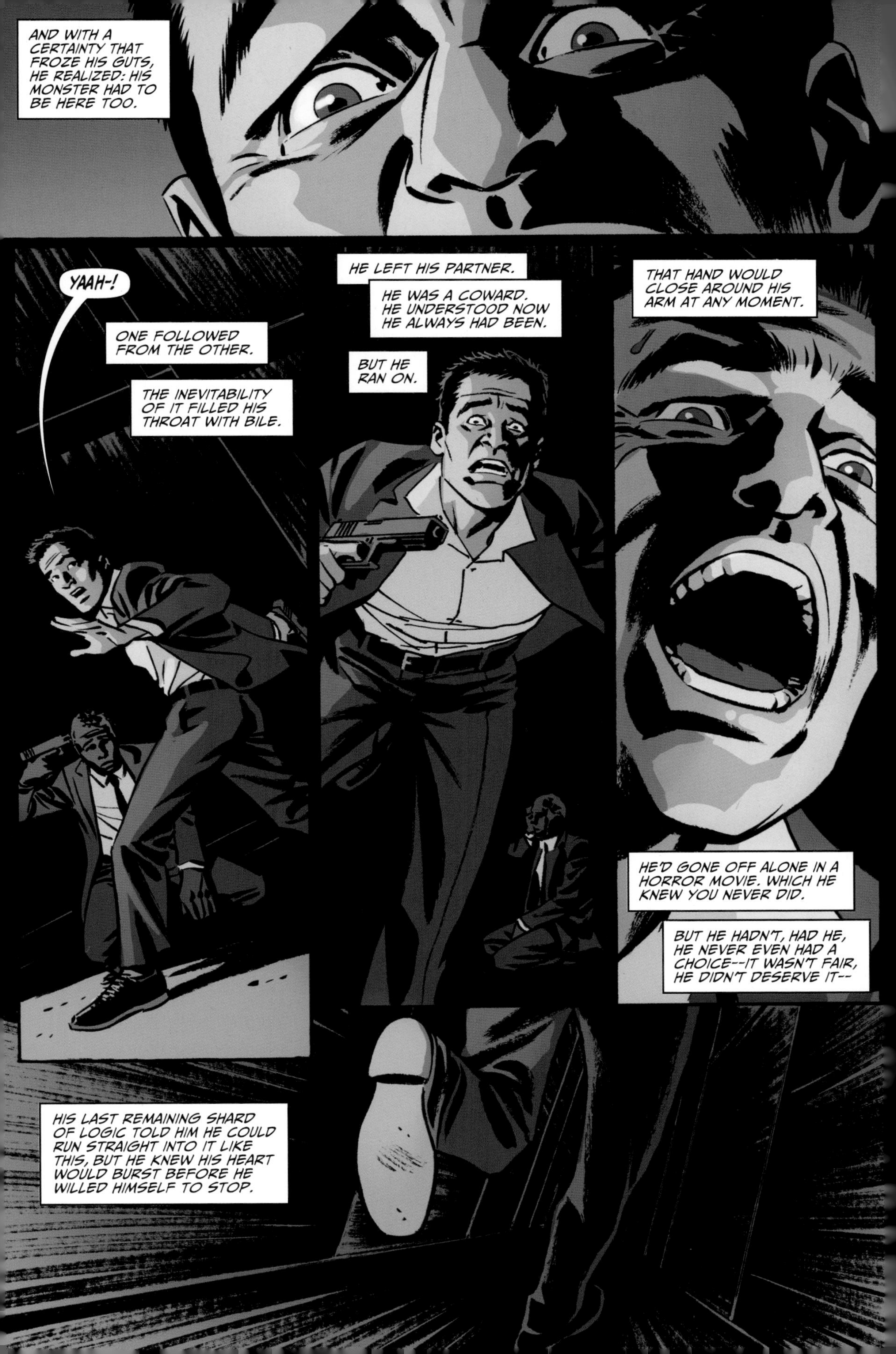
AND WITH A CERTAINTY THAT FROZE HIS GUTS, HE REALIZED: HIS MONSTER HAD TO BE HERE TOO.
YAAH-!
ONE FOLLOWED FROM THE OTHER.
THE INEVITABILITY OF IT FILLED HIS THROAT WITH BILE.
HE LEFT HIS PARTNER.
HE WAS A COWARD. HE UNDERSTOOD NOW HE ALWAYS HAD BEEN.
BUT HE RAN ON.
THAT HAND WOULD CLOSE AROUND HIS ARM AT ANY MOMENT.
HE'D GONE OFF ALONE IN A HORROR MOVIE. WHICH HE KNEW YOU NEVER DID.
BUT HE HADN'T, HAD HE, HE NEVER EVEN HAD A CHOICE--IT WASN'T FAIR, HE DIDN'T DESERVE IT--
HIS LAST REMAINING SHARD OF LOGIC TOLD HIM HE COULD RUN STRAIGHT INTO IT LIKE THIS, BUT HE KNEW HIS HEART WOULD BURST BEFORE HE WILLED HIMSELF TO STOP.

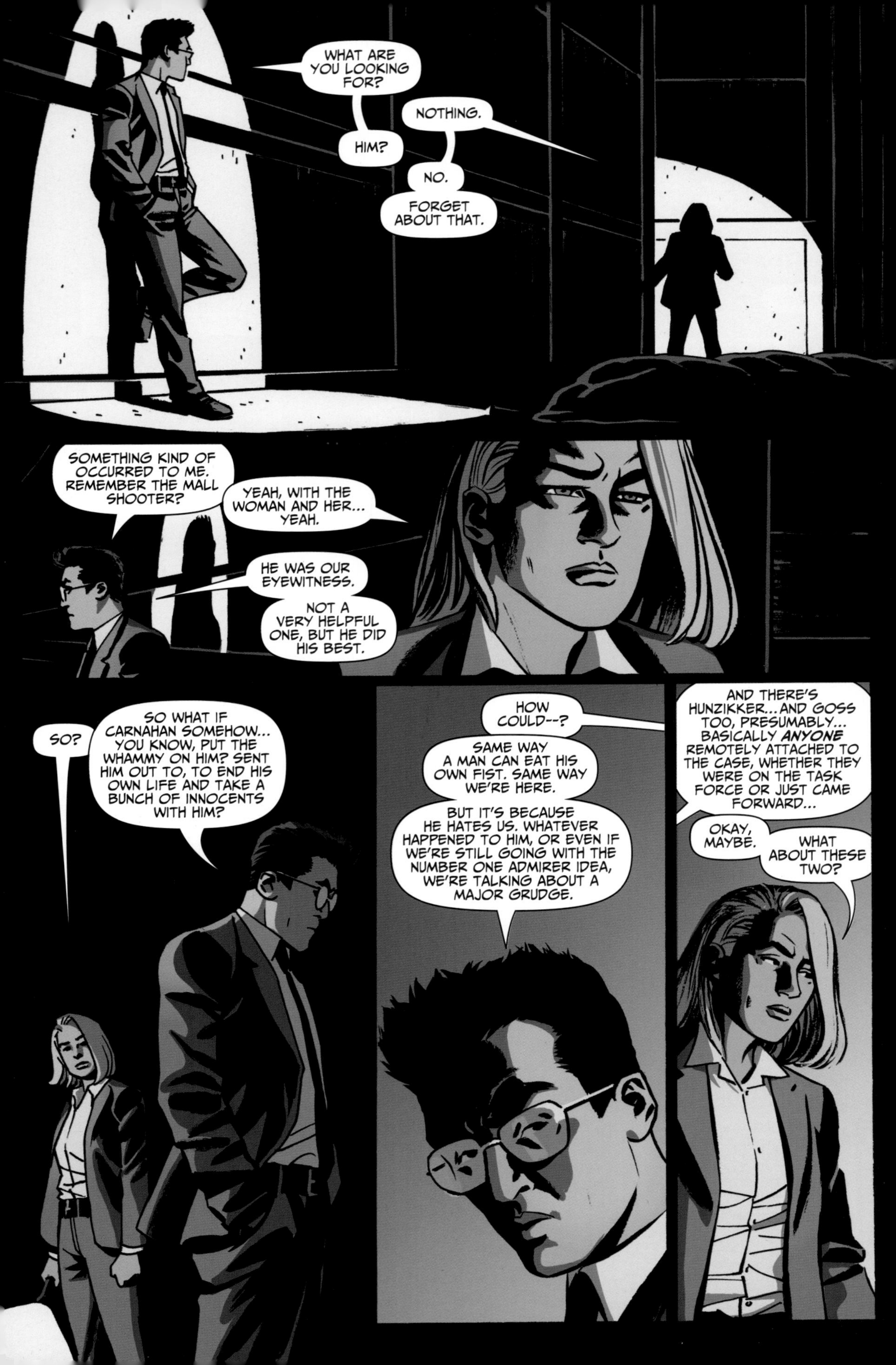
WHAT ARE YOU LOOKING FOR?
HIM?
NOTHING.
NO.
FORGET ABOUT THAT.
SOMETHING KIND OF OCCURRED TO ME. REMEMBER THE MALL SHOOTER?
YEAH, WITH THE WOMAN AND HER... YEAH.
HE WAS OUR EYEWITNESS.
NOT A VERY HELPFUL ONE, BUT HE DID HIS BEST.
SO?
SO WHAT IF CARNAHAN SOMEHOW... YOU KNOW, PUT THE WHAMMY ON HIM? SENT HIM OUT TO, TO END HIS OWN LIFE AND TAKE A BUNCH OF INNOCENTS WITH HIM?
HOW COULD--?
SAME WAY A MAN CAN EAT HIS OWN FIST. SAME WAY WE'RE HERE.
BUT IT'S BECAUSE HE HATES US. WHATEVER HAPPENED TO HIM, OR EVEN IF WE'RE STILL GOING WITH THE NUMBER ONE ADMIRER IDEA, WE'RE TALKING ABOUT A MAJOR GRUDGE.
AND THERE'S HUNZIKKER... AND GOSS TOO, PRESUMABLY... BASICALLY *ANYONE* REMOTELY ATTACHED TO THE CASE, WHETHER THEY WERE ON THE TASK FORCE OR JUST CAME FORWARD...
OKAY, MAYBE.
WHAT ABOUT THESE TWO?

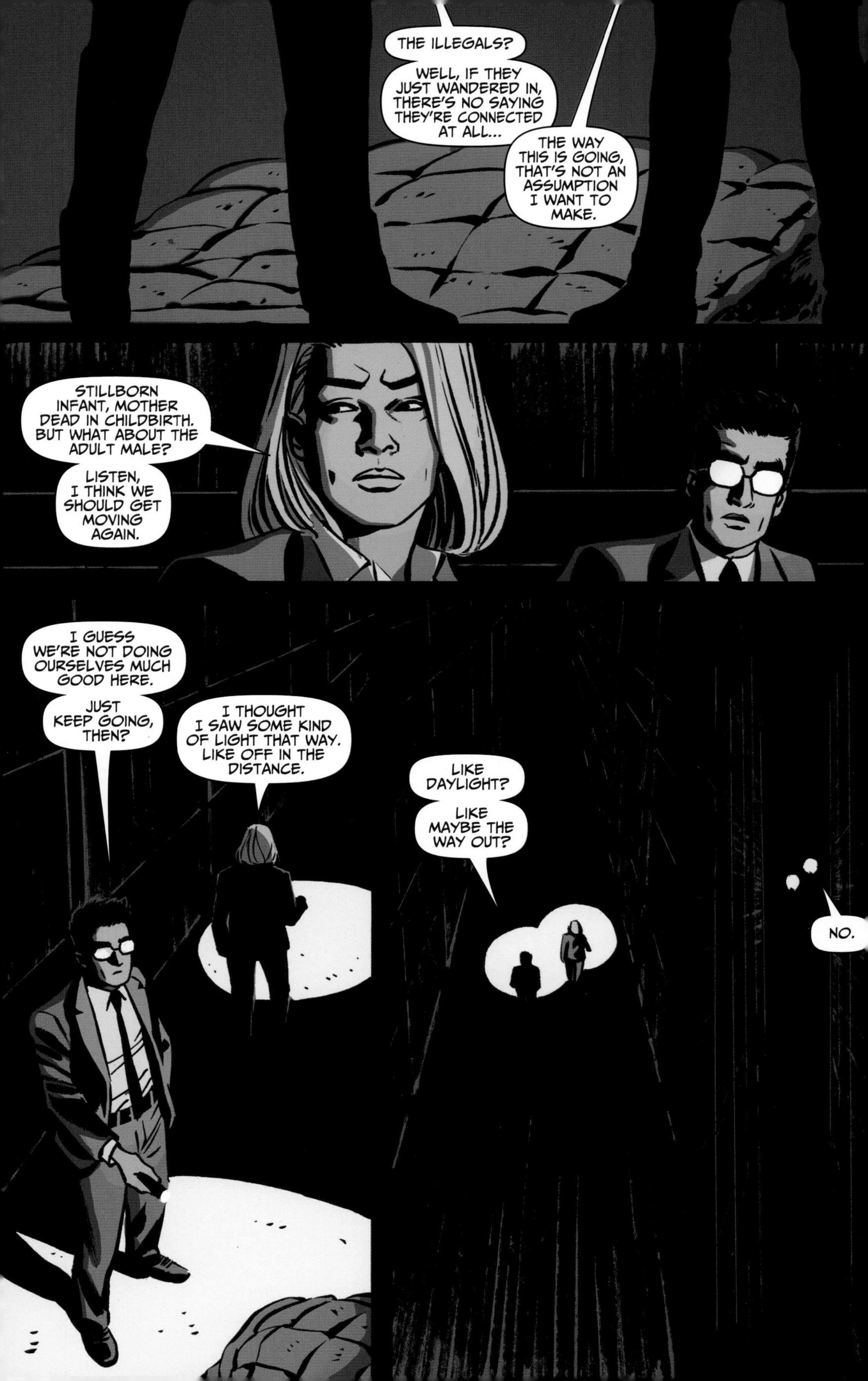

THE ILLEGALS?
WELL, IF THEY JUST WANDERED IN, THERE'S NO SAYING THEY'RE CONNECTED AT ALL...
THE WAY THIS IS GOING, THAT'S NOT AN ASSUMPTION I WANT TO MAKE.
STILLBORN INFANT, MOTHER DEAD IN CHILDBIRTH. BUT WHAT ABOUT THE ADULT MALE?
LISTEN, I THINK WE SHOULD GET MOVING AGAIN.
I GUESS WE'RE NOT DOING OURSELVES MUCH GOOD HERE.
JUST KEEP GOING, THEN?
I THOUGHT I SAW SOME KIND OF LIGHT THAT WAY. LIKE OFF IN THE DISTANCE.
LIKE DAYLIGHT?
LIKE MAYBE THE WAY OUT?
NO.

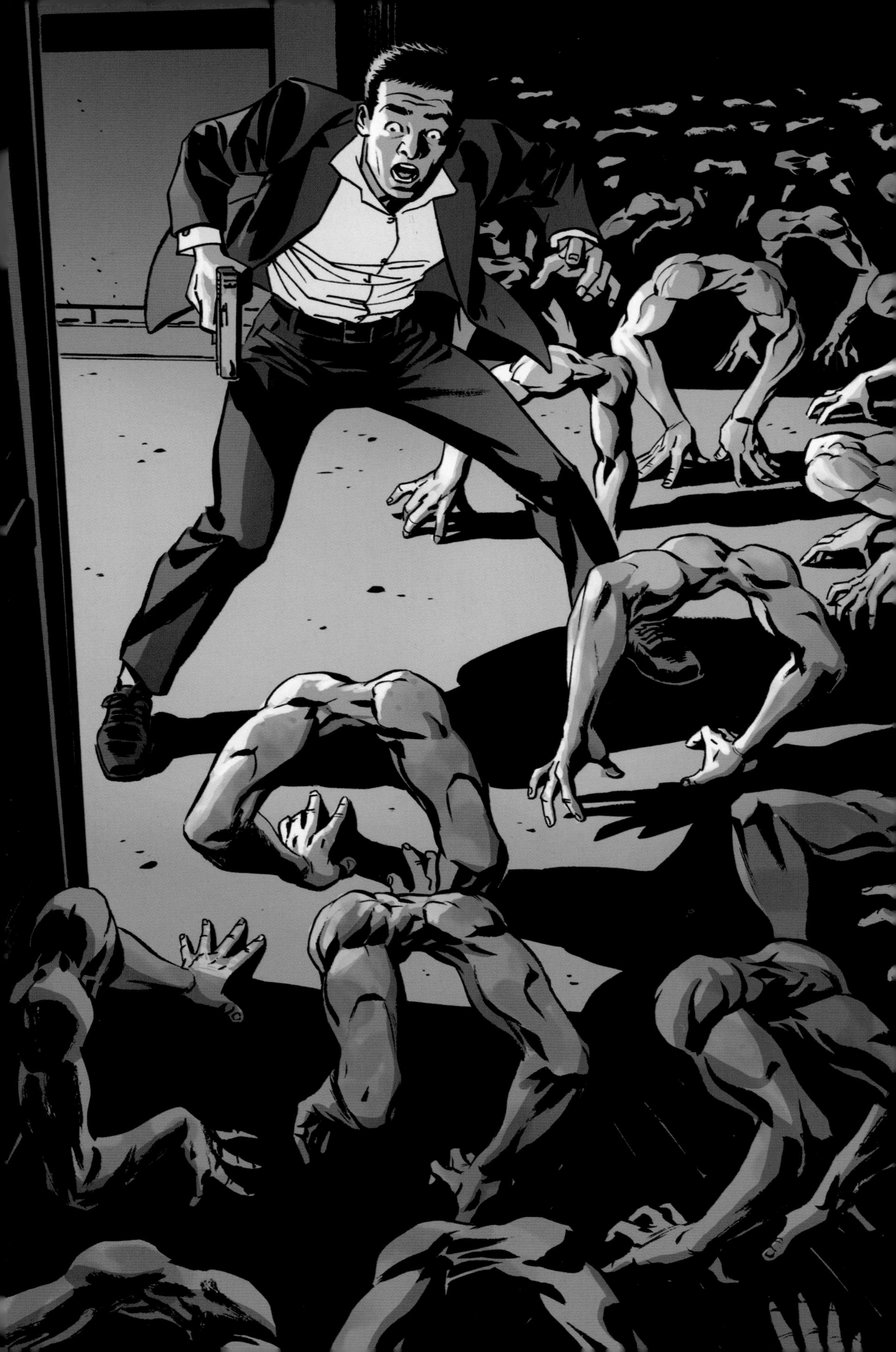

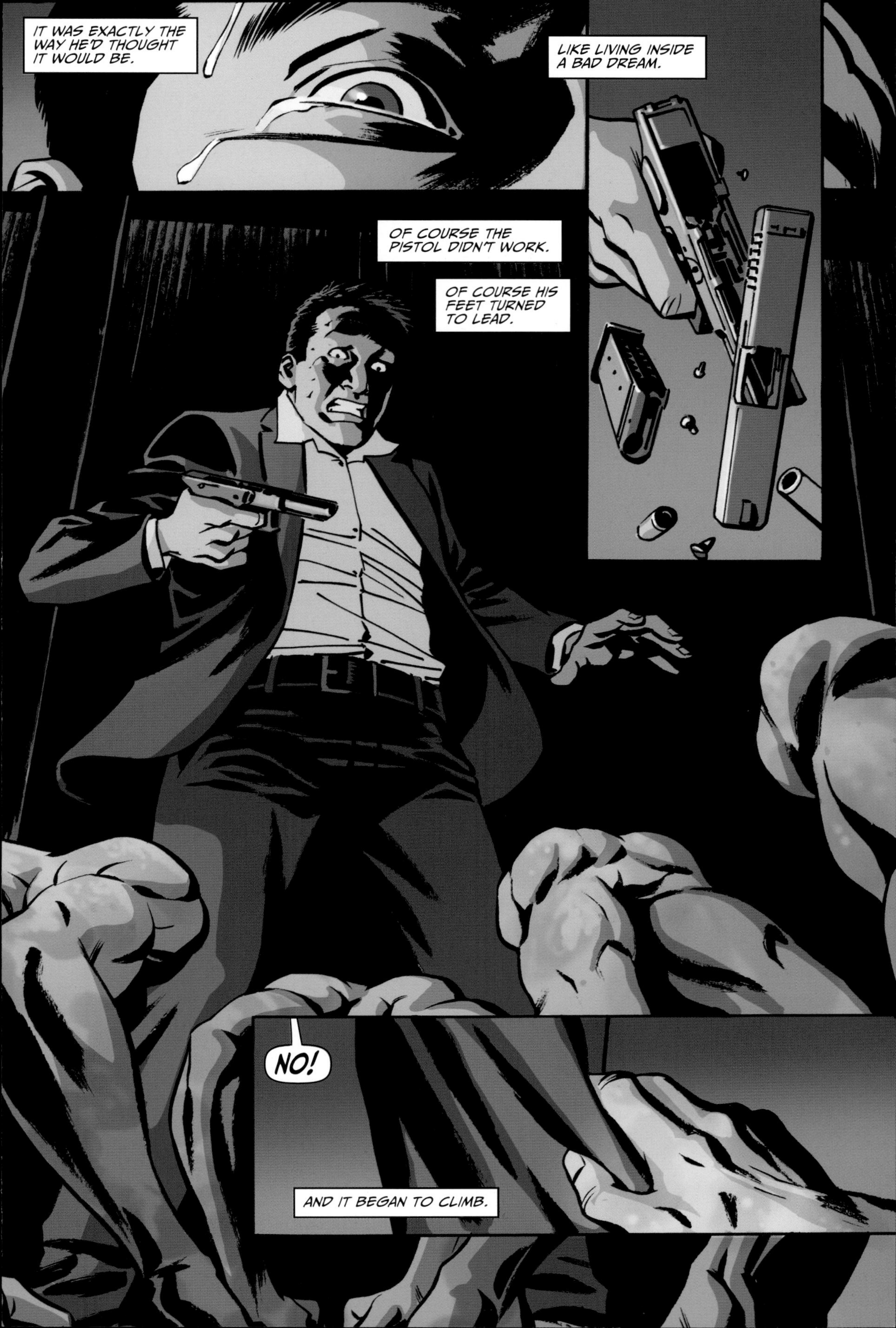
IT WAS EXACTLY THE WAY HE'D THOUGHT IT WOULD BE.
LIKE LIVING INSIDE A BAD DREAM.
OF COURSE THE PISTOL DIDN'T WORK.
OF COURSE HIS FEET TURNED TO LEAD.
NO!
AND IT BEGAN TO CLIMB.

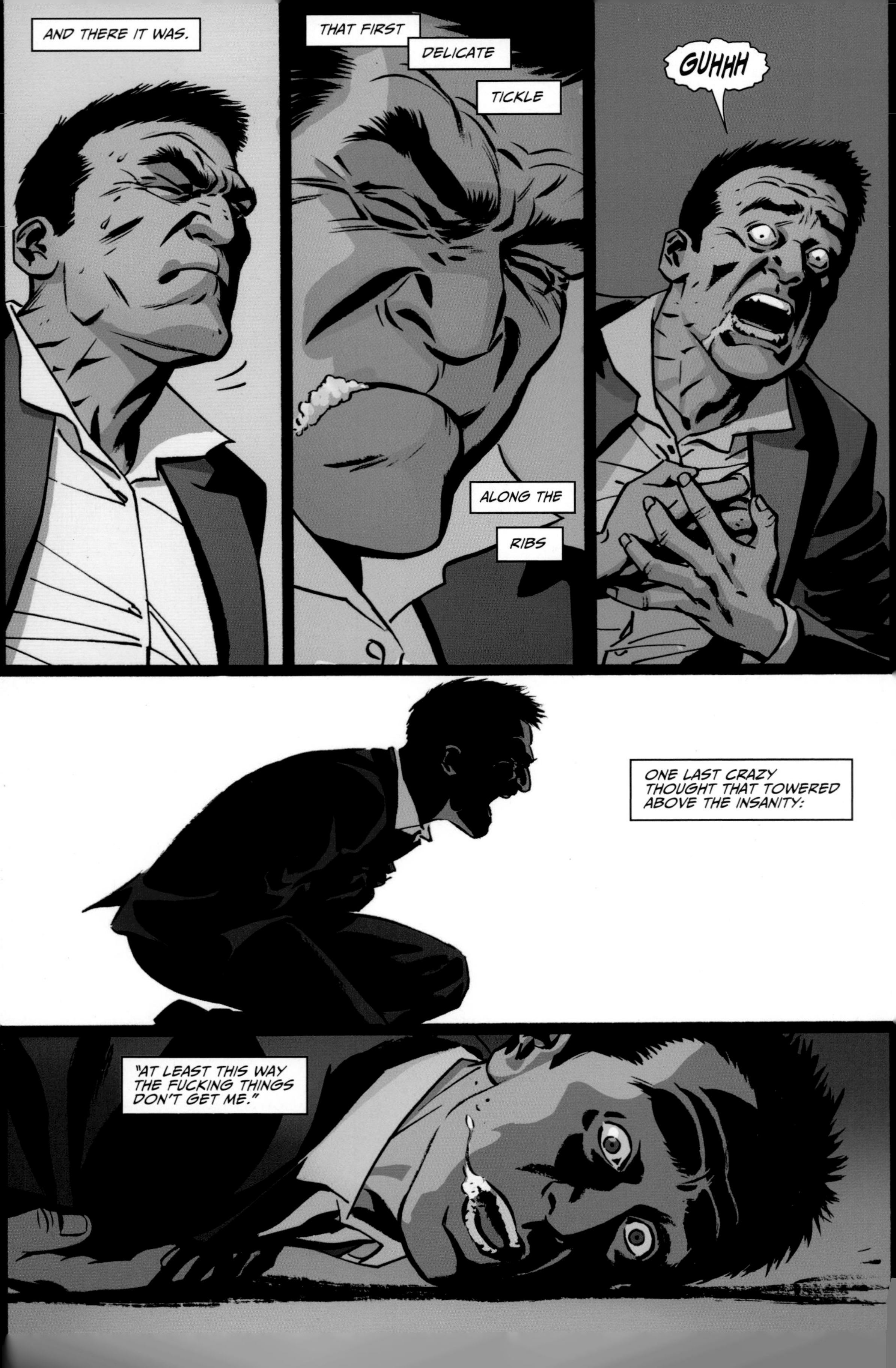
AND THERE IT WAS.
THAT FIRST
DELICATE
TICKLE
ALONG THE
RIBS
GUHHH
ONE LAST CRAZY THOUGHT THAT TOWERED ABOVE THE INSANITY:
"AT LEAST THIS WAY THE FUCKING THINGS DON'T GET ME."

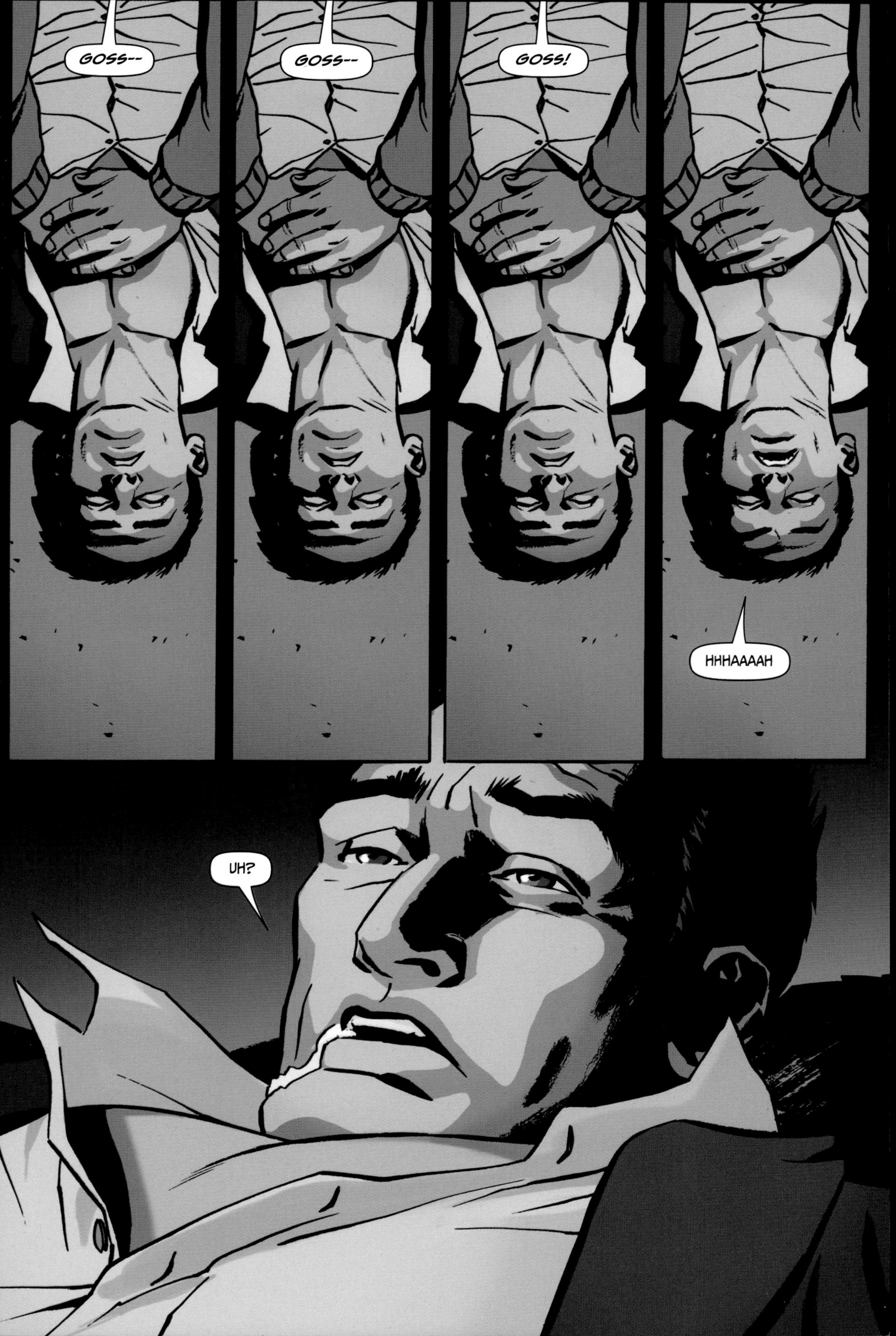
GOSS--
GOSS--
GOSS!
HHHAAAAH
UH?

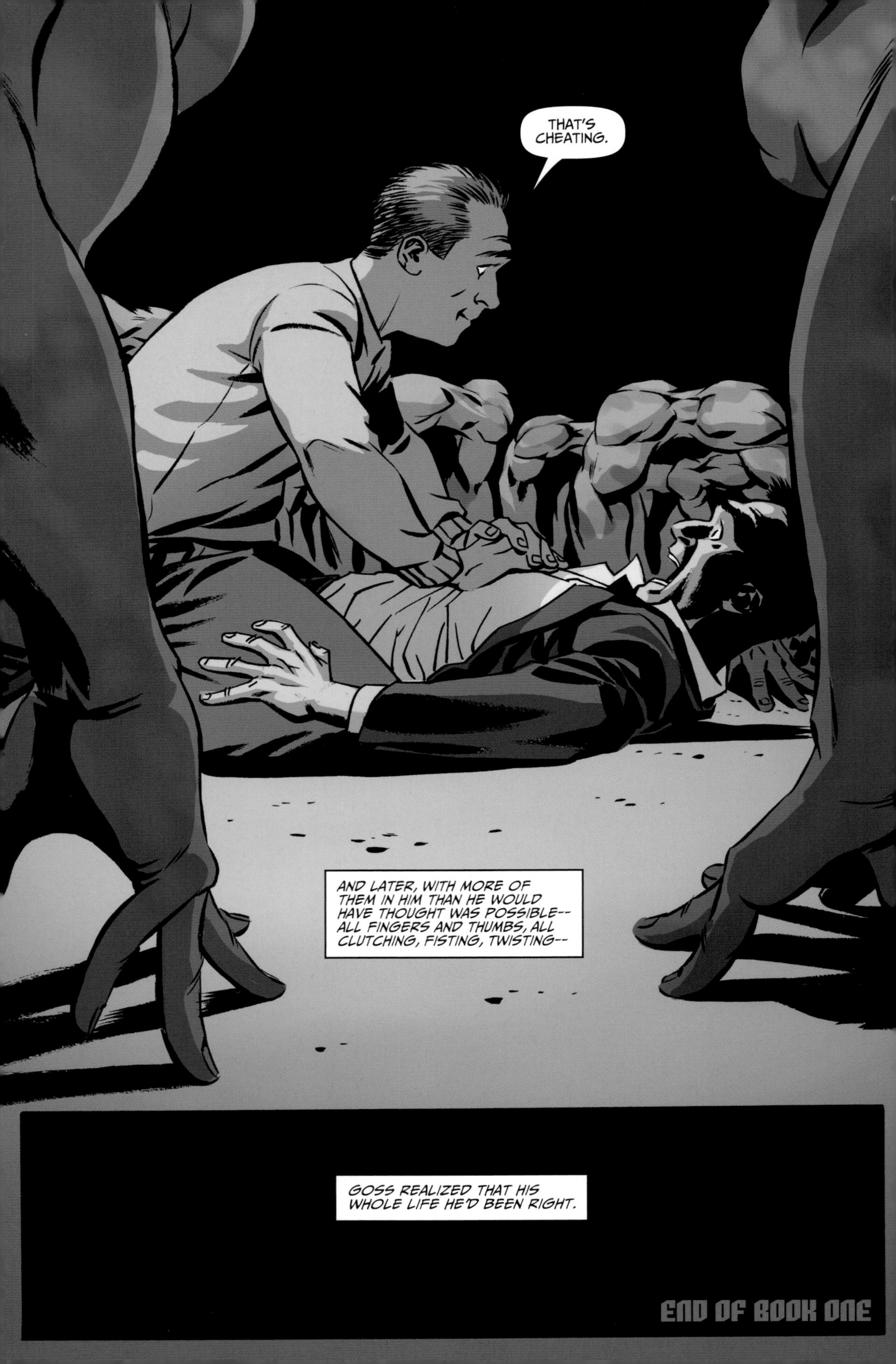
THAT'S CHEATING.
AND LATER, WITH MORE OF THEM IN HIM THAN HE WOULD HAVE THOUGHT WAS POSSIBLE-- ALL FINGERS AND THUMBS, ALL CLUTCHING, FISTING, TWISTING--
GOSS REALIZED THAT HIS WHOLE LIFE HE'D BEEN RIGHT.
END OF BOOK ONE

Issue 1
FRANCESCO FRANCAVILLA
Comics Elite variant cover

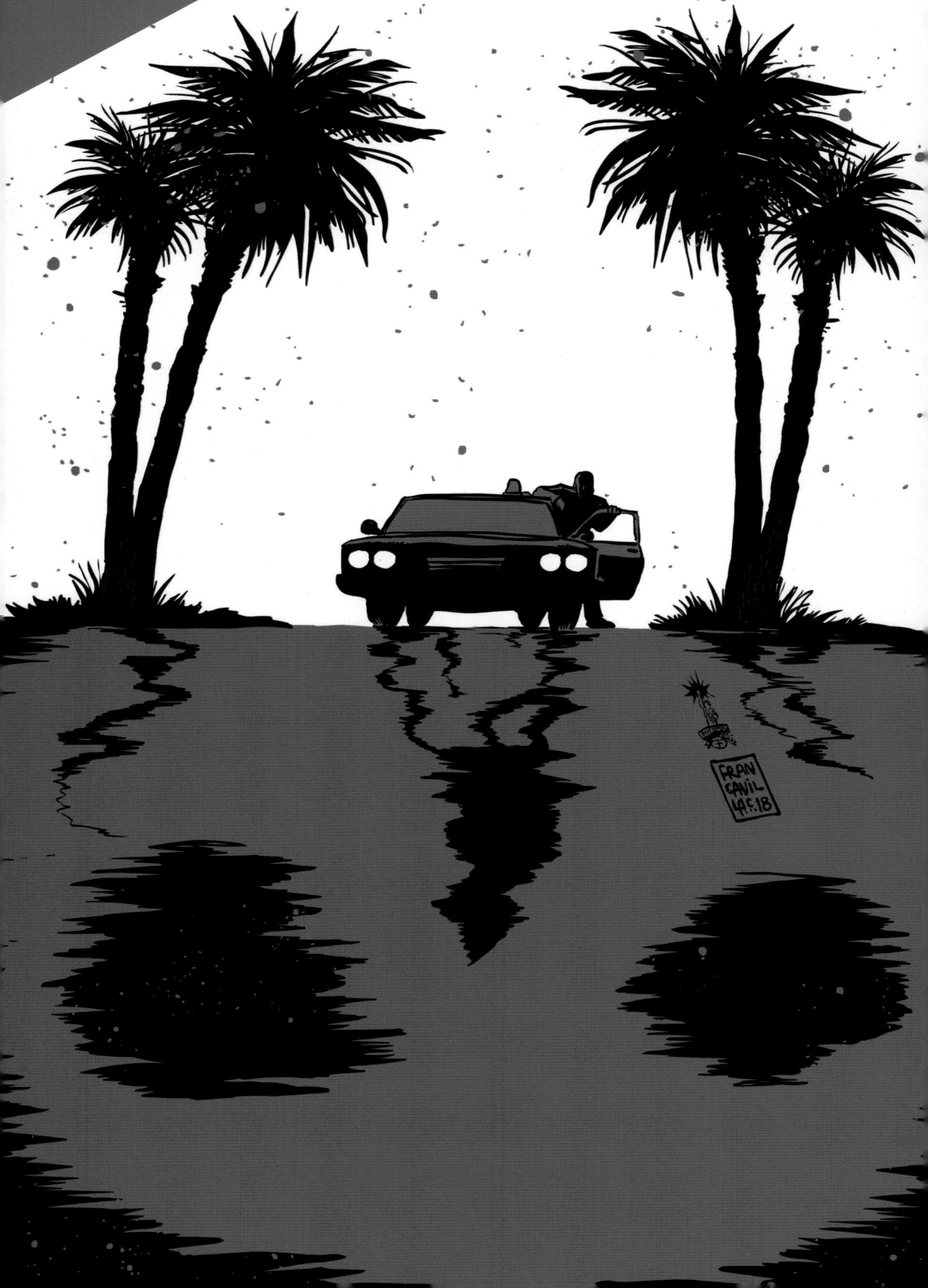

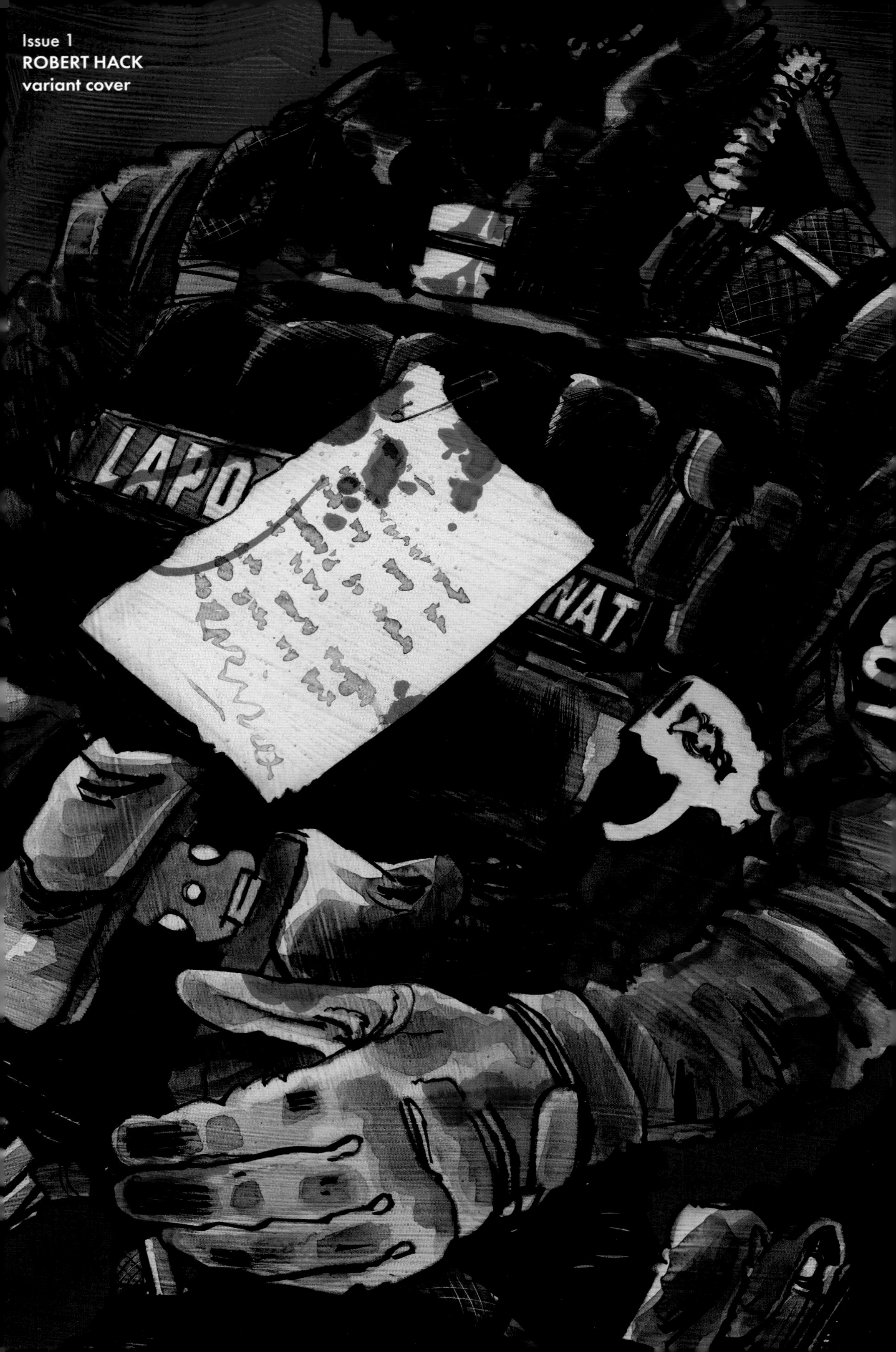
LAPD
NAT

Issue 1
ROBERT HACK
variant cover

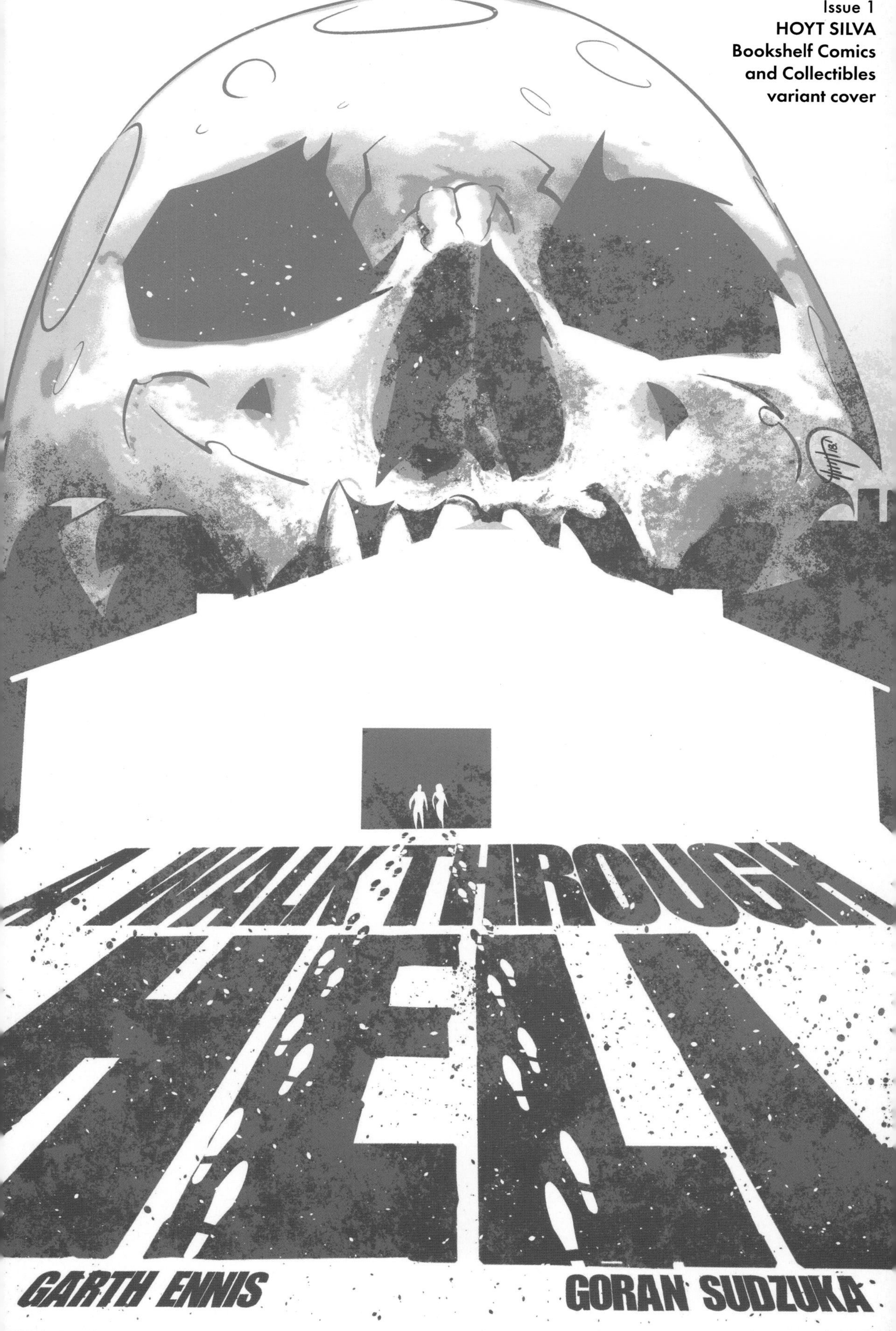
A WALK THROUGH
HELL
GARTH ENNIS
GORAN SUDZUKA

Issue 1
HOYT SILVA
Bookshelf Comics
and Collectibles
variant cover

Issue 1
GORAN SUDŽUKA w/ IVE SVORCINA
Rogues Gallery variant cover

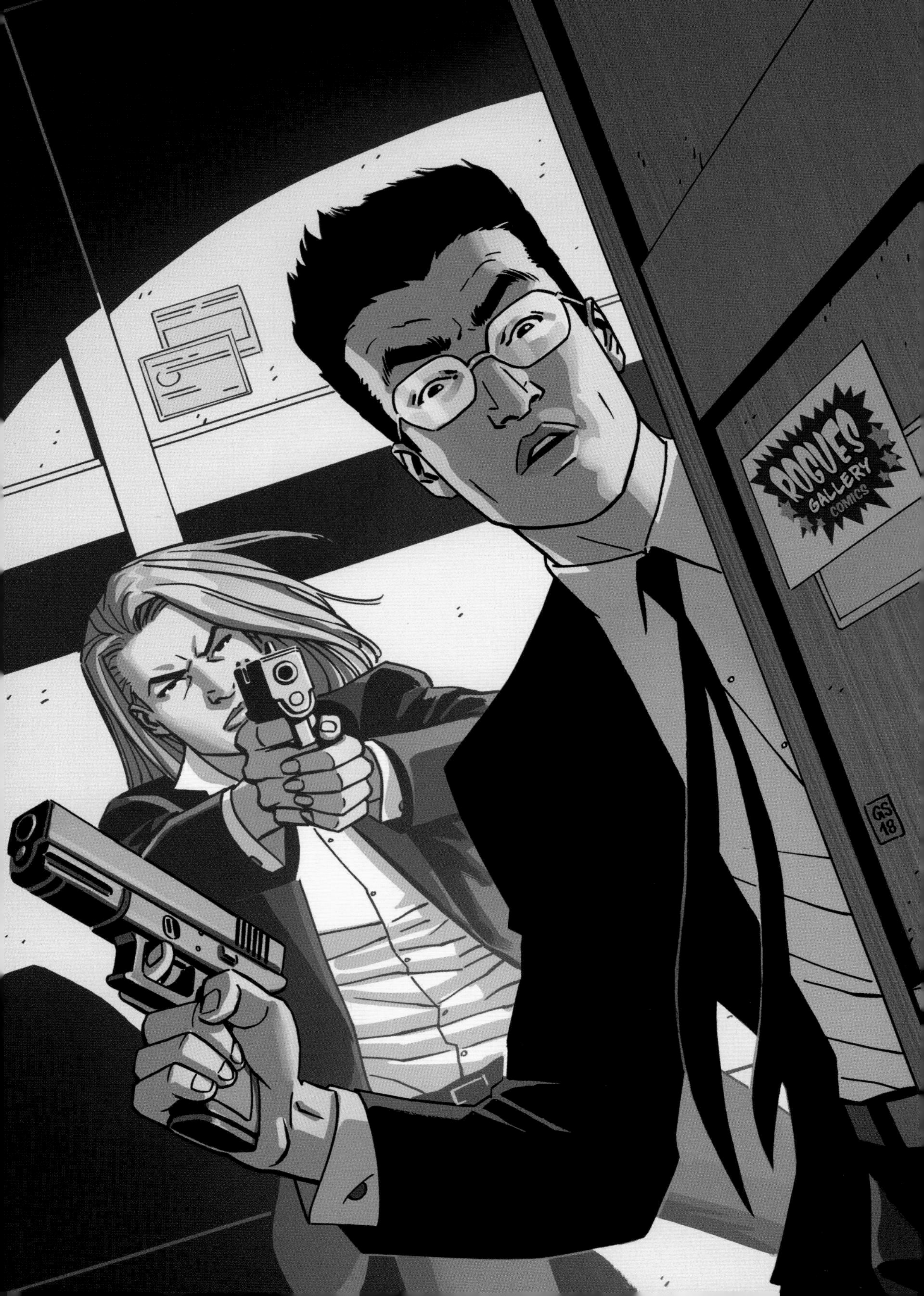
ROGUES
GALLERY
COMICS
GS
18

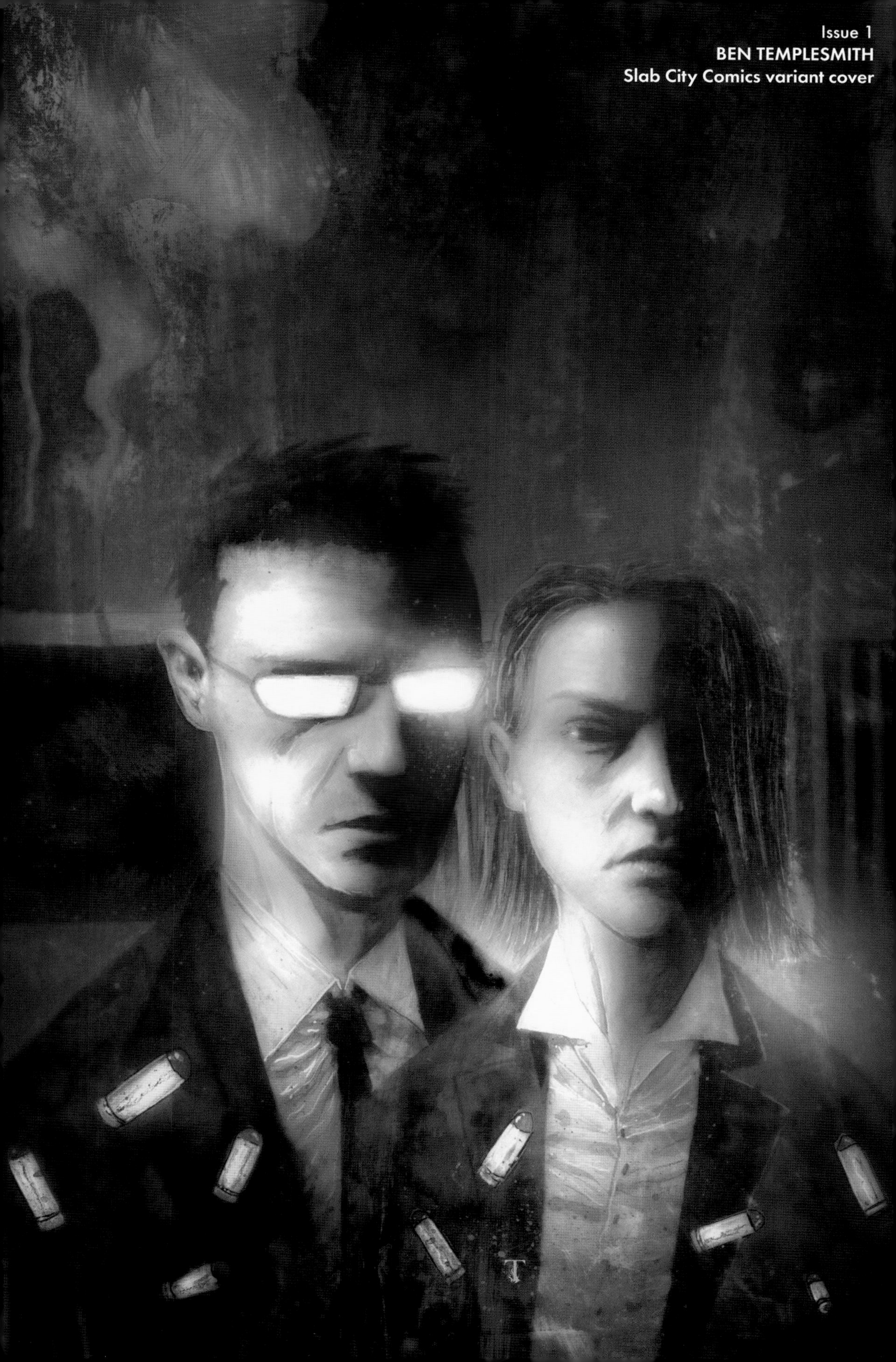

Issue 1
BEN TEMPLESMITH
Slab City Comics variant cover

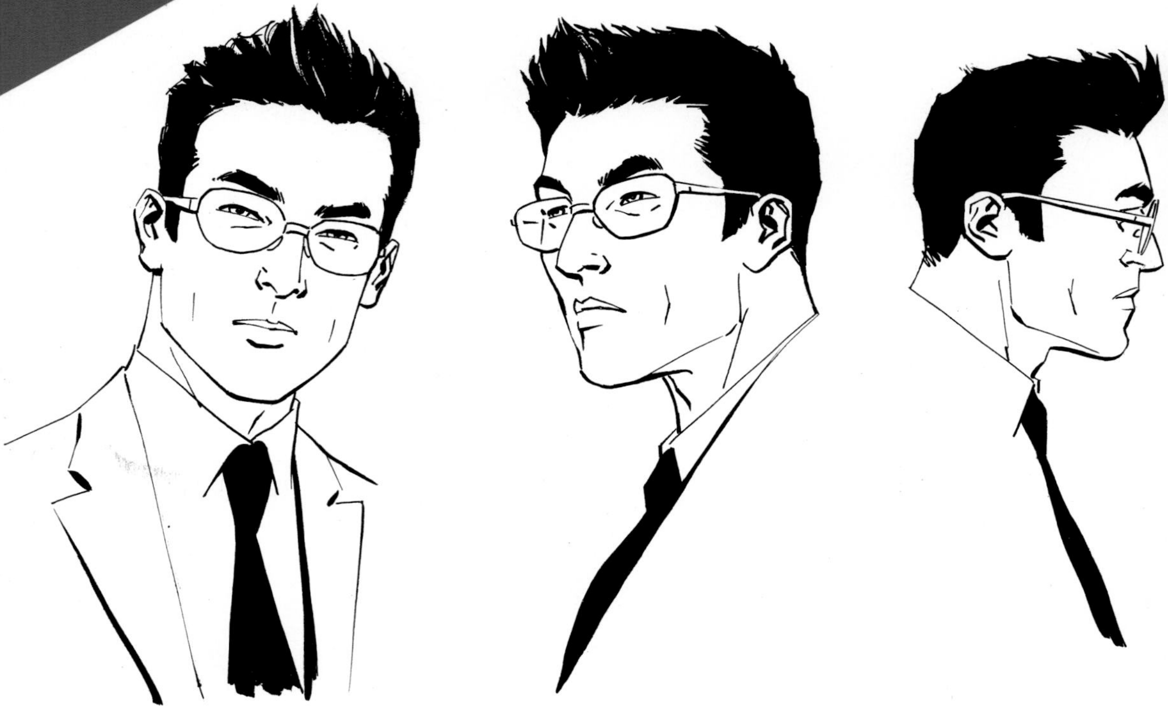

McGREGOR

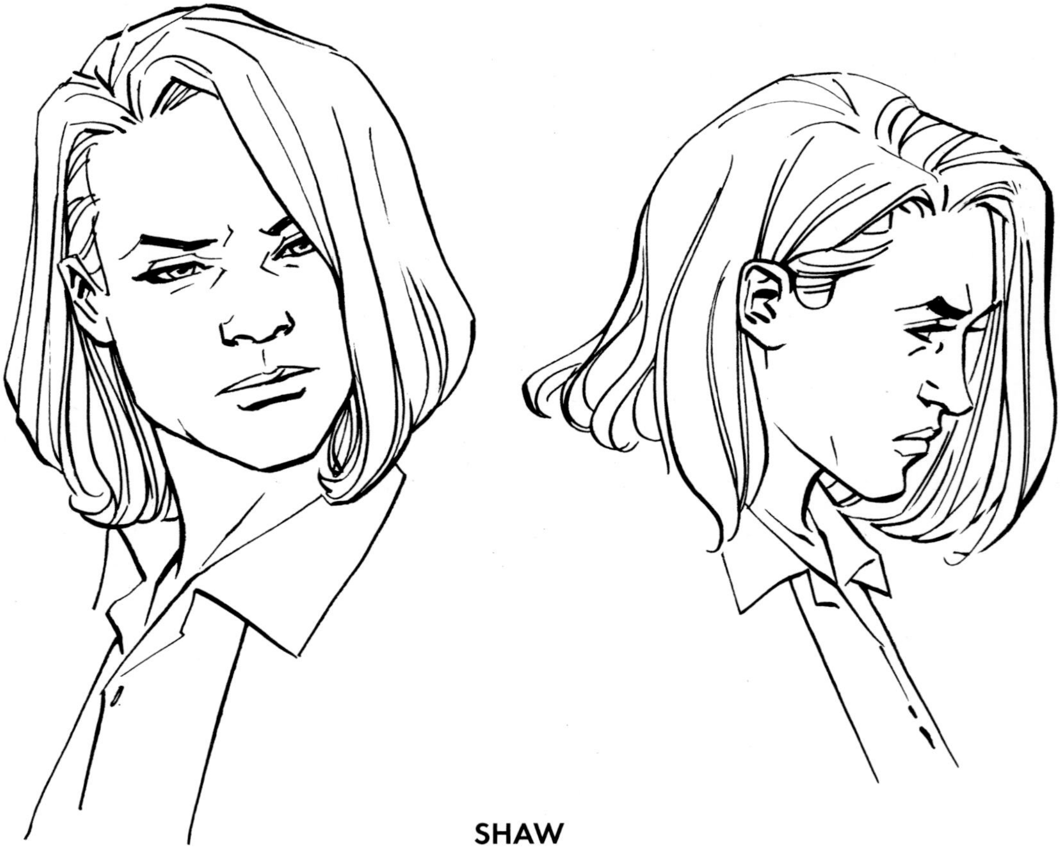

SHAW

by GORAN SUDŽUKA

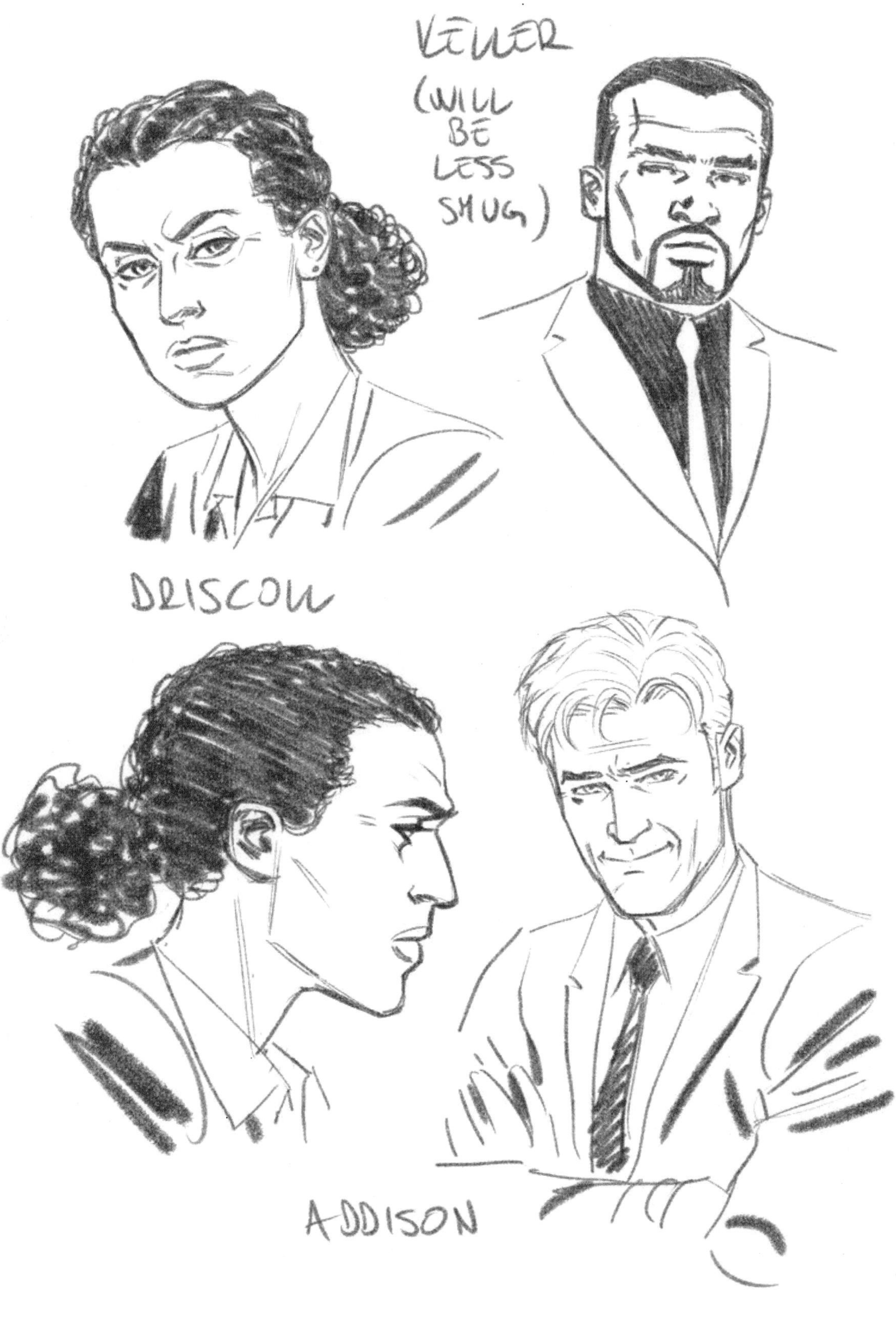
KELLER
(WILL BE LESS SMUG)
DRISCOLL
ADDISON

A WALK THROUGH HELL™ #1

A WALK THROUGH HELL 1 GARTH ENNIS

PAGE EIGHTEEN

1. Big. Each man draws his pistol- all regular service Glocks- and puts it to the forehead of the man sitting opposite him. A couple close their eyes, a couple steel themselves, but all have the same look of sad acceptance on their faces. Apart from the there's no drama to their body language at all, they remain seated. This would be one second before they fire.

2. The aide and the Lieutenant stop short in mid conversation, turning towards us in alarm- presumably the gunfire. The aide shits himself, the Lieutenant glares in confusion. Further back the other cops turn too.

3. They've opened the van doors wide and the aide is staring in at us in appalled horror, gasping- never seen anything this bad in his life, an administrator like him has probably never even seen a dead body. We don't see what he sees, not even a drop of blood on the van. The Lieutenant has already turned and is sprinting away.

Lieutenant: **JESUS!**

script by
GARTH ENNIS

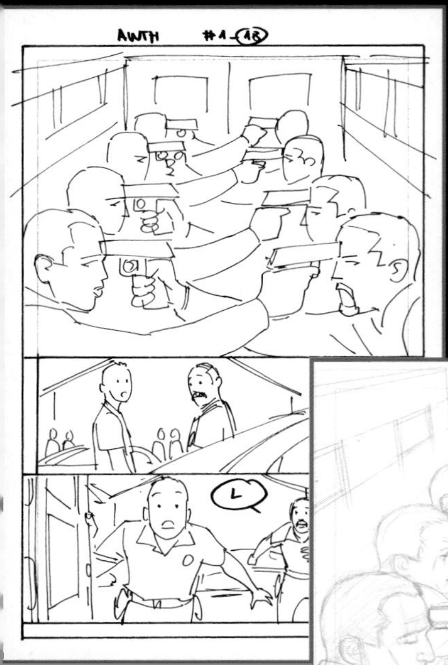

AWTH #1-18
L

layouts by
GORAN SUDŽUKA

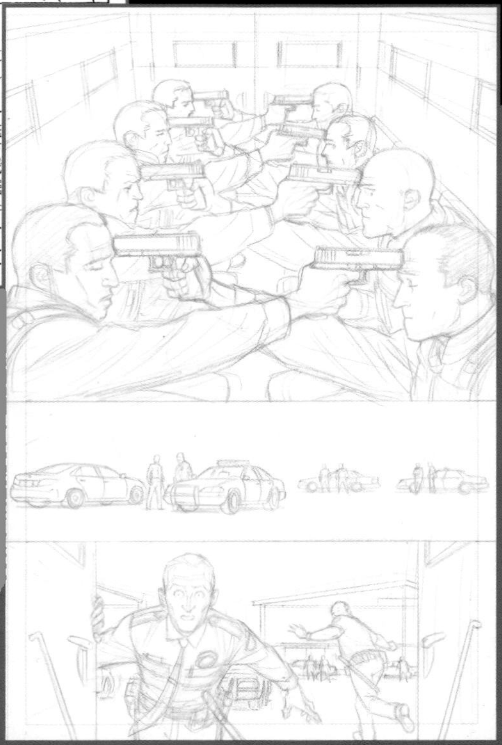

PAGE 18 PROCESS

pencils by
GORAN SUDŽUKA

inks by
GORAN SUDŽUKA

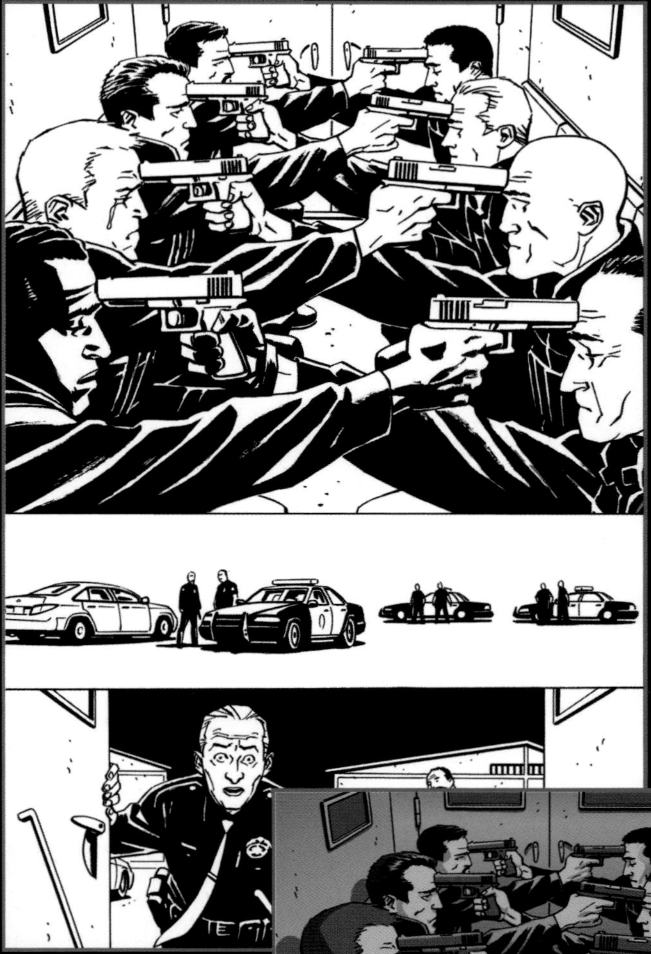

colors by
IVE SVORCINA

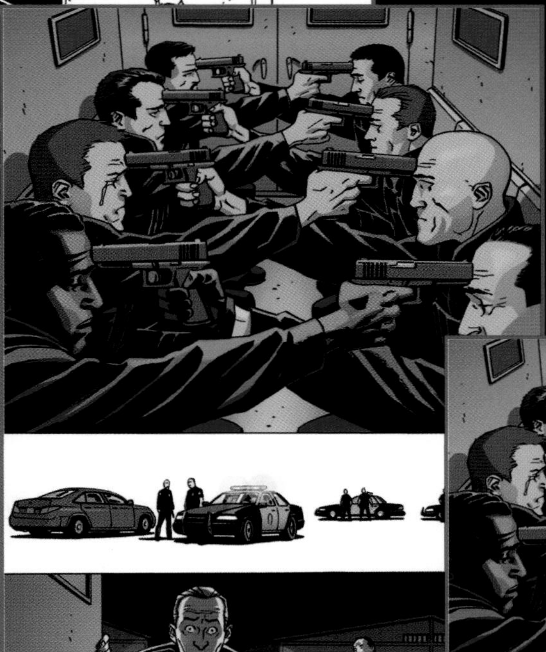

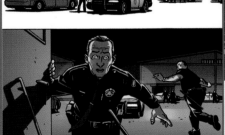

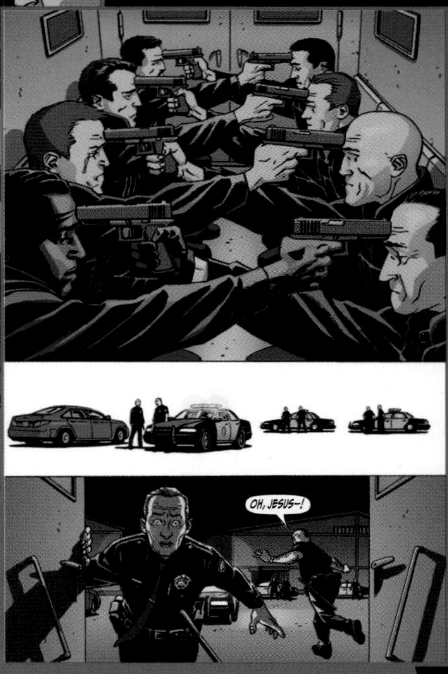
OH, JESUS—!

lettering by
ROB STEEN

A WALK THROUGH HELL™

#2

A WALK THROUGH HELL 2 GARTH ENNIS

PAGE SEVEN

1. Shaw and McGregor stare at us- she keeps her pistol aimed and her face goes completely still, eyes a little wider but muscles taut and mouth tight shut. McGregor, though, is completely horrified- eyes bulging, jaw almost on the floor, lowering his pistol in spite of himself.

McGregor: HUH

" " HUH

2. View past the ragged gash that used to be the back of Hunzikker's head, silhouetted in the Maglite beams. The other two are just dark shapes.

McGregor: **HUNZIKKER...?**

3. Pull back as McGregor slowly stands, lowers his pistol, moving closer to the kneeling Hunzikker. Shaw keeps her pistol dead-aimed at the poor guy.

McGregor: ARE—ARE YOU—

Shaw: DON'T TOUCH HIM--!

4. Close up. Hunzikker fires once, directly into his ear, and a shard of skull flies off the other side of what's left of his head. We don't see his face, but we do see the casing fly from the breech of the pistol.

Off: **JESUS CHRIST!**

Off 2: **GODDAMMIT!**

5. Pull back a little, their pov as Hunzikker slowly turns to look at us. His eyes are full of torment and misery, a distant but terrible despair. Quietly but utterly wretched, a sense of a man who wants help when he already knows he's doomed.

6. His pov on them staring back. This time even Shaw can't completely control herself, her eyes widen further, her gritted teeth show- just- as she angrily struggles to control herself. McGregor is far worse, his eyes almost fly from his skull as he slams his hand across his mouth to keep from screaming.

script by
GARTH ENNIS

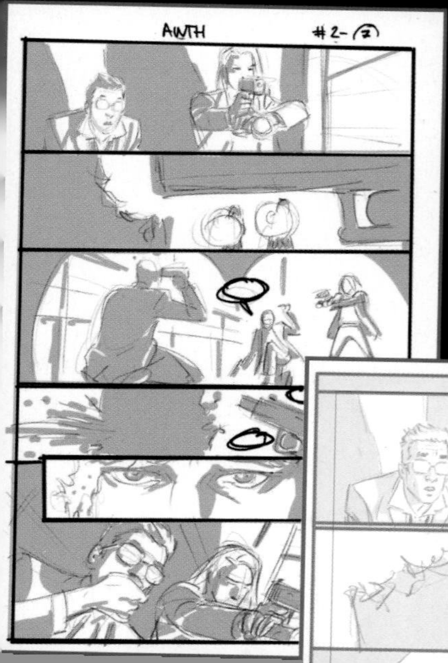
AWTH #2-(7)

layouts by
GORAN SUDŽUKA

PAGE 07 PROCESS

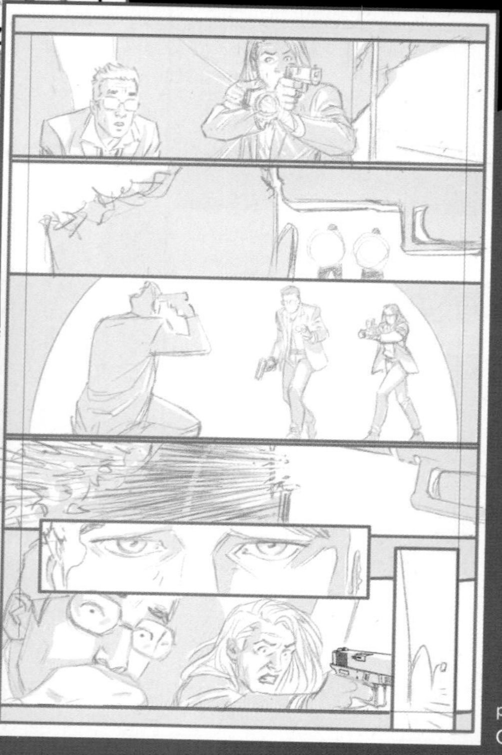

pencils by
GORAN SUDŽUKA

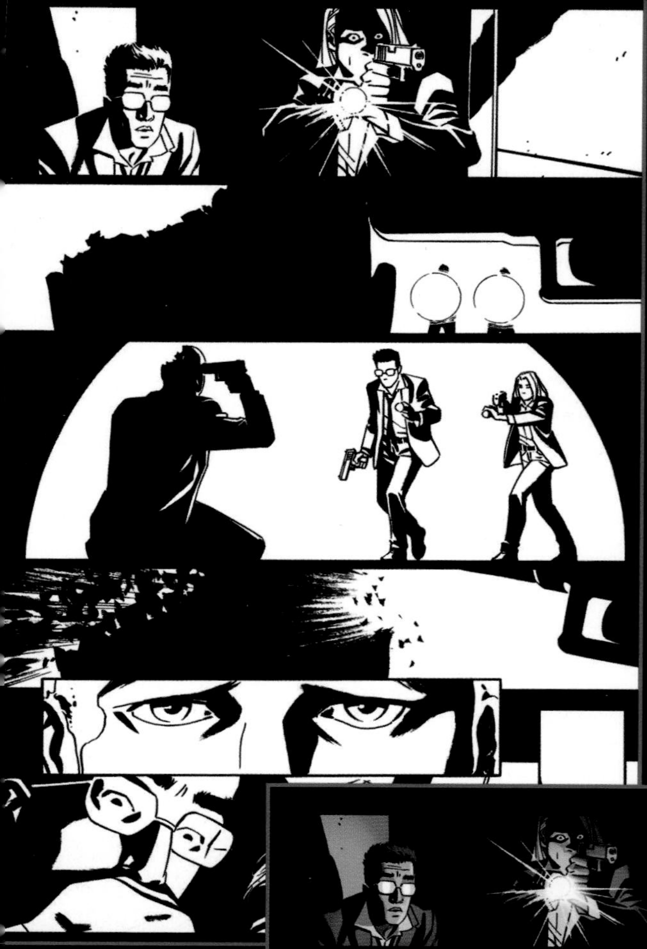

inks by
GORAN SUDŽUKA

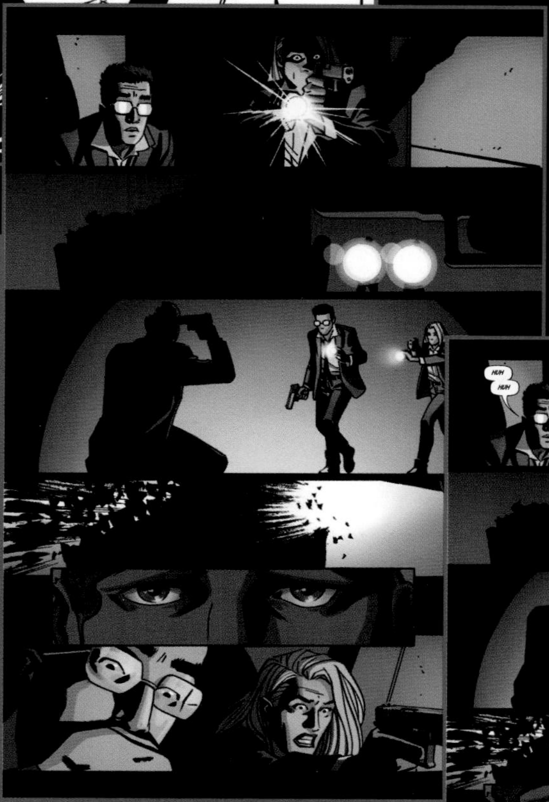

colors by
IVE SVORCINA

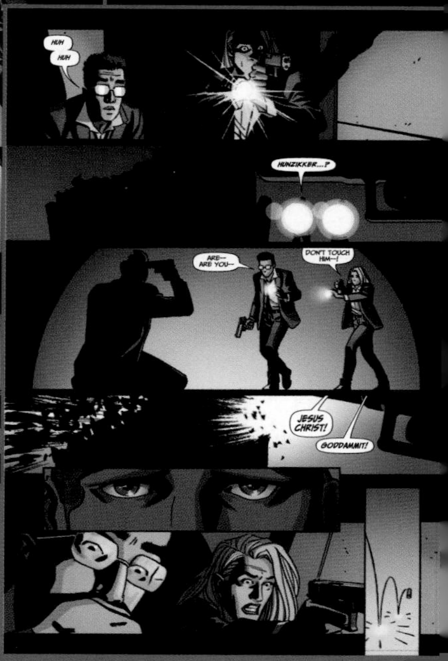
HUH
HUH
HUNZIKKER...?
ARE— ARE YOU—
DON'T TOUCH HIM—!
JESUS CHRIST!
GODDAMMIT!

lettering by
ROB STEEN

A WALK THROUGH HELL™

#5

A WALK THROUGH HELL 5 GARTH ENNIS

PAGE EIGHT

1. Close. Shaw places her left hand firmly on top of his head and puts a little .38 revolver over his ear, fires once. A squirt of blood shoots from the opposite side of his head, no more than that. We only see Shaw from the shoulders down, so no view of her face- but Carnahan is looking right at us, eyes suddenly wide, mouth opening.

2. Out of flashback, warehouse interior again. Shaw and McGregor sit side by side. She faces front, tired, not much fight left in her. He has his elbows leant on his knees and his fingertips clamped to his forehead, not looking up, quietly but totally appalled.

Shaw: NOBODY HEARD.

3. Flashback again. Shaw crouches by Carnahan, whose body sits slumped in the chair, carefully placing the .38 in his dead hand. Not too close on her here, just enough to see what she's doing.

Caption: "THE NEXT DAY I CAME INTO WORK, AND WHEN THE NEWS BROKE NO ONE EVEN LOOKED AT ME SIDEWAYS.

" " "I EXPECTED THERE MIGHT BE SOMETHING FROM HIS LAWYER ABOUT AN INQUIRY, YOU KNOW, **THE F.B.I. HAVE BEEN HOUNDING MY CLIENT AND BLAH-BLAH-BLAH**, BUT... ZERO.

" " "I GUESS I WAS..."

4. She's folded the legal pad in half- not just the three pages- and is tucking into the back of her pants next to her Glock nearest us. We don't see her face. Carnahan sits slumped in his chair on the other side of the desk, dead, face shadowed. It really does look like a suicide.

Caption: "CAREFUL NOT TO OVERDO IT."

script by
GARTH ENN

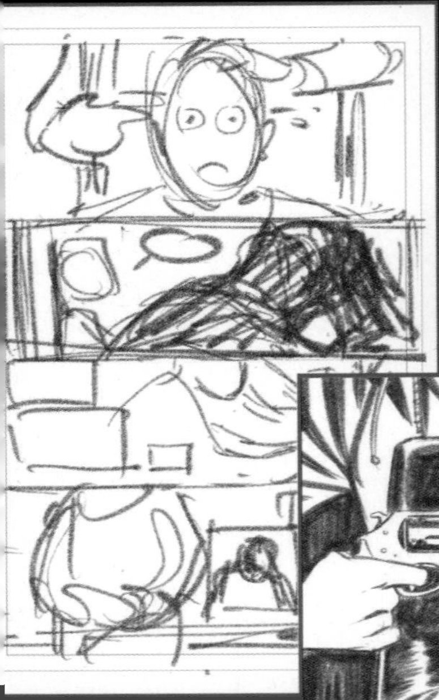

layouts by
GORAN SUDŽUKA

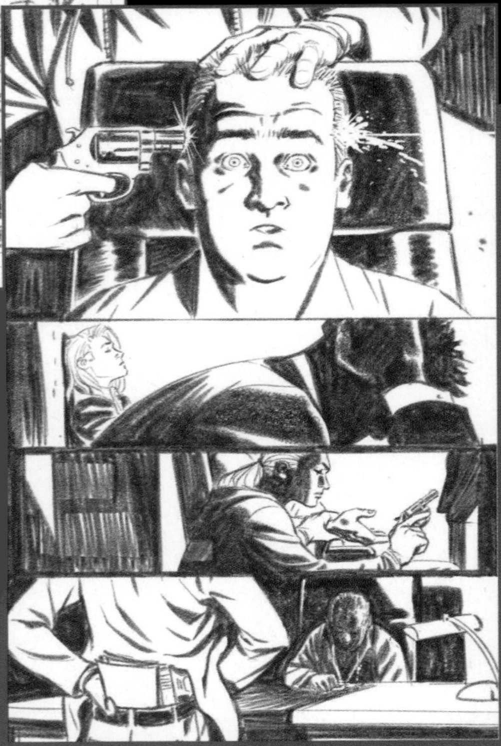

PAGE 08 PROCESS

pencils by
GORAN SUDŽUKA

inks by
GORAN SUDŽUKA

colors by
IVE SVORCINA

lettering by
ROB STEEN

ABOUT THE CREATORS OF A WALK THROUGH HELL™

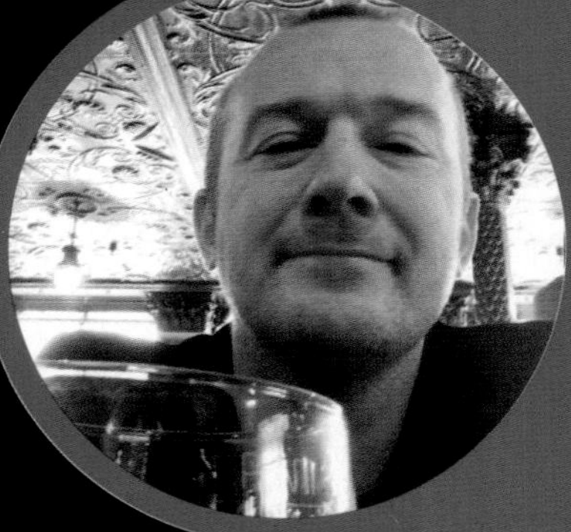

GARTH ENNIS writer

Garth Ennis has been writing comics since 1989. His credits include *Preacher, The Boys, Crossed, Battlefields and War Stories*, and successful runs on *The Punisher* and *Fury* for Marvel Comics. Originally from Belfast, Northern Ireland, he now lives in New York City with his wife, Ruth.

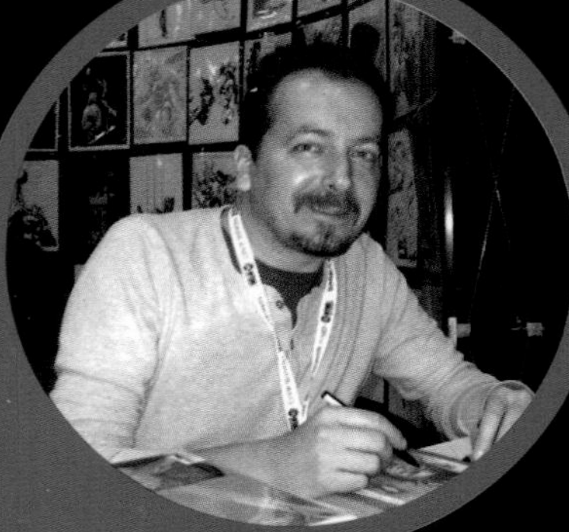

GORAN SUDŽUKA artist

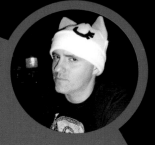

Goran Sudžuka was born in Zagreb, Croatia in 1969. After years of publishing comics in Croatia and Germany, he started working for American markets. His first work was *Outlaw Nation*, co-created with Jamie Delano for DC Comics/Vertigo, which earned him the Russ Manning Most Promising Newcomer Award in 2001. He stayed with Vertigo for ten years, working on some of their flagship titles like *Y: The Last Man* and *Hellblazer*. Later, he worked on titles like *Wonder Woman* (DC Comics), *Ghosted* (Image), *Wolverine, Thor, Deadpool* and *Daredevil* (Marvel). Since he read *Hellblazer #70* in 1994 he has wanted to work with Garth Ennis—twenty-three years later, a dream comes true.

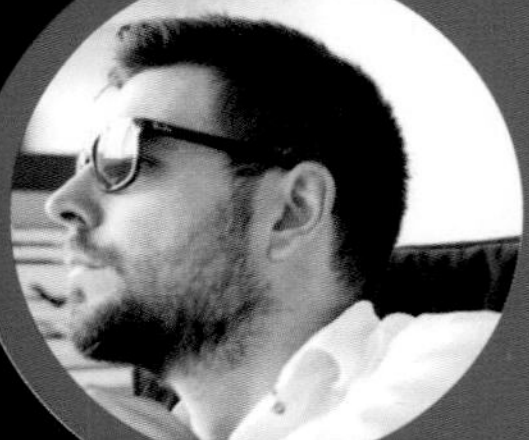

IVE SVORCINA colorist

Ive Svorcina was born in 1986 on a small island in the Adriatic sea in Croatia. Being self-taught, he somehow managed to start his professional career in 2006 and since then he has worked for such publishers as Marvel, DC, Delcourt, Image and smaller publishers in Croatia. Notable achievements include getting kicked out of the computer science college and getting nominated for an Eisner award for his work on *Thor*. Currently he resides in Zagreb.

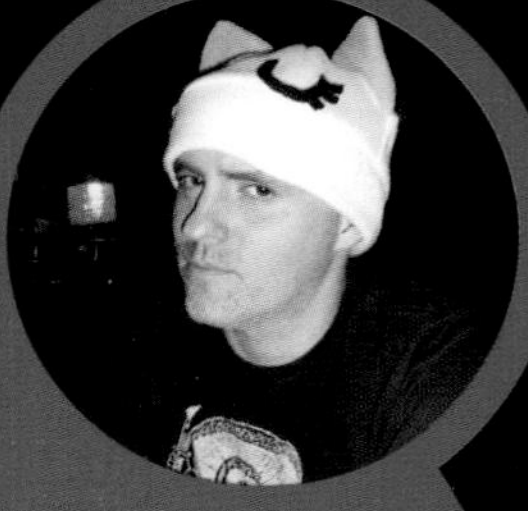

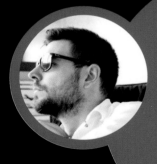

ROB STEEN letterer

Rob Steen is the illustrator of the *Flanimals* series of children's books written by Ricky Gervais and the Garth Ennis children's book *Erf*. He is also the colorist of David Hine's graphic novel *Strange Embrace* and letterer of comic books for AfterShock, Marvel, Dynamite, Image and First Second.